T0303920

ROUTLEDGE LIBRARY EDITIONS:
THE ECONOMICS AND BUSINESS OF
TECHNOLOGY

Volume 19

COMPUTERS IN COMPANY TRAINING

COMPUTERS IN COMPANY TRAINING

DAVID HAWKRIDGE, WENDY NEWTON AND
CAROLE HALL

Routledge
Taylor & Francis Group

LONDON AND NEW YORK

First published in 1988 by Croom Helm

This edition first published in 2018
by Routledge
2 Park Square, Milton Park, Abingdon, Oxon OX14 4RN

and by Routledge
711 Third Avenue, New York, NY 10017

Routledge is an imprint of the Taylor & Francis Group, an informa business

© 1988 D. Hawkridge, W. Newton and C. Hall

British Library Cataloguing in Publication Data
A catalogue record for this book is available from the British Library

ISBN: 978-1-138-50336-6 (Set)
ISBN: 978-1-351-06690-7 (Set) (ebk)
ISBN: 978-0-8153-6729-1 (Volume 19) (hbk)
ISBN: 978-1-351-25760-2 (Volume 19) (ebk)

Publisher's Note
The publisher has gone to great lengths to ensure the quality of this reprint but points out that some imperfections in the original copies may be apparent.

Disclaimer
The publisher has made every effort to trace copyright holders and would welcome correspondence from those they have been unable to trace.

COMPUTERS IN COMPANY TRAINING

DAVID HAWKRIDGE, WENDY NEWTON AND
CAROLE HALL

CROOM HELM
London ● New York ● Sydney

© 1988 D. Hawkridge, W. Newton and C. Hall
Croom Helm Ltd, Provident House,
Burrell Row, Beckenham, Kent BR3 1AT

Croom Helm Australia, 44–50 Waterloo Road,
North Ryde, 2113, New South Wales

Published in the USA by
Croom Helm
in association with Methuen, Inc.
29 West 35th Street
New York, NY 10001

British Library Cataloguing in Publication Data

Hawkridge, David G.
    Computers in company training.
    1. Employees, Training of — Computer-
    assisted instruction
    I. Title   II. Newton, Wendy
    III. Hall, Carole
                      IIF5549.5.T7

415007550

Library of Congress Cataloging-in-Publication Data

Hawkridge, David G.
    Computers in company training/David Hawkridge, Wendy Newton, and
    Carole Hall.
        p. cm.
    Bibliography: p.
    Includes index.
    ISBN 0-7099-4778-X
    1. Employees, Training of — Data processing. 2. Occupational
    training — Data processing. 3. Computer-assisted instruction.
    I. Newton, Wendy. II. Hall, Carole. III. Title.
    HF5549.5.T7H357   1988
    658.3'12404 — dc19   87-30417

Filmset by Mayhew Typesetting, Bristol, England
Printed and bound in Great Britain by Mackays of Chatham Ltd, Kent

Contents

Figures

Preface

WHAT THIS BOOK IS ABOUT

This book is about a new wave. Its pages are full of the names of world-famous companies. Why have these companies used computers, interactive video and telecommunication technology for training? What has been their experience with this new training technology so far? Should other companies follow their example?

To answer these questions, we carried out two studies, one in the United States and one in Britain, of industrial and business training in companies using this new technology.

We knew that business concerns, including banks, insurance companies and retailers, had introduced microelectronic technology into numerous financial, clerical and inventory control processes, to increase their efficiency. And that industrial corporations were rapidly turning to this technology for improving design, manufacturing, storage and distribution.

We also knew that introducing new technology creates new training needs. This has been freely acknowledged at meetings such as NASA's 1984 Symposium on Productivity and Quality (Gerard and Edwards, 1984), in the European Economic Community's initiatives, and in reports such as *A Challenge to Complacency* (Manpower Services Commission, 1986).

We asked the question: Can these new needs be met by training through the technology, as Eurich (1985) proposed in her study of training in US corporations? In 1984, the American Society for Training and Development conference was told that only 5 per cent of companies questioned were using computer-based technology in their own training (Stacey, 1986, personal communication). Now, four years later, it is clear that in many corporations those responsible for traditional training are seriously considering how to exploit the new training technology to make training more effective and cheaper.

We wrote this book because we believe that when company training policy is changing it is time to analyse critically existing and potential training uses of the technology. This kind of critical analysis, set in context, is not readily available elsewhere.

Our book reports what the companies have done with the new training technology. We do not claim to cover every single company, but this book contains much material published for the first time and draws together many widely scattered publications. We found only a little useful material in the research literature, and although several hundred US and British companies are experimenting with applications, few have been researched and written up. Where accounts have been published, they have often been written by employees of provider or vendor companies, rather than by users, whose voices have seldom been heard.

OTHER PUBLICATIONS IN THIS FIELD

Among the books in this field, Kearsley (1983) provides a discussion of computer-based training (CBT) in the United States. Dean and Whitlock (1982) offer a British trainers' primer, but say little about users' experience. Heaford (1983) and Beech (1983), in their books on computer-based learning, describe CBT in a handful of companies. All four books draw mainly on company experience in the 1970s, before microcomputers were widely used. Newer publications are emerging about using CBT and interactive videodiscs with microcomputers. Gery (1987), for example, provides details of implementation.

Interactive videodisc technology came on the scene in the 1980s. Iuppa (1984), Iuppa and Anderson (1987), and Parsloe (1984a) touch on how to develop company training with this technology. Duke (1983) undertook an early survey, and Bayard-White (1985) reviews three British companies' use of the discs for training.

We found that the journals are erratic in dealing with CBT. United States and British journals concerned with instructional systems usually focus on developments in education but also deal sometimes with company training, for example,

British Journal of Educational Technology
Educational Technology
Instructional Innovator
Instructional Science
Journal of Educational Technology Systems
Journal of Instructional Development
Performance and Instruction Journal
Programmed Learning and Educational Technology

Training journals deal regularly with corporate training, and occasionally report on applications of the technology, for example,

Data Training
Training
Training News
Training and Development Journal
Training Officer

Two introductory packs for trainers are on the British market: *An Introduction to Computer-Based Training* is sold by the Open University, and Eurotech sells *Understanding Technology Based Training*.

TRAINING NEEDS: THE BASIS FOR OUR ANALYSIS

Our own analysis starts from training needs and problems now faced by industry and commerce. In addition to what we say about needs in Chapter 1, each of Chapters 7–13, dealing with company experience, begins with a discussion of needs. We feel it is important to explain the new training technology in plain language (Chapters 4–6). We describe and analyse how the technology is actually being used for business and industrial training in the two countries (Chapters 7–13). We discuss in detail the problems and constraints (Chapters 14–17), and finally we look at trends and the future up to 2000 AD (Chapters 18–20).

This book is not a manual to tell trainers how to prepare training using the technologies. Nor is it strictly a research report, although we draw heavily on our collected data. Instead, we set out to provide a full description of company experience, plus analysis of the context against which decisions must be taken regarding introduction of training based on computers.

We do not attempt to 'sell' the new training technology, but we do set out to inform all those who, between them, spend billions each year on training in our respective countries.

OUR CREDENTIALS

Writing this book was an exciting professional task for us, and we should explain our own backgrounds. Since 1970, David Hawkridge has been Professor of Applied Educational Sciences and Director of the Institute of Educational Technology at the British Open University (which uses the new technology in teaching over 100 000 students). He was previously at the American Institutes for Research, Palo Alto (where he worked on one of the first computer-based education projects and developed training for AT&T), and has been a Visiting Professor at Stanford and Syracuse. He is chairman of the International Advisory Panel for staff training in the Television Universities and Polytechnics of China. In 1986 he advised the World Bank and Unesco on training. He has written three other books about using technology in education and training (Hawkridge and Robinson, 1982; Hawkridge, 1983; Hawkridge, Vincent and Hales, 1985).

Wendy Newton is a Programme Manager at the Council for Educational Technology for the United Kingdom, based in London. She is responsible for developing projects in Open Learning, including those geared specifically to meet the needs of small businesses. After working as Leverhulme Trust funded Project Officer on the British study, she spent six months as a Research Consultant to the Open University on a project developing a demonstrator computer-based expert system for the analysis of the training needs of small businesses. Her experience has included running an Adult Education Programme at one of Britain's first Tertiary Colleges in the 1970s and wide experience of lecturing and tutoring in institutions as diverse as prisons and the Open University. Her previous research was of interethnic relations among Indian South Africans in Natal.

Carole Hall is a training consultant whose company, HallTech, in Pleasanton, California provides training and marketing services for the high-tech companies of Silicon Valley, as well as major banks, insurance companies and educational institutions. She has 20 years' experience in designing, developing and implementing a wide variety of technical training and educational programmes. Her company's clients have included Ampex, Convergent Technologies, Fairchild, Hewlett-Packard, Lockheed, Memorex, PMI and Raytheon. She began work on computer-assisted instruction when she joined a nationwide mainframe project at the American Institutes for Research, and is now involved with microcomputer-based systems.

OUR METHODS

Our methods were straightforward. We conducted telephone interviews with trainers in many companies in both countries. In this way we were able to build up a computerised database and a collection of documents about the use made of new training technology. Our aim was not to conduct a comprehensive survey but to identify and analyse in depth a large number of cases. We visited about 50 selected companies that are using the technology to talk face-to-face with training managers, trainers and, where possible, trainees. What we say about companies we visited has been cleared for accuracy by the companies themselves.

ACKNOWLEDGEMENTS

We want to thank publicly all those who gave us their time and attention during the US and British studies. We decided not to risk embarrassing them by including a directory of addresses. Some talked to us on the telephone, some answered our letters, others received us at their companies' premises. Some were working for companies that provide the hardware and software, but many were actually using the technology for training. A few were staff of national societies or centres that were general sources of information. Each made a contribution to this book.

In the United States: Steve Allen (Allen Communications), Don Abshire (Chevron Information Technology), Robert Barnes and Mary Evans (Drexler), Maureen Beausey (Eastman Kodak), Roland Bechtel (Cincinatti Milacron), David Berenhaus (Association for Educational and Communications Technology), Henry Berman (Interactive Medical Communications), Irene Blumenkranz, Shawn Richardson and Russ Grant (Mervyn's), Paul Braden (US Department of Commerce), Sharon Brown and Janet Perdzock (NCR Corporation), Peggie Campeau and Judith Appleby (American Institutes for Research), Bob Chapman (Learning Resources Network), Dianne Clarke-Kudless (Dunn and Bradstreet), Phil Corman (Digital Equipment Corporation), Jim Curtin (Minolta Corporation), Mike Dell'olio (UNUM Life Insurance Company), Richard Dinwiddie (USLIFE), Aldo Dossa (Pacific Bell), Larry Eps (Coca-Cola USA), Sue Espinosa, Jeff Vasek and Dave Cram (Apple Computer), Danny Filter, Jeff Ballard and Pam Evans (IBM), Frank Fisher (Harvard University), Bill Fountain (General Electric),

Raymond Fox (Society for Applied Learning Technology), Shelley Friedman, Kent Dimmick, Tina Giles and Patrick Mage (Bank of America), Lou Gonzales, Judie Gordon and Susan Price (Pinnacle Courseware), Karen Gustafson (Nissan Motor), Carol Harbin (Syntex Laboratories), Brighton Harris (Pratt and Whitney), Larry Israelite (Scientific Systems), Ted Khan and Ed Emke (Picodyne), Susan Lewis (Zale Corporation), Arthur Melmed (New York University), Rockley Miller (Videodisc Monitor), Helen Moore (Lockheed Missiles and Space), Ron Nugent (Nebraska VideoDisc Group), Stephen Paroby (Ernst and Whinney), Peter Pipe (Pipe Associates), Travis Piper (Creative Approaches Inc.), Deborah Plumley, Joe Ercolani, Tom Watson, Judee Humburg, Olga Towstopiat, Robert Coulter, Skip Norman and Nick Iuppa (Hewlett-Packard), Leah Rampy, Rick Hill, Steve Hendryx (American Express Travel Related Services), Gary Quinlan (Wilson Learning), Rob Robles (Allen Bradley), Charline Seyfer (Mountain Bell), Jay Silber (FlightSafety International), Kerry Sissons (Goal Systems International), Margaret Stewart (Bell Canada), David Stone (Computer Teaching Corporation), Carole Tomczyk (Xerox), Bruce Warren (Warren-Forthought), Nancy White, Vershelle Jarmon, Richard Gess, Linda Shatzer and Karen Tomlinson (AT&T Technologies), Joanne Willard (Creative Training Concepts), Bill Ziemba and Don Robbins (Ford Motor Company).

In Britain: Jenny Alderman (Open Learning, Sainsbury's), Peter Allen (Agricultural Training Board), Trevor Ashworth and Mike Brown (College of Telecommunications Training), John Barker (Format PC), Maggi Barker (BACIE Library), Margaret Bell (Open Learning, British Telecom), Mary Benwell (Road Transport Industry Training Board), Tony Bewley (British Telecom), John Coffey (Open Tech Training and Support Unit), Liz Copeland (CAP Scientific), Peter Copeland (Futuremedia), Mary Corbett (Mentor Interactive Training), John Cox (Datasolve Education), Matthew Dixon (National Computing Centre), Roger Dobson and Keith Judson (B&Q Retail), Gina Dooley and Ian Brooker (Boots), Angus Doulton and Claire Bayard-White (National Interactive Video Centre), George Eccles (Ferranti Computer Systems), John Elmitt (Maritz Training), Leslie Goodman (Manpower Services Commission), John Hatfield (Rediffusion Simulation), J.L. Haynes, C.D. Walden and Pam Keen (Barclays Bank), Michael Hawes (British Gas), John Heaford and Glenn Bartholomew (Deltak), John Heppell (White Rose Systems), Terry Hinton (University of Surrey), Cheryl Hitchcock and Julian Wakeley (Abbey National), Maureen Holland

(Intra Systems), Stephen Kirk (Convergent Communications), David Macey, Stephanie Hirst, Keith Dagwell and Peter Sharman (British Caledonian Airways), Kate McColl (WH Smith), Jan Menzies, Janice Holden and Rita Surgey (Rank Xerox), Diana Laurillard, Tim O'Shea and Ouida Rice (Institute of Educational Technology, Open University), Robin Mair (Cameron Communications), Derek Moore (STC-IDEC), John Naughton and Keith Williams (Technology Faculty, Open University), Eric Parsloe (EPIC Communications), Tony Randall and Tony Tyrrell (SEGAS), Brian Rudge and David Andrews (Central Electricity Generating Board), Clive Shepherd (VPS Interactive), Graham Smith, Peter Leese and Alan Ellis (British Rail), John Stratford (British Broadcasting Corporation), Calvin Thomas and Keith Stevens (SWGAS), Ken Thompson and Laurie Shields (College of Air Traffic Control), Peter Welch (American Express), Quentin Whitlock (Dean Associates), John Williams and Diana Yeomans (Austin Rover).

We are grateful to the Leverhulme Trust and the Open University for financial support that enabled us to carry out the British and US studies respectively.

WHO SHOULD READ THIS BOOK

We believe that corporate decision-makers, training managers and trainers, including present users of the technology, will find it interesting and thought-provoking. We also hope that they, and trainers of trainers, will find it useful because, although claims and anecdotes abound, there is little analytical information in this field. This book is a critical analysis of the new wave. We want it to stimulate discussion in many companies.

David Hawkridge, Milton Keynes, Buckinghamshire
Wendy Newton, Midsomer Norton, Avon
Carole Hall, Pleasanton, California

Part One

The Setting

1

Company Training Needs

INVESTING IN HUMAN RESOURCES

Companies spend huge sums of money each year on training. Training is a gigantic and expanding enterprise. IBM is reputed to spend $1 billion a year on training, worldwide. American Telephone and Telegraph (AT&T) is said to spend the same amount in the United States alone. Boyer (1985) put the figures for the United States at nearly 8 million trainees costing upwards of $40 billion annually. These sums are increasing. The American Society for Training and Development (1986), after surveying 750 large companies, reported that over half had increased their training budgets for the coming year. In Britain in 1984, the amount spent on training by industrial firms was only 0.3 per cent of annual turnover, compared with 3 per cent in the United States, but it amounted to 53 million worker/days spent on training (Manpower Services Commission, 1985), and the figure is rising.

This is investment in human resources on a grand scale. Much of it happens outside the formal education system, through on-the-job training and special off-the-job courses. One US study estimates that informal training amounts to 80–90 per cent of all job-related training (Lusterman, 1985).

Companies are not fully aware, however, of how much they are spending on training, as an important US study shows (Eurich, 1985). Holland (1986) points out that very few British companies have a budget line that includes all training costs. Training goes on in so many parts of most companies that the true cost is hidden. The largest single hidden item is without doubt the salaries and wages of employees while being trained. Calvert (1986) reports that only 7 per cent of the banks surveyed in his US study knew how much they

3

had spent on salaries paid to employees while being trained. Very few companies add up the cost, as Craig and Evers (1981) suggest they might, of trainers' and consultants' salaries, costs of hardware and software, rental of training facilities, administrative expenses, evaluation costs, costs of developing and printing training materials, and a proportion of company overheads. In other words, the size of the investment in training is even greater than it appears to be.

Why are companies spending so much on training? What needs are being met? Companies want employees whose training has given them the skills, knowledge and attitudes required to do their jobs well and safely. This is true whether these employees are managers, accountants, clerks or artisans, and whether their jobs are on the factory floor, in the office or the store. New employees often need training before they can be reasonably effective within a company. Existing employees require retraining because companies and jobs are changing and new technology is being installed: many workers now find their knowledge is out of date within a year or two if they have no retraining. In a 1984 study in Britain, Rajan (1985) found that there had been significant technical changes since 1980 in about 80 per cent of the 1650 manufacturers and 100 distributive companies he surveyed. New and existing employees may suddenly require training in how to use technology not accessible to universities and colleges, as Eurich (1985) mentions, nor perhaps to other competitor companies. Career development and promotion from the ranks cannot go ahead without company training.

There is also a realisation dawning on many companies that training can lead to increased sales. Training of a company's own employees leads to better quality products and services to customers, improving the image of the company with these customers. In some fields, such as computer manufacture, a company that provides good training to its customers, so that they can use its products efficiently (and sooner), improves its relationship with these customers and boosts its future chances of sales.

EXAMPLES OF COMPANY TRAINING NEEDS

Consider, for example, a company operating a large continuous processing plant, such as a nuclear power station or a petrochemical plant producing ammonia. Such a plant is still being designed while it is being built, to incorporate latest technical developments, yet employees must be fully trained to operate each plant efficiently and safely the moment it starts up. Once started, it cannot be stopped without the company incurring very heavy expense, therefore any employees who leave must be replaced immediately by fully trained newcomers. Employees must be trained to deal with modifications to the plant, such as the introduction of computerised controls aimed at saving energy or improving output. They must quickly acquire any new knowledge that comes to light about the plant's operations as a result of research or even as a consequence of disasters. Safe operation of the plant is vital, yet employees must be trained in complex emergency procedures without these emergencies actually being triggered, and without danger to other employees or expensive equipment. These employees cannot be trained on the plant itself, however, because the risks are too great.

Or consider a company, such as a bank or building society (savings and loan association in the United States), with many branches offering computerised financial services to thousands of clients. The Bank of America, for example, must train its employees because it sells services that incorporate new procedures, based on the technology, and aimed at providing greater benefit to the client and greater profit to the company. Mistakes can mar the reputation of the bank as a responsible financial institution. Mistakes, because they are costly to rectify, damage profits. Training is needed to improve the bank's image and increase profits.

In the machine-shops of manufacturing companies, there have been drastic technological changes. Simple numerical control (automation) of the 1950s gave way to computer numerical control in the 1970s, which was then displaced by direct numerical control and flexible manufacturing systems, all computer-based and largely outside the immediate control of operators on the shop floor (Brady, 1984). Such companies need to retrain operators for other jobs or in using their old craft skills in programming the new systems. Without retraining, bankruptcy may ensue.

Companies manufacturing electronic and other hi-tech products must cope with even more drastic changes, as their technology is upgraded each year. For example, besides IBM, US companies such as Apple Computer, Control Data Corporation, Digital Equipment Corporation, Hewlett-Packard, Texas Instruments, Wang and Xerox, must all retrain a large percentage of their employees. They do so to keep pace with products of their own scientific research and development and to retain employees who have acquired knowledge, experience and expertise that would be valuable to competitors. These companies have an extra training task, too: they must provide

5

training to employees of their customer companies, who will manage and use the hi-tech products.

Retail or distributive companies are not exempt from the need to train employees. There have been great changes in storage and distribution methods (Rajan, 1985). For example, B&Q Retail is a large British company selling do-it-yourself and gardening supplies. In 1986 it committed £2 million to a company training strategy. B&Q has special training needs because its retail stores are scattered all over the country. There is a high employee turnover, including weekend employees required for B&Q's six or seven days a week opening hours, and new employees must be quickly trained in the operation of each store, including such aspects as safety and spotting potential solvent abuse. Or take another example, Boots, a large British company that originally manufactured and marketed pharmaceutical products only. Boots has diversified its range of products, which are sold through a chain of high street retail stores. Boots has large numbers of retail employees, scattered in many branches, who must be trained in various systems and procedures. Bazeley (1985) identified training needs such as customer service, cash register training, health and safety, stockbooks, despatch and delivery. Many of the activities included in these topics are due for computerisation, therefore she expected a heavy demand for retraining. Electronic point of sale (EPOS) and electronic funds transfer (EFT) technology, as it is adopted in retail companies such as B&Q and Boots, will raise new training needs, not least in how to cope with malfunctions (Rajan, 1984).

Very large transportation companies such as British Airways have special training needs arising from the vast geographical spread of their systems and the rapid introduction of new and more complex technology. Safety is at a premium, and the cost of operational delays is high. Training must often fit within their employees' abnormal working hours.

At the other end of the scale, small companies also must train their employees, to enable them to cope with changing processes, procedures, technologies and markets. In a British study of small and medium-sized companies, however, Dorsman and Griffith (1986) found that training was thought of as an added cost rather than an investment and that these companies knew very little about new training technology. Another British study, by the Institution of Production Engineers (1986), found that most small manufacturing companies had no training policy at all and provided the minimum training. Even medium-sized companies (with 100–1000 employees) often did not employ a training officer or manager. A common problem mentioned by companies surveyed in this study was that they could not spare employees from everyday work, for training.

Regrettably, if these small and medium-sized companies fail to train, they lose their competitive edge, unless they can poach trained workers from larger companies. They particularly need training in such areas as management, interpersonal skills, safety, dealing with legislation and introduction of new technology.

Finally, agricultural companies deserve a mention. Farmers need training in decision-making with regard to their animals or crops. For example, they need to understand the year's cycle of work and the likely effects of different actions at various points in the year. They need to train themselves without leaving the farm, and must be able to update their knowledge at any time when decisions are required, rather than the time when a particular college course is being offered.

CLASSIFYING TRAINING NEEDS

Company training needs are classified in various ways. For example, many employees need training in skills and procedures, but these two categories are not very clearly defined. Thus a typist must learn the skills of using the keyboard, but some of these undoubtedly include learning procedures, that is, what to do in what order under what circumstances. A bank clerk has to learn many procedures, but few skills. Skills can be defined narrowly as requiring the skilful use of one's body, but in practice they are defined broadly, to include psychological as well as motor or muscular aspects. Seymour's (1986) skills analysis techniques focus on points at which the trainee must make difficult discriminations, as when a quality control inspector on a production line is required to spot small flaws that would be ignored by most people, or when a pilot is required to distinguish between responses of his aircraft to the controls.

Other categories of employees may require training in product knowledge or management. Again, these terms are interpreted somewhat vaguely. A 'product' may be a physical object made by the company, or it may be a service offered. For example, a telephone company's sales staff, and some of its other employees, must know about a new type of exchange being marketed by the company, and about a new telephone conferencing service available to customers. 'Management training' is an even fuzzier term.

Training of managers, and of people who will become managers, has numerous aspects, ranging from how to motivate employees to how to read a balance sheet and analyse complex situations. Commonly, the training needs include problem-solving, decision-making, time management, interviewing skills, leadership skills, managing meetings, and so on.

Needs analysis, task analysis and written task specifications should be and often are the prelude to a new training scheme, and, in the process, training needs are identified. But here too definitions are seldom clear enough to indicate beyond doubt the kind of training that should follow. Later, if evaluation is based on task specifications, difficulties can arise because the actual work often departs from what has been written down (see Chapter 17).

Do employees need to be trained in-house? Although companies send many employees to other agencies to be trained, there is evidence that most training in large companies is in-house, conducted within the company. This training may be on-the-job or off-the-job. Carnevale and Goldstein (1983) quote a figure of about 60 per cent for US in-house training, with a range from 43 per cent for service companies to 77 per cent for the mining industry. That is to say, in US companies, about 40 per cent of training is conducted off-the-job and off the companies' premises. We cannot quote equivalent data for British companies.

Quite apart from training their own employees, many companies also face the need to train their client's employees. This is particularly true of companies selling technically complex products and services, or where they extend their new technology systems of communication beyond their own boundaries. In Part Three, we describe the experience in this field of the Bank of America (see Chapter 7) and of computer manufacturers like Hewlett-Packard and Apple (see Chapter 9).

One further category of training need is to train the trainers. In this study, it became clear that many companies need to train their trainers how to exploit computers for training. There is a dearth of well-trained trainers, as even a very large company like British Steel recognised. Regrettably, small and medium-sized companies, if they have training officers at all, probably have comparatively untrained trainers.

Classifying training needs is a somewhat academic exercise, of course. Company managers and trainers tolerate well the difficulties of finding and using accurate descriptions and classifications for training needs. In everyday practice, terms like 'skills training' and

8

'procedures training' serve their purpose of giving a broad hint of trainers' aims in a particular course. Meyerson and Zemske (1985) claim that there has been a shift in the United States from technical to 'behavioural' training: this may be so, but the analysis depends on how these categories are defined.

UNION AND GOVERNMENT ATTITUDES

Large modern companies generally want their employees to be trained, and so do the unions. In the United States and Britain, unions have insisted on funds being set aside by employers for retraining their members to manage and use new technology. The US and British governments have thrown some weight behind the training effort, too, because they see training as a key to improved productivity and reduced unemployment. If proof is needed, a British study found that among private sector companies high business performance was strongly associated with a high level of training, on every single measure (Manpower Service Commission, 1985). The US Bureau of Labour Statistics (1982) predicts that by 1990 US industries that do much training will have grown faster than the rest. New laws now require employees to be properly trained. The US Department of Labour and the British Manpower Services Commission actively promote training, the latter the more so because Britain is far behind other industrialised countries in its general training provision.

SEARCHING FOR COST-EFFECTIVENESS

It seems certain that company training needs will continue to expand rapidly, as they have over the last few decades, according to Eurich (1985). This will be true for large, medium and small companies.

Training costs will rise at least as fast as training expands to meet these needs, unless ways can be found to increase the cost-effectiveness of training. Unfortunately, training costs are relatively higher for small companies, yet training must be done in any company that expands or changes its range of products and services.

The search is on, therefore, to find more cost-effective training. That is to say, companies want to exploit training techniques that either cost less for the same degree of effectiveness, or achieve greater effectiveness for the same cost. Techniques that cost more

9

must yield proportionately greater returns.

More cost-effective training brings a variety of benefits, not simply increased company profits. Ineffectual training is rightly despised by employees and rejected by managers, and damages company morale. Expensive training may seem prestigious at the time, but is only worthwhile when it is highly effective. What employees want is training, and retraining, that enables them to do the job well and safely. Only then can they gain greater job satisfaction. Of greatest value to the company is training that makes employees well-motivated and more competent.

Company policy-makers and decision-takers, not least the training managers, search ceaselessly for more cost-effective training techniques and tools. Low-technology, instructor-led or 'stand-up' training is still very widespread, accounting for more than 80 per cent of the training time, but providers of training technology are offering many products and services. Significantly, these providers have become themselves a hi-tech growth industry, part of the new wave — computer-based training and its associated technology — that is hitting the company shores.

2

Company Views of New Training Technology

DEFINING NEW TRAINING TECHNOLOGY

The new wave of training is based on new training technology. What do we mean by 'new training technology'? On the software side, the term encompasses an important new range of authoring tools that offer trainer-authors the chance to bring the hardware to bear on company training problems. The term encompasses the hardware, too. Trainers can draw on mainframe computers, with more or less 'intelligent' terminals and telecommunication systems, even including satellites. Trainers can also exploit microcomputers, which are becoming particularly valuable for training, because they can be used singly or linked in local networks, or together with videodisc or videocassette players.

Trainers see the arrival of computers and new communications systems as important because they hope the technology will make training more effective. As Kearsley (1983) stresses, computers offer training in which trainees must be active, not passive. Training through the new technology is different from conventional training through lectures, television or printed manuals. But is it more effective?

IS NEW TRAINING TECHNOLOGY MORE EFFECTIVE?

Companies look at training effectiveness in several different ways. In general, they want training to be appropriate to the individual, of course, but they also want it to produce more or less the same standard of performance in all employees doing a particular job. They are interested in any system that seems likely to control training by

11

standardising it. At the same, they may want to set about *decentralising* training, for a variety of reasons. Because time costs
money, and because it is seldom convenient to have their employees
training off-the-job, they are interested in *reducing time required* for
training. This may well lead to *saving on training costs*. In a few
cases, companies may judge training effectiveness in terms of its
success in *meeting sudden large-scale training needs*. Overall,
companies want training to result in *improved job performance*.

Standardising training

In training, increased standardisation is often equated with increased
effectiveness. Conventional 'stand-up' or instructor-led training is
notoriously unstandardised, varying with the trainer and training
centre.

Computer-based training, commonly known as 'CBT', appears to
offer standardisation. Eastman Kodak, for example, decided to use
microcomputers to standardise its training of field service engineers.
The trainees were widely scattered, worldwide, yet the training had
to be done quickly and in standardised form (Duc Quy and
Covington, 1982). Texaco Tankerships' trainees are even more
widely scattered, on board ships moving across the oceans. Yet
tanker crews need standardised and frequent training in safety and
emergency procedures. CBT is providing this.

CBT cannot guarantee standardisation of performance, as
opposed to standardisation of training, because ultimately, of
course, on-the-job performance depends on the individual as well as
the training. But it can increase the chances of performance being
up to a particular standard. Kearsley (1983) suggests that some
companies want increased control over training. With printed
manuals, branch offices use the existing material differently or
neglect it altogether, with very uneven results. Unstandardised training can be expensive in company systems that demand uniformity
(such as banks and insurance companies). Standardised training can
be introduced through CBT because the software can be developed
to include frequent testing and recording of progress and scores.

Decentralising training

Many companies are interested in the new technology because they think it will help them to decentralise training. Centralised training is expensive and difficult to organise, particularly in companies with far-flung branches, yet is necessary for conventional training if only a few trainers and training facilities are available. It can also be untimely. Training is always likely to be seen as more effective if it is available where and when needed. General Motors decided to put the training right on its island assembly system (see Chapter 8). Eastman Kodak decided to decentralise its training of field engineers (see Chapter 8). Again, the Texaco Tankerships case study (see Chapter 11) is a good example of CBT meeting these needs. In some companies, CBT may result in reduced demand for central training facilities and personnel. Fewer trainers may be needed.

Reducing training time

All companies want to reduce the time employees need to become properly trained, as this will reduce overall labour costs and increase profits. The more desperate ones either cannot afford to have employees away from the job or their staff turnover is so high that they need to reduce the ratio of training time to actual working time. Some have many part-time employees who need to be trained just as much as the full-timers. CBT has shown some remarkable savings: Orlansky (in Hart, 1983) reported an average saving of 30 per cent in the United States and, among the case studies in Part Three, Zale Corporation reported savings of 50 per cent. Austin Rover and Barclaycard are the most often quoted British examples of CBT reducing training time.

Saving on training costs

Companies hope the technology will produce savings. This is particularly true in large companies, which hope to reap economies of scale by training many employees using the same computer program. In this way, the high initial cost of CBT is set off against large numbers of trainees. In the United States, RSA/Information Design conducted two surveys of Fortune 500 (large and very large) companies in 1983 and 1984. Although less than a quarter of the companies replied, the data revealed increased actual and planned use of CBT, based on hopes of reduced costs for training in many fields. In a 1985 British survey, Intra Systems asked 90 organisations

13

(each with over 1000 employees) about the advantages and benefits of CBT. Of the 30 already using CBT, some claimed very significant savings. A larger survey in the same year by the Open University obtained 371 replies and showed that two-thirds of the 90 or so companies claiming to use CBT had more than 1000 employees. More than 70 per cent of these 90 companies wanted to know about the case for and against expenditure on CBT (Laurillard, 1986).

Meeting sudden large-scale training needs

Some companies face dramatically increased training needs because their functions or operations have been changed by legislation or deregulation. In Britain, the building societies came into this category in 1986 and had to consider carefully whether CBT could be used to train and retrain large numbers of staff scattered in many branches. When the Government introduced new sick pay regulations, Remploy needed to teach these to all its employees, most of whom are disabled (see Chapter 8). In American Telephone and Telegraph, CBT was developed and used to train employees, following a change in the structure of the company, brought about by new laws. A different kind of emergency arose at Allied Carpets, a company with a chain of stores in Britain. With more than two dozen new stores likely to open each year in an ambitious expansion programme, the company needed CBT to provide standardised training to new branch staff, and installed microcomputers with a 6.5 hour course developed for Allied Carpets by Mentor Interactive Training.

Improving job performance

Overall, companies are looking to training for improving job performance. If the new technology can train people to do their jobs better, then almost any company is likely to become interested in it. Kearsley (1983) offers several examples of companies wanting to use CBT to improve job performance or eliminate job problems. To quote Eastman Kodak again, the company knew that graphics and simulations would be valuable in teaching field service technicians. Motivating training was needed that would not simply sit on the shelf (Duc Quy and Covington, 1982). British Steel took the same approach: when the company decided to use interactive video for training workers on the 'pickle line' (see Chapter 8), it was looking for better performance on the job.

TRAINING THROUGH THE TECHNOLOGY

The coming of the new wave has been speeded up, of course, by companies installing computers and communications for purposes other than training. For example, banks already had terminals linked to a mainframe computer for accounting and administrative purposes. To use the terminals for training as well seemed to some managers and trainers to be an obvious step. Where training is built into the hardware used for such purposes, this is called 'embedded training', in the jargon of trainers.

Many early projects, such as British Airways' seat reservation system, were of this kind, the most obvious example of training through the technology. Many people using computers for their work, such as insurance agents and airline reservation clerks, can expect some embedded training now. At the very least, the computer systems offer them a range of job aids, and often there are CBT lessons available too.

COMPUTER MANUFACTURERS AND EMBEDDED TRAINING

Companies have responded very differently, however, to opportunities for introducing embedded training. Computer manufacturers are a specially interesting category in this respect. Confidently, IBM took the lead, years ago, with its own mainframe computers. The company regarded proper training of its employees as essential if it were to sell its hardware. Branscomb (1980) reported that about 10 000 IBM employees were using 400 terminals for training in IBM's US offices. Companies operating IBM mainframe computers could until recently purchase an IBM authoring system (see Chapter 4) with which to prepare their own in-company embedded training. IBM later adopted the same policy in marketing its microcomputers (personal computers or PCs). Field engineers, dealers and users of IBM products can therefore be trained partly through computers. Recently IBM has developed training that uses interactive videodisc packages with an IBM personal computer, with which IBM systems can be simulated.

Other US mainframe computer manufacturers have followed

15

IBM, offering embedded training to help buyers to learn to use their hardware and software. For example, the Xerox Documenter workstation incorporates embedded training. All Apple micro-computers are sold with embedded training. Hewlett-Packard sell to buyers of their computers embedded training for certain applica-tions. Digital Equipment Corporation offers interactive videodisc training material to purchasers of its mainframe computers.

What about companies that do not manufacture computers? Some have brought in embedded training. We have already mentioned British Airways as a prime instance, and the banks as pioneers. The Bank of America, to enhance the attractiveness of its computerised systems to potential client companies, offers embedded training to these clients as part of the deal.

DOUBTS ABOUT EMBEDDED TRAINING

There are other companies, however, that are much less certain of their policy on embedded training. In a British company that sells a wide range of products through retail stores, a feasibility study revealed confusion and scepticism. One manager pointed out that computer-time for embedded retail training would get a low priority, because training was seen as less urgent than, say, inventory control or budgeting for salaries. Another suggested that the single terminal to be provided in each store would be quite inadequate for training purposes. A third questioned whether the company knew how to produce computer programs for training its employees. Yet another wanted to be told the advantages of embedded CBT, when employees in stores were already ignoring the printed training manuals and videos put out by his company!

Or take the case of a British bank that has terminals in every one of its hundreds of branches, all linked to mainframe computers. The bank experimented with a videotex system that delivered embedded interactive training by telephone line to over 100 of these terminals. Within five years, it labelled videotex a 'zero-stretch' training technology, outside the mainstream of the bank's general informa-tion technology development, therefore not a long-term proposition. Not surprisingly, its own computer management services division looked askance at videotex, which eventually turned out to require a separate network of lines, a separate mainframe computer and separate maintenance and back-up. In 1987, this bank was at a crossroads, undecided about which forms of training technology to adopt for the immediate future. Its first criterion for choosing new technology was whether the new would replace the old training methods at the same or lower cost, and be at least as effective.

DEDICATED SYSTEMS

Not all companies, by any means, train through computers and communications they have installed for other purposes. Many companies have decided to buy separately the hardware and software required to carry the training. They have rejected the idea of embedded training and prefer to use systems that are dedicated to training.

One important reason for their different policy is that embedded training is often anathema to data processing departments, who do not want to support training within the service they provide to their companies. Even where a mainframe computer has plenty of spare capacity, data processing staff may find the training system intrusive. The reasons they give may sound somewhat like excuses, but they see training sessions as difficult and expensive to schedule and possibly even dangerous to data held in the computer. Training consequently receives low priority, and may in due time be pushed off the computer altogether as the spare capacity diminishes due to business expansion.

In Chapter 14 we discuss other reasons why embedded training is not for everyone. Some of these may seem trivial, like 'Where shall we put the terminals?', but they are very real to company staff, and stand in the way of adopting this form of CBT. Fortunately, dedicated systems offer an alternative, to meet different needs.

EXAMPLES OF COMPANIES USING DEDICATED SYSTEMS

For example, a British chain of do-it-yourself and gardening stores, B&Q, decided to spend £220 000 in 1986 on videodisc players and discs, for training use only. The initial feedback was 'It is so much better than what we were doing before', and some of the 70 store managers reported that advance bookings of the machines were running as much as five to six weeks ahead.

Another British company with a chain of stores, W.H. Smith, was more cautious in introducing the technology for training in-store travel agents. To start with, the company bought interactive videodisc

17

players for only three training centres and prepared a disc on travel package transactions as a pilot. The success of this pilot may well become the lever for changing company policy towards greater use of the new training technology, especially as EPOS (electronic point of sale) equipment is introduced.

GOVERNMENT INFLUENCE ON COMPANY VIEWS

Company views of new training technology have been influenced to some extent by actions and events beyond the commercial and industrial sphere. In the United States, the federal government has not directly intervened to encourage companies to take up new training technology. What is noticeable, however, is that very large sums of government money go into defence-related training in the United States and that many of the providers have developed training applications for the military. This places some providers in a strong position, as Kearsley's (1983) book shows. Their expertise and experience gained in defence contracts can be used to persuade companies to install the new technology for civilian training.

In Britain, government encouragement and intervention has been more direct. Since 1981, companies willing to experiment with new training technology have been able to obtain grants from the Manpower Services Commission towards the cost of well-designed projects, and providers have benefited accordingly. This has doubtless influenced company attitudes towards the technology, although some companies, such as Austin Rover and Barclays Bank, had embarked on using it well before government funds became available. The Commission has also fostered awareness through sponsoring a series of national conferences and vendors' exhibitions, and has paid for several surveys and studies aimed at improving companies' understanding of what the technology can offer.

COMPANY AWARENESS OF NEW TRAINING TECHNOLOGY

In 1987, at the time of writing, most companies in Britain and the United States seem to be still at the stage of becoming aware of the new training technology. A minority, almost all large companies, have gone beyond awareness to active interest and steps towards adoption (see Chapter 14). Thus Hirschbuhl (1986) was able to report that a 1985 survey of large US corporations indicated that 66 per cent of those responding were using CBT in one or more training areas. Datasolve Education (1987), a major British provider of CBT, reported that about 120 British companies had sent employees on its computer-based courses in 1986. Small and medium-sized companies prefer off-the-shelf training of this kind to developing their own. Development, testing and implementation of CBT (see Chapters 7–13, 15 and 16), however, are in full swing in several hundred companies. Evaluation, a particularly difficult process for any company (see Chapter 17), is being pursued with care and determination by only a handful.

The next chapter examines briefly the strategies companies use as they explore and move towards, or away from, the new technology for training.

3

Company Strategies

FINDING OUT ABOUT NEW TRAINING TECHNOLOGY

How do companies get to hear about new training technology? It seems as though companies have some difficulty in obtaining the information they feel they need for corporate decision-making about the new technology.

This information is available from several sources. Vendors freely circulate information about the products and services they offer, ranging from ready-made software packages and complete systems to consultancy on the needs of a particular company. Conferences and exhibitions of hardware and software bring vendors into contact with company trainers. Some providers maintain their own demonstration centres, and in Britain the National Interactive Video Centre is a good example of an information centre sponsored jointly by government and providers. Meetings of professional societies of trainers offer opportunities to exchange views. Books, journals and magazines (see Preface) convey information to managers as well as trainers. Contacts with other companies, at manager and trainer level, can be very important. Companies actually using the technology may be willing to talk about their experience. Those that have not yet adopted it can certainly learn from others in the same situation. Informal networks are vitally important.

In fact, companies obtain their information in quite a haphazard way, according to a US study by McLean (1985) of how 20 large US companies sought information about using interactive videodisc technology for training. Most of her respondents could not recall exactly when and where they had first heard of interactive videodisc, although providers were probably the main initial source. She found that trainers in these companies thought the publications then available were uncritical and not very useful. Trainers told her that the most valuable sources of information were other trainers, though these could be elusive. They said that adoption then occurred through chance factors. One company had already decided to invest in interactive videotape, rather than videodisc, when the manager met, by accident, a representative of a firm dealing in videodisc-based training. Following a reappraisal, the company invested $4 million in videodiscs.

Companies are faced with a fairly bewildering array of information, once they find it. For example, there are well over 100 authoring tools (see Chapter 4) on the market, not quite the same 100 in the United States as in Britain, but with substantial overlap. Even if the choice has been narrowed down because the buying company is already committed to a particular hardware manufacturer, many options probably remain. There are also over 100 providers in the market (both countries combined). Experienced providers seldom have only older hardware and software to offer, because they update and adapt their systems. Those who have recently joined the market lack experience in implementing their products. US vendors may have only American-style training products that possibly irk British trainees, and vice versa. In fact, very few British providers operate in the US market but, conversely, many British providers sell US products and some are subsidiaries of US vendor companies.

Five basic strategies are available to companies that want to find out about new technology in training in a systematic way. Advice is available from both consultants and vendors. Visits to other companies using CBT or considering using it can be very valuable, as can joining a user group. Lastly, the company's own resources may prove surprisingly useful. These strategies are worth examining in more detail.

ASKING CONSULTANTS

Many companies ask one or more consultants for advice. Consultants in this field, as in others, do not know about all the options available, however, because they have their own problems in getting up-to-date information. What a consultant can do for the client is to analyse the company's needs, in consultation with the managers and trainers, and propose at least one solution, which may well include training hardware and software of a particular provider with whom the consultant has worked satisfactorily before.

Some consultants will offer to prepare a report containing:

(a) a training needs analysis;
(b) a design specification, including objectives;
(c) a schedule for development of CBT in the company;
(d) a staffing and resources plan;
(e) a costing;
(f) a cost-benefit analysis that compares at least two alternatives, based upon predicted throughput of trainees;
(g) advice on maintenance and support of the system, once installed;
(h) names of possible suppliers.

The company will normally receive the consultant's best estimates, founded on his or her knowledge and experience, but forecasts in this field are notoriously inaccurate. In particular, in-company development times and costs are frequently underestimated by both the company and the consultant.

ASKING SEVERAL VENDORS

Another company strategy is to ask several vendors to provide details and demonstrations of their products and services. Before a company can adopt this strategy, it must have a good idea of what it wants. If it has not drawn up a training needs analysis and possibly a design specification, then the providers are likely to press for one. Up to a point, they may be willing to assist the company without charge in arriving at a written statement, but they can reasonably ask for consulting fees if the assessment of training needs really has not been done by the company. A company that calls for bids in the hope that it can get plenty of free consulting will be unpopular among providers, for sound reasons. Yet providers recognise that there is a learning process for both sides: providers must learn about the company, and the company about the providers. Sometimes consultants will suggest an even more fundamental step, a company analysis, before training needs are analysed. Not all company problems can be solved by training!

Some vendors provide consultancy services, but needless to say they advocate their own products. One brochure, for example, declares that the provider will conduct a short study 'to determine how your particular application fits the technology'. Vendors may offer technology-driven solutions. Some years ago, a US survey research group did a market survey for the Corporation for Public Broadcasting to identify potential training applications for interactive videodisc (Butterfield Communications Group, 1983). This was certainly a case of a solution looking for a problem, whereas companies want solutions based firmly on their training problems and needs.

One natural consequence of asking several vendors may be that the company is pressed to adopt a particular system. We discuss issues at stake in Chapter 14.

VISITING OTHER COMPANIES

A third company strategy is to visit other companies in the same line of business, both ones using the technology and those merely considering it. There is much to be learned from their successes and failures, particularly the latter. Companies using older systems may be able to warn about problems that have arisen, as well as exhibiting their successes.

Of course, if these companies are competitors, they may be unwilling to talk much. Or they may have proprietary products which they are unwilling to demonstrate. Even vendors have to be careful about saying too much about the details of development and implementation in some of the companies they sell to, particularly if something very new is being tried out.

Alternatively, it may make sense to visit a wide range of user companies. As these are less likely to be in direct competition, exchange of information may be freer. The systems of different providers can be observed in operation and the user companies may be willing to talk about the advantages and disadvantages of each.

Visiting conferences, trade shows and exhibitions, where other user companies are present together with providers, is an excellent source of information. In both the United States and Britain each year there are several national gatherings of this kind on computer-based training and/or interactive videodisc. Vendors demonstrate their products and offer seminars, and so do some user companies.

JOINING A USER GROUP

A fourth strategy, open to some companies, is to join a user group. All its members will be using one provider's products and services, and at meetings of the group there is usually full and frank discussion of new developments and of problems, often with a representative of the provider present. Although these groups are particularly useful to companies that have already adopted systems, they can be helpful to those trying to obtain information.

Unfortunately, only the larger providers have set up user groups. For example, Goal Systems, which markets the *PHOENIX* authoring system, sponsors a number of regional user groups in the United States. In Britain, Mentor Interactive Training in 1986 set up a user group of more than 30 companies training with its products.

USING THE COMPANY'S OWN RESOURCES

Finally, a fifth strategy is to use the internal services of the company. Companies that have large data processing and training departments may well have employees who are qualified to assess vendors' products. Instead of buying in services, a company may decide to establish a team across departments, taking into account interdepartmental politics, and charge it with the task of advising management of the options.

As always, using the company's own resources has important payoffs in terms of motivation and involvement of employees. There is less danger of a technology-based training solution being foisted onto trainees. If the company lacks particular skills in its team, it may be possible to second one or two employees for specialised crash training. Ultimately, the team may become an in-house CBT development group, as happened at Standard Chartered Bank, for example, when interactive videodiscs were being made for training purposes.

COMBINING STRATEGIES TO REDUCE RISKS

These strategies are seldom used singly. Most companies decide to use two or three, in parallel or in sequence, before deciding whether to invest money in the new technology for training.

Some companies want to start with a small, cheap system over which they feel they have a good deal of control. In other words, they want to minimise the risks. For example, Rank Xerox trainers found it easy to convince the managers to invest in a low-cost £3000 system, *Take Five*, based on well-known hardware (the BBC-B microcomputer and a videotape recorder). This was partly because Rank Xerox already had its own video studio and favoured having its own employees, rather than actors, on the tapes. It was also because the trainers themselves could produce, test and revise the packages in a reasonably short time, without calling in an outside team.

Chevron Information Technology Company reduced the risk of a poor investment in CBT by carrying out two assessments rather than one before making its choice. First, its trainers visited a major CBT conference where they could see the range of offerings available and talk to many providers and users. Second, they evaluated several different authoring systems before choosing one that was still under development, *ADROIT* (see Chapter 6).

PILOT STUDIES

Other companies want to reduce risks by first conducting a pilot, perhaps making use of an existing mainframe system with terminals. For example, British Gas South East (SEGAS) set up in 1979 quite a large two year pilot during which about 25 basic training packages were developed and tested through some 200 terminals. The company decided to try CBT because there was a general demand for increased training efficiency, and because reduced manning levels were making it difficult for units to release employees for training at a specified time. Standardised but individualised and highly effective training was required. Many of SEGAS's prototypes had to be shelved or modified, but over 100 packages are now in use, introduced in a carefully planned way and available through some 2000 terminals. Whereas computer-based training was at first seen to be mainly for employees at lower levels, now it is being used by managerial staff as well (Randall, 1986).

Another British company, the Abbey National Building Society, carried out a pilot project using microcomputers in just thirteen of its branches (see Chapter 7). Not all the branches participated fully, yet 84 per cent of the trainees who used CBT felt positive about it, and the company is expanding its computer-based training. Similarly, the Midland Bank commissioned development of a pilot

25

interactive videodisc, using existing training materials, to explore the feasibility of this training medium.

In the United States, Syntex, the pharmaceutical company, moved through several stages in its relationship with a provider, Picodyne, before adopting CBT developed by Picodyne for its sales representatives (see Chapter 10). Zales, a retail jewellery chain, developed interactive videotape on a small scale, then expanded the system to offer more than 40 courses.

Each company has to develop its own assessment process before deciding whether to adopt the technology, as McLean (1985) found in her US survey. Laurillard (1986) does not favour small-scale pilot projects, however, saying that a 'minimum critical mass' is needed before CBT becomes visible in a company. A company that assigns a budget and staff, and decides on objectives and a time-scale is much more likely to find CBT working well for it. She suggests that CBT has to become an integrated part of a company's organisation, not simply an optional extra. In one very large US company we visited in California, CBT had been given to a single member of staff to 'explore', and we were told that her position in the company was not secure.

WHY DO COMPANIES REJECT THE NEW TRAINING TECHNOLOGY?

The single factor that most often leads companies to turn away from the new technology after a period of interest in it is the loss of a board member or manager who was enthusiastic about it. When the drive from the board or management suddenly stops, company strategy falters, pilot projects die unnoticed and trainers can seldom follow up successfully the initiative the board member or manager took.

There seems little doubt, however, that computer-based training in a company needs a strong training department, with staff who are willing to be innovative. If there is no such commitment, then the company is likely to turn away from the technology.

Occasionally, management must bear the responsibility for a company gaining a poor opinion of CBT. Sometimes trainers are given little or no role to play in the decision-making process. For example, one British company decided, at top level, to introduce a local area network to provide electronic mail for managerial staff. The system's American-made software included an embedded help and training package, much like a training manual. The company's trainers had no say in the matter, and the embedded training was poorly used by the managers who, not surprisingly, thought it was less than helpful.

Providers and consultants must sometimes take the blame. Even with a strong training department that includes one or more experienced trainer-authors, a company may decide against adopting computer-based training for reasons related more to a provider's approach than to inherent qualities of the technology. Providers, in their enthusiasm for their product and driven by the need to make a profit in a highly competitive market, may occasionally sell an inappropriate authoring system, say, to a company. Consultants may misjudge the company's situation and offer recommendations that cannot be implemented. Nothing is so damning to computer-based training as pieces of hardware and software merely gathering dust, therefore experienced providers and consultants do their best to ensure that the system is appropriate.

Companies that have already invested large sums in computer-based training may find, with the passage of time, that they cannot sustain the effort required to maintain the system. There are certainly cases where a mainframe system had spare capacity, available for training purposes, that was gradually used up. After a few years, training was low on the priority list, employees were frustrated at having to wait for a convenient time for training and the programs were used less and less.

THE COST OF WAIT-AND-SEE

Inevitably, we found companies in our study that had decided to adopt a wait-and-see attitude. They were hoping that something better would come along, without the major problems that still surround CBT (see Parts Three and Four). Some were well-informed. Others were not, though they showed interest in what we were going to write.

What is the cost of waiting? Or to put it the other way round, what is the cost of plunging in, of not waiting? Both are very difficult to assess in a general way, although we offer some suggestions about what lies ahead in Part Five. A great deal depends on the particular company, and we certainly do not believe that all companies should be adopting CBT. Instead, we strongly affirm that all companies should analyse their training needs and be aware of what CBT is and what it can do.

In the next three chapters, we discuss the full range of what the providers have to offer, and at the same time we introduce much of the technology.

Part Two

The Technology

4

Authoring Tools

THE SOFTWARE OPTIONS

Making the decision to move into computer-based training is not easy for any company, as this book clearly demonstrates. Our aim in Chapters 4, 5 and 6 is to provide an overview of the chief software and hardware options. We deal first with software because company experience shows repeatedly that correct software choices are more vital even than choosing the best hardware, although naturally the two must be compatible. Understanding what the software can and cannot do is the first step in making a sound decision in this field.

There are four basic choices regarding the training software, that is to say, the programs that actually do the training. A company can:

(a) *Buy the software off-the-shelf*, already developed, from a provider (Rothwell, 1987, offers advice). This kind of software is often called 'generic', because it usually provides training in skills commonly needed in many companies. Providers like Computer Systems Research, Comsell, Control Data Corporation, Datasolve Education, Deltak, Education Technology, Interactive Information Systems, Maxim Training Systems, NCR, Rank Training, White Rose Systems, to mention only a few, all sell generic software, suitable for straightforward CBT on mainframes and/or micro-computers, and/or for interactive videodisc CBT. Within the data processing market, Digital Equipment Corporation, Hewlett-Packard, IBM and others also sell generic software (see Chapter 9).

(b) *Commission development of generic software by a provider for company use and for sale to other companies*. For instance, Jaguar Cars decided to commission from the National Computing Centre an interactive videodisc, *Introduction to Industrial Robots*,

31

now on open sale. The Electrical, Electronic, Telecommunications and Plumbing Union commissioned a disc from Epic Industrial Communications on solid state electronics. National Westminster Bank made this choice when it asked Interactive Information Services to produce the interactive videodisc *Smile — You're on the Telephone*. In the United States, IBM offered interactive videodiscs for training to its 2000 dealers.

(c) *Commission development of software by a provider, solely for its own use*. This kind of software is sometimes called 'company-specific', or even 'non-generic'. Kellogg, the US petrochemical group, commissioned software for a simulation of ammonia processing plant operations. TransWorld Airlines commissioned software covering operating procedures for flying McDonnell-Douglas DC-9 aircraft by autopilot.

(d) *Develop company-specific software using its own trainers* and, if necessary, programmers, possibly in collaboration with a provider. Remploy, for instance, developed its *Statutory Sick Pay* software in collaboration with PMSL Mentor (now Mentor Interactive Training). British Nuclear Fuels developed 36 software packages, covering training activities from induction to management, in collaboration with Marconi Instruments.

DEFINING AUTHORING TOOLS

Whichever choice is made during the adoption stage (see Chapter 14), developing CBT software requires authoring tools. What are these tools?

Authoring tools, as Heaford (1985) calls them, consist mainly of programming languages and computer programs written in these languages. He puts them into four categories: general programming languages, authoring languages, authoring systems, and integrated authoring systems. These four represent a progression over the last 25 years and the differences between them are worth looking into.

General programming languages

Not surprisingly, authoring tools have evolved considerably, more or less in parallel with the evolution of other software (O'Neal, 1986a). Early authoring systems of the 1960s used well-known general purpose programming languages, such as FORTRAN

(FORmula TRANslator), BASIC (Beginners' All-Purpose Symbolic Instruction Code) and COBOL (COmmon Business Oriented Language), to develop computer-based training.

Regrettably, these languages did not easily handle the text and graphics needed to carry out training. Nor did they deal well with trainees' answers. If a company insisted on preparing training materials using these languages, it had to employ at some expense a very competent programmer, and found its options limited.

Today there are operating systems (the software that runs a computer's basic operations) that offer certain built-in facilities. For example, MS-DOS (*Microsoft's Disk Operating System*), *Unix* and Digital Research's *GEM* all permit a degree of authoring, as do sophisticated languages such as Forth, Pascal and C. But using operating systems in all but very simple ways is still a task for programmers, not trainers, a point overlooked by Blackburn (1986) in advocating their use. He is right, however, in pointing out that companies which already have computers usually have such systems available and do not necessarily have to buy other authoring tools.

Authoring languages

Although general programming languages are still used to prepare CBT, the next advance was to develop special commands and syntax, or what came to be known as authoring languages. IBM's *Coursewriter* and Control Data Corporation's *TUTOR* were among the first, and required a mainframe computer. Such authoring languages offer short-cuts and save time, as Dean and Whitlock (1983) show. There is no need for a programmer to write the subprograms required for introducing text, graphics, questions, answers, or other training components. Depending on the complexity of the language, the programming for these is built in, ready to be used by a trainer who knows only a little about program writing. Even in the late 1960s these languages made it possible for a trainer-author to replicate simple patterns within the instruction, such as question-and-answer. Programmers were no longer essential for producing CBT. Productivity began to rise sharply among the producers.

Authoring systems

Building up these relatively simple languages into authoring systems took a great deal of development effort, and in the United States the government provided assistance. Large, powerful computers, called mainframes (see Chapter 5), have been used widely in industrial and commercial settings since the 1960s, and by the early 1970s several mainframe manufacturers were offering authoring systems for computer-based training. For example, IBM's *Coursewriter* was assimilated into the IBM *Interactive Instructional System* (*IIS*). Yeates (1986) was able to report that over 2000 installations worldwide were using *IIS*, with another 1200 using the compatible Westinghouse software.

These systems were mainly for training data processing employees. In the United States, Control Data Corporation (CDC) developed *TUTOR*, the Hazeltine Corporation had authoring systems for *TICCIT*, and in Britain International Computers Limited produced its little-used *ARIES*. All of these were developed initially for mainframe computers (see Chapter 5).

Integrated authoring systems for mainframe computers

WICAT first used the *CDS* authoring system, which offered trainer-authors a choice of strategies, through menus and prompts on the screen. Later, WICAT moved on to develop *WISE* and the Hazeltine Corporation brought out *TICCIT's Adapt*. These are integrated authoring systems, with three tiers. First, they use an advanced authoring language to offer a choice of strategies and many aids. Second, they enable trainer-authors to resort to more basic authoring languages to modify the strategies if desired. Third, they also allow trainers to direct the trainees to go to any general purpose programs that can be run on the computer being used. This means that trainees could find themselves using a word-processing or database program as part of the training. If necessary, a subprogram can be written for the trainer-author by a programmer, to carry out something unusual that is not catered for by the system (O'Neal, 1986a).

Integrated authoring systems are now being considered for use with new microcomputers that have substantially increased memory. A few companies are developing this type of integration for CBT through linking microcomputers and mainframes. American Express is one of the most successful, having programmed an IBM System 36 minicomputer to do some of the more memory-intensive work required by an expanded authoring system (see Chapter 7).

Several authoring systems for mainframe computers have been

redeveloped for use on microcomputers, as Drinkall (1985) points out. The most recent innovations in authoring are almost all geared to microcomputers, permitting use of full colour graphics and interactive video, which have not been incorporated into most main-frame systems. The range of authoring tools developed specifically for microcomputers is discussed in Chapter 6.

ROTHWELL'S CLASSIFICATION OF AUTHORING SYSTEMS

Rothwell (1983b) suggests a fourfold classification of authoring systems, though she accepts that there are now many hybrid varieties.

(a) *Form-driven systems*: the trainer using these is doing little more than filling in a 'form' that appears on the computer screen (and may be completed on paper beforehand), in determining the course structure, question-and-answer sequences, branching and so on, for example *IIS* and *TICCIT's APT*.

(b) *Prompting systems*: instead of a form, questions appear on the screen, and the trainer answers them to construct the training program according to a predetermined training strategy, for example, *Easywriter*.

(c) *Macro-based systems*: the trainer can use commands to present text, specify branching, incorporate data and so on.

(d) *Menu-driven systems*: by selecting commands from successive menus, the trainer can employ a variety of training strategies, for example, *ADROIT*, *Mandarin*, *Mentor II*, *Micro-PLATO* and *WISE*.

The hybrid or integrated systems that, for instance, combine prompts with menus, are really multilevel, says O'Neal (1986b), because authors leave the menus and, provided they can program, use general purpose programming languages to develop the detailed training sequences they want.

CONCURRENT AUTHORING SYSTEMS

Among the most recent authoring systems are those that are termed concurrent. Pacific Bell uses one to train employees to use applications software. This is a system that runs *with* the software it teaches about, effectively 'wrapping' the software program to control trainee interaction. Concurrent systems save considerable development time by eliminating the need to re-create the entire application program for a simulation. In 1987, other examples were *CAS* (*Concurrent Authoring System*) by Evergreen Technologies, *ADROIT*, the *Trillian Concurrent Authoring System* by Trillian Computer Corporation, *Auto Trainer* by Software Recording Corporation of America, and *Shelley* by ComTrain.

As Judd (1986) points out, there are three types of concurrent authoring system, distinguished from each other by the way in which the applications software is related to the authoring software. Embedded systems entail the authoring software having 'hooks' to the applications software, allowing continuous monitoring of performance. Co-resident systems hold both sets of software in memory simultaneously, so that the author has to swap from one to the other explicitly and cannot monitor performance. Shell systems (see Part Five) provide continuous monitoring and require no hooks.

CHARACTERISTICS OF AN IDEAL AUTHORING SYSTEM

Ideally, an authoring system should help trainers to decide on the content and sequence of training. Such a system does not yet exist, although Mudrick (1986) describes what he perceives as desirable features. In our opinion, it might be linked to a databank of content (for example, training needs specifications, task analyses, etc.) which would help trainers to review what was needed. CDC's *TUTOR* offers a simple way of organising content hierarchically, but in doing so presupposes that hierarchies can be found in all content, which they cannot. *Mandarin* (see Chapter 6) provides a way of laying out the course structure on the screen, and stores the content accordingly, which is helpful.

The ideal system should be able to cope with several training strategies, including those modified by information about an individual trainee's characteristics. *Mandarin*, one of the most recent products on the British market, has no capabilities of this kind. In Chapter 19 we discuss Naughton's (1986) views on how artificial intelligence may be able to help develop more responsive CBT programs. Artificial intelligence research may yield the basis for an ideal authoring system that is capable of analysing and responding to trainees' plain language (in their own words) questions and answers. At present, CBT systems ask all the questions and allow trainees only a limited range of answers (Dean and Whitlock, 1983, provide examples).

The ideal system should be 'transparent' to the trainer-author: it should not demand the learning of elaborate codes and procedures. It should be in plain language. Nordberg (1986) points out that popular spreadsheet programs, such as Lotus 1-2-3, have the virtue of allowing business people to see their data in the way they are used to, in columns (and rows), and to see what changing data in one column does to the other columns. He neglects to mention, however, that even these programs employ codes that require time to master. Perhaps what is needed is something closer to Apple Macintosh programs, which use small symbols on the screen (icons) and plain language menus instead of code letters. Working with them is more intuitive than logical.

Many present-day authoring systems lack good word processing capabilities, and they offer only rudimentary advice on screen design. Ideally, a system should offer the trainer-author facilities at two or three levels: a basic word processor should be available for roughing out the course, then more sophisticated levels for polishing it.

The ideal system should assist in the evaluation of the programs made with it, by having sophisticated facilities to collect data from students and to identify the programs' weak points. Many existing systems do little more than keep a record of trainees' progress through modules, and may keep test scores for the trainer to scrutinise periodically. Using such data for evaluation is not easy, since weak performance by trainees does not necessarily mean weak training by the computer (see Chapter 17).

Finally, the ideal authoring system should enable the trainer-author to improve and update the programs as often as necessary, without having to throw away programs because a new microcomputer has appeared and the old one is obsolete. Regrettably, no such system exists. There have been proposals for a 'virtual' definition: such a definition would state the minimum technical requirements of the hardware and software, in the hope that quite inexpensive systems could meet the standard. The fact is, however, that many different authoring systems have appeared, in competition with each other, and the providers feel obliged to make each one unique, to protect their rights.

THE CASE OF MOUNTAIN BELL

Mountain Bell, located in Colorado, is part of the US telcommunication network. Its training and education department is developing on Wang computers a system aimed at facilitating the entire instructional design process. Expected to be fully functional in 1987, the system is for use by Mountain Bell's technical and management training staff.

The authoring system will aid trainers at various ways. It will provide for data collection and sampling, store data with the appropriate training task, establish a task hierarchy, provide skill knowledge statements and objectives, based on its data, determine the appropriate format and suggest job aids, decision tables and general training materials.

The aim is that the course developer using the system will have computerised tools for completing any phase of his or her work. For example, as part of a needs analysis, the system produces a comprehensive interview guide. After the interview, the developer will put the data collected into a database ready for future use. All later data is added to the system and used wherever appropriate during implementation and evaluation. Thus the developer can use data to determine the cost-worth ratio of any CBT prepared.

This ambitious project may lead the way towards an ideal authoring system, and we await publication with interest. At the same time, we have to add that new authoring systems are coming onto the market by the score each year, and almost as many are disappearing!

5

Mainframe Systems

EARLY CBT AND MAINFRAME SYSTEMS

In a sense, CBT is not new. In some form, it has been available for more than 20 years, almost since mainframe computers were first installed in industrial and commercial companies. These computers used to occupy very considerable amounts of space, but now occupy rather less. As a rough guide, mainframe computers (which, confusingly, include minicomputers) require a room, rather than a desktop or two, and their size of memory and processing power still distinguishes them from microcomputers, though the gap is closing. They still serve large organisations, often through terminals located in widely scattered offices.

Early forms of CBT were developed entirely on mainframe computers, because CBT required the power then only available on large systems and microcomputers did not yet exist. But Beech (1983) notes that mainframes in those early days were cumbersome. Putting data into them was done by means of punched cards or paper tape, and the output was on screens with poor definition or on slow, noisy printers. Mainframes were also expensive. O'Neal (1986b) estimates that costs in the 1960s were about $50 000 per workstation. Today, the power of mainframe machines is still very useful for CBT, particularly when a company already has one with a large number of terminals that share the mainframe's time. The cost per workstation has dropped significantly, too.

TYPES OF MAINFRAME SYSTEMS

We ought to distinguish the main types. *Piggyback* systems are so called because they run on already installed computers, usually large mainframes manufactured by well-known providers such as IBM. If a piggyback system is used to train employees to use the mainframe, this is called *embedded* computer-based training. Embedded CBT runs on hardware that is used daily for other purposes besides training. Mayer (1967) was probably one of the first to report on programming a mainframe to train employees to use it.

Mainframes also permitted the development of large integrated systems of mainframes and terminals that do not offer embedded CBT and are not piggyback systems. These are systems *dedicated* to education and training tasks and used for nothing else. The only applications software used on them is education or training software.

Piggyback systems

These systems were among the earliest to be developed, being used initially to train data processing employees. For example, IBM developed its *Interactive Instructional System* (*IIS*), and Boeing Computer Services brought out its *Scholar/Teach 3* system, which also runs on IBM mainframes. Neither could provide graphics, yet IBM developed a useful range of CBT for data processing employees, and Boeing did the same for its own employees and for airline personnel. Digital Equipment Corporation (DEC) had its *Dimension* authoring system, Honeywell the *CAN* instructional system and *NATAL* authoring language, and Sperry Univac the *Advanced System for Education and Training*, but all three were less developed than *IIS* or *Scholar/Teach 3* (Kearsley, 1983).

IBM's *Interactive Instructional Authoring System* (*IIAS*) requires trainers to use various worksheets, on which they enter the CBT components, such as instructions, questions, answers and so on. From these, the course is developed, frame by frame. Alternatively, IIAS can cope with simulations of segments of other IBM applications, such as operating a system that searches a database. Full colour graphics are feasible, depending on the type of terminal available. The presentation system (*IIPS*) can keep full records of each trainees's progress.

Probably the best known piggyback system is Goal Systems International's *PHOENIX*, which is based on IBM's *IIS* but has more authoring and training facilities. It was developed for IBM mainframes but some non-IBM equipment can be tied into it too. According to Hickey (1985, 1986), *PHOENIX* is the leading mainframe

CBT system. Over 1200 organisations (not all companies) were using it then in the United States and about 160 in Britain. In 1987, Goal Systems claimed over 3000 users in 1600 locations. Deltak has provided a version known as *PHOENIX/DS*.

The *PHOENIX* authoring system is called *EASE* (*Easy Authoring System for Education*). *EASE* (Version 6.0) has good word processing capabilities and some graphics. Colour can be added. It provides a good variety of choices through menus. Drill and practice sequences are straightforward to develop. Tutorial sequences are simple enough to write if they consist of not more than branching from multiple-choice questions. Simulations and complex problem-solving are more difficult, although Dean and Whitlock (1983) say that there is no difficulty in using algebraic and trigonometric formulae in the training material.

PHOENIX includes various facilities needed to guide and record the progress of trainees. Thus a trainer can inspect trainees' scores and note which materials they have not yet studied or mastered. The system also records times, dates and sessions of study.

PHOENIX's original popularity was based on its suitability for use on IBM mainframes, the workhorses for many large US companies such as American Express (see Chapter 7), and on the simplicity of its authoring system, which provided for many of the conventional training strategies commonly used by US trainers. Goal Systems now markets generic software for it, on business-related topics. A *PHOENIX* version suitable for IBM personal computers (PCs) was published in 1986. Authoring can now be done on either a mainframe or a personal computer, although there is not, as yet, complete transportability between the two. The mainframe cannot accommodate PC graphics and the personal computer cannot handle the memory-intensive record-keeping dealt with by the mainframe.

One further type of piggyback system running on mainframe computers is to be found in the large-scale simulators that are used in training airline pilots and power-station controllers (see Chapters 11 and 13). The size of memory and speed of processing required to simulate operation of such complex machinery and systems is beyond present-day microcomputers, and instead the systems run on mainframe computers installed for other purposes.

Embedded systems

Embedded CBT has four main elements, accordingly to Bentley (1986): the training system, the operations system, the interactive help system, and a training database. Take, for example, a bank employee using a new computerised ledger system. The ledger system is the operational system. Overlaid upon it is the training system, to which the employee can move easily by pressing a function key. The training system offers a menu with several options. On selecting one, the employee begins training and can call up portions of the operational system's programmes to carry out exercises in, say, entering certain types of financial data. For these exercises, the computer calls up the training database, rather than using the real database containing customers' accounts. Within the training *and* on returning to the operational system, the employee can use the interactive help as required. Airline check-in counter and ticket clerks use a similar embedded training system as, for example, at British Airways (see Chapter 11).

Embedded training on mainframes must be publicised within the company: employees may not even know it is there, says Reid (1985), unless it is advertised and unless employees are expected to take time to use it. We should also note here that one type of concurrent authoring system, used in developing embedded training, is (confusingly) termed embedded.

Dedicated systems

Bitzer (1977), who led the early research and development work for *PLATO* (see below) envisioned a system for schools, colleges and universities with a million terminals; more recently Gooler (1986) has described a proposed nationwide North American system based on mainframes linked by satellite at night to microcomputers in schools. This proposal was backed by American Telephone and Telegraph, but at the time of writing this book it was being implemented only in a small part of Canada.

Such giant schemes might just be technically feasible for education, but they are not for trainers in business and industry. The nearest trainers come to using such far-flung yet integrated systems is when they turn to videotex (viewdata, or Prestel in Britain) to deliver CBT. Videotex consists of television sets or other quite simple terminals, linked by telephone line to a central mainframe.

In Britain, Barclays Bank installed a large network of this type to train employees in more than a hundred branch offices (see Chapter 7), and British travel agents are experimenting with a similar system (see Chapter 11).

On a smaller geographical scale, dedicated mainframe systems are used to support CBT that is separate from the operational systems (not embedded) and runs on the developers' own computers (not piggybacking on already installed machines). Four US companies have developed CBT systems of this type, and these deserve further mention (see Chapter 4 for details of their authoring systems). They are *PLATO, TICCIT*, WICAT's *WISE* and Regency System's *USE*, all marketed in both the United States and Britain.

PLATO (Programmed Learning for Automated Teaching Operations) started in 1959 as an educational research project at the University of Illinois with grants from the US Government. In the 1970s it was taken over by Control Data Corporation (CDC), which has developed and marketed it, claiming in 1987 that it was the world's most successful training system. *PLATO*'s hardware consists of a time-sharing mainframe computer (for many years the CDC Cyber 70) with a large number of terminals connected to it by telephone lines. Each terminal has a keyboard and a high-resolution monitor with a touch-sensitive screen. Most CBT developed for *PLATO* calls for considerable touching of this screen by trainees as they respond to questions. *PLATO*'s original authoring system was *TUTOR*, which has evolved into *PAL* (*PLATO Authoring Language*). *PLATO* enables trainers to present text and analyse trainees' answers, but they can also use graphics (with a special editor), animation, change the size or style of the text, all with assistance from 'help' screens and consultants available through the system itself. For example, Kearsley (1983) mentions that Commercial Credit Corporation, a US subsidiary of Control Data Corporation, used *PLATO* to develop a simulation of sales calls, to train its sales staff. When *PLATO* is in action, the *PLATO Learning Management (PLM)* system administers tests, collects the marks and sends trainees to the next module (Beech, 1983). There is a central software 'bank' of 10 000 hours' worth of instruction, much of it academic.

Companies that want to make use of the mainframe *PLATO* system have three training options. They can send trainees to a CDC study centre in which there are terminals linked to the central bank of courses. They can set up their own terminals, so that trainees study on the companies' premises, or they can develop their own courses, using *TUTOR* or *PAL*, on their own complete *PLATO* system, as did Travenol Laboratories (see below), Plessey Microsystems (see Chapter 8) and Toledo Edison Power (see Chapter 13).

PLATO has a sophisticated management system (*PLATO Learning Management or PLM*) which records trainees' progress in detail and enables trainers to specify what particular trainees should study next (Kearsley, 1983, provides a detailed account). British Airways introduced the complete *PLATO* system for training aircrew (see Chapter 11). Travenol is part of a large company that develops, manufactures and markets hospital products, according to Rothwell (1983a). To meet its training needs, the company decided to experiment with CBT. It selected off-the-shelf *PLATO* courses and hardware, and, using the *TUTOR* authoring language began to develop its own packages for trainee induction. With only one terminal, development and training were slow, but trainees liked CBT.

The *TICCIT* (*Timeshared Interactive Computer Controlled Instructional Television*) system was developed for education and training by the Mitre Corporation, again with grants from the US Government. In 1976, it was handed over to the Hazeltine Corporation, which now markets it. *TICCIT* runs on a dedicated time-sharing Data General minicomputer, designed to serve no more than 128 terminals, compared with *PLATO*'s much larger timesharing capabilities. Its terminals have a light-pen for inputs, and the system is capable of showing videotapes from a central store, hence the word 'Television' in its title. *TICCIT* originally had an authoring system named *APT* (*Authoring Procedure for TICCIT*) that incorporated a strategy based on psychological research: trainer-authors worked within a rigid framework of rule, example, practice, help. They were expected to insert on blank screens the learning objective, the rule to be learned, some examples of the rule's application and a series of practice items for the trainee to master. They could select to some extent the kinds of questions they wanted to ask and were not restricted to multiple-choice questions. Easily edited but quite limited colour graphics were available and authors could introduce plenty of variety in presenting material on the screen.

Some years later, the higher-level *TAL* (*TICCIT Authoring Language*) was developed. This does not restrict authors to the rigid framework of rule, example and practice. It avoids using hundreds of commands by providing a small number that authors themselves can modify to obtain the results they want. *APT* and *TAL* led to *ADAPT*, an authoring system with four levels. The simplest level

44

prompts the author and provides a standard format that can be changed if necessary. Higher levels provide for more complex procedures, using the same syntax. Authors can also revert to *APT* or *TAL* within *ADAPT*. *ADAPT*'s colour graphics can be enhanced by inserting pictures or diagrams captured electronically by a television camera and then edited on the screen. Thus the Hazeltine Corporation continues to develop *ADAPT* (Mudrick, 1986) by adding further options, while retaining the rule–example–practice pattern as a training strategy.

In the United States, the Hazeltine Corporation also markets *MicroTICCIT*, a dedicated CBT system based on an IBM personal computer backed up by a Data General minicomputer that can serve up to 64 workstations simultaneously, each with a colour monitor, special keyboard, light-pen, touch-sensitive screen and other accessories as required. The same product is marketed in Britain by STC Technology. Using *ADAPT*, it can be programmed to carry out all the functions of the mainframe *TICCIT* system, and more (Wilson and Bracken, 1984). *MicroTICCIT* was used by the College of Telecommunications, of the Civil Aviation Authority, in a British pilot study (see Chapter 11).

MicroTICCIT, like *TICCIT*, employs a basic training strategy that cannot easily be varied, although the complexity of the modules can be varied according to the trainer-author's experience and skill.

Particularly unusual in *MicroTICCIT* is the inclusion of a readability test. During development, authors can automatically test the readability of a module by using the Flesch–Kincaid formula, which is the US Department of Defence standard. The formula gives a result expressed in terms of a US grade level, rather than a reading age.

MicroTICCIT has a typical trainee management system that provides evaluation information of three kinds. Trainees can find out which training modules they have passed, failed, are still working on, or have yet to begin. Within a module, they can see which pieces they have studied, the number of practice items they have answered, how many they have answered correctly and the number they must pass to master the module. Trainers have equally detailed information about each trainee. They can also look at the progress of the group as a whole, in terms of time taken and attainment. They can find out which pieces of each module are causing trainees difficulty. Trainer-authors receive statistical information about what trainees are doing with each practice item they encounter. If they wish, authors can get a log of every key press made by each trainee. This may help them to trace the track a trainee has taken through a difficult mode.

The World Institute for Computer Assisted Teaching (WICAT), based in Utah, developed the *WICAT Interactive System for Education (WISE)*, and a program for management trainee records (*SMART*). These run on WICAT's own mainframe minicomputers, which can handle a number of terminals at once on a timesharing basis. The terminals have high resolution graphics, and can interface with videodisc players.

WISE offers trainers the use of eleven kinds of frame for constructing lessons, according to Rothwell (1983b), who calls *WISE* a powerful system that appears to be capable of tackling any CBT problem that previously required programming in a computer language. An author using the system sees a menu of choices from which to select a training strategy. Once a strategy is chosen, the system controls inputs by requesting from the author what is needed for each screen display. *WISE* assesses students' responses against various criteria, such as spelling, word order, arithmetical accuracy, inclusion of keywords, matching of synonyms and so on, and can analyse statistically the data it collects. Through *WISE*, the author can provide feedback for right as well as wrong answers (Duke, 1983). American Express (see Chapter 7), Lucas (see Chapter 8) and American Telephone and Telegraph, British Telecom and Cable and Wireless (see Chapter 12) are examples of companies that have used *WISE*.

Regency Systems markets a dedicated interactive training system based on the *USE* authoring language, developed by the Urbana Software Enterprise in Illinois, and running on the Regency RC-2 minicomputer. *USE* is sometimes called a dialect of *TUTOR*. The hardware for each workstation includes a keyboard and a monitor with a touch-sensitive screen, and interactive video can be integrated with it. The system has very well-developed graphics, suitable for simulation. It is sold in Britain by Rediffusion Simulation, which also markets a microbased version. In the early days, Mobil Chemical (see Chapter 8) made good use of a Regency Systems RC-1, and the Central Electricity Generating Board chose a Regency RC-2. British Caledonian (see Chapter 11) is another example of a company making excellent use of Regency Systems.

SELECTING A MAINFRAME AUTHORING SYSTEM

The task of selecting a mainframe authoring system (see Chapter 4), is far from easy. A company training manager cannot be expected to acquire detailed knowledge of several systems before recommending one. Providers naturally stress the technical advantages of their products, and of the hardware that runs them. A system that can cope with graphics in more than 4000 colours is not necessarily one suited to the training needs of a particular company. It may turn out, during development, that the training strategies which the company desperately wants to use cannot be implemented with that system. That is what happened at Abbey National (see Chapter 7).

In general, the trend in CBT is away from mainframe systems and towards using microcomputers, which offer more flexibility. Although a company may initially want to employ its existing mainframe in training, the added cost of microcomputers may be justified. The decision about using a mainframe or not is unlikely to turn on the authoring system, because there is plenty of choice for both mainframes and microcomputers.

The best advice we can give is that any company considering CBT should assess thoroughly its training needs, select a short list of those that can be met by CBT and then search for the programs that meet the highest priority needs on the short list. This was the highly successful approach used by Chevron Information Technology for training its data processing personnel (see Chapter 13), and by the accounting form of Ernst and Whinney (see Chapter 7) to train its auditors in electronic data processing concepts.

Interestingly enough, the result of this process in each company was to use microcomputers to train personnel in mainframe concepts and operation. This is a fairly new approach, but one that is appealing to many companies, especially those in which microcomputers have proliferated. Now that courses can be readily authored and implemented on microcomputers, companies are finding that they desire more than 'plain vanilla' mainframe CBT (see Mervyn's in Chapter 10), and prefer not to use costly mainframe time to develop and implement courses.

In the United States, Creative Approaches of East Bloomfield, New York, has developed an innovative method for removing authoring from the mainframe to the microcomputer, if that is required. A word processor is used for input, and the file is transferred to an IBM personal computer or a lookalike. A program called *Creative Course Writer* converts the text into executable code, transferable directly to the mainframe if needed. Two other programs allow screen simulations and course listings to be converted similarly. Although designed for companies using either *PHOENIX* or *IIS*, it can be adapted for other systems.

Interactions of this kind between microcomputers and mainframes are a valuable technological development in CBT.

6

Microcomputer Systems and Interactive Video

THE HARDWARE

CBT systems based on microcomputers are a very strong challenge to mainframe systems, which they may well supersede within a few years. As speed and memory increases in these smaller machines they are becoming very suitable for developing and delivering training. Many a trainer-author would like to be independent of mainframe computers, as Lloyd (1985) points out, because to be so is probably to be independent of the company's data processing department. The latest microcomputers, with hard-disc drives, have sufficient speed and memory to run integrated authoring systems that reach towards the ideal discussed in Chapter 4.

No particular microcomputer is specially well-suited to incorporation into a CBT system, but some makes and models are quite *unsuitable* because they lack capacity. Some are more popular than others, with a greater range of authoring tools available for them and better interfaces for attaching other equipment, such as an interactive videodisc player.

DOMINANCE OF IBM PERSONAL COMPUTER STANDARD

Because of the worldwide dominance of the microcomputer market by the IBM PC (Personal Computer) standard, the commonest hardware is more or less compatible with the PC, and more software, including authoring software, is available for PC-compatible hardware than for any other. Among US authoring systems that are PC-compatible are *TenCORE*, which was derived from *TUTOR*, the language for the *PLATO* system, and *BITS* (*Boeing Intelligent*

49

Terminal System) Scholar/Teach 3, which also evolved from a mainframe version. The *TICCIT* authoring system, *ADAPT*, runs on an IBM PC, too, in the *MicroTICCIT* form, although a Data General is the mainframe backup. Others developed in the United States specifically for microcomputers and implemented on IBM PCs are *ADROIT* (ADR), *Authology* (CEIT Systems), *Authority* (ITS), *CDS/Genesis* (EIS), *The Educator* (Spectrum Training), *PC-PILOT* (WCS, discussed by Beech, 1983), *QUEST* (Allen Communications), *SABER* (Pinnacle Courseware) and *SAM* (Learncom).

IBM itself recently launched *InfoWindow*, described as an interactive computer-based system made up of an IBM PC with monitor, touch-sensitive screen and up to two videodisc players. Two authoring programs run on this system: the *Learning System* is for the educational market and *Video/Passage* is for business and industry. Other PC authoring packages are likely to be modified to run on the system.

Authoring systems developed for the IBM PC standard are constrained somewhat by the hardware, which has not been able to handle high quality graphics without special enhancement (EGAs, or enhanced graphics adapter cards, are sold by IBM and others). It remains to be seen whether good-quality authoring systems will emerge for IBM's new standard, the Personal System/2.

Besides IBM PC machines and their lookalikes, in the United States other makes of microcomputer have been used in CBT. For example, the Apple II range of machines has been used with several authoring systems including *PASS* and *Apple PILOT* (the latter being described by Rothwell, 1983b, as one of the best implementations of *PILOT*), and, more recently, *SuperPILOT*. Authoring tools for the Macintosh have now appeared in the United States, such as *Course of Action*, developed by Autoware, and Apple itself has sponsored *VW/I* (see below), geared to the highly graphic display and increased memory of Macintosh II and SE computers, and the Apple IIGS. Another exciting authoring system, *CreationStation*, from Warren-Forthought, needs Macintoshes as part of its hardware.

In Britain, in addition to American-developed authoring tools, trainers can obtain for IBM PCs and similar machines several British authoring systems, such as *COMBAT, Domino, Easywriter, Mandarin, Microwriter* and *ProCAL2*.

50

SELECTED AUTHORING TOOLS FOR MICROCOMPUTERS

Full technical details of US and British authoring tools on the market are available from their vendors. Here we comment on the range of capabilities offered by some selected programs, to supplement our earlier discussion of authoring tools in Chapter 4. Our list is far from complete, but it includes most of those we mention as being used by particular companies in Part Three. There are many others competing in this market.

ADROIT

The *Applied Data Research Online Interactive Training (ADROIT)* authoring system, developed and marketed in the United States, is menu-driven, with a full range of lesson design options. One of its chief strengths is that it can simulate mainframe software. In other words, it can capture or copy programs from a major operational system, such as a bank's accounting system, complete with real data, for use in training on a microcomputer, away from the real system. Trainers can add questions (and answers) to the captured programs, and if necessary integrate them with interactive video. Like many authoring systems, it is accompanied by a trainee records system, for managing training. *ADROIT* was used to develop CBT for the Bank of America (see Chapter 7) and for the Chevron Information Technology Company (see Chapter 13).

Authority

Authority was developed by Interactive Training Systems in the United States and is a menu-driven system providing for flexible CBT authoring, with varying types of instruction and use of peripherals such as a touch-sensitive screen or a video player. It has full graphics and a course management component to keep track of trainees' progress. It can run on the IBM personal computer, XT or AT, or compatible machines. *Authority* contains six editors, for events, effects, video/audio, graphics, text and overlays. ITS supplies an interface, the *ITS 3100 Interactive Video Kit*, claimed to be the most technologically advanced peripheral subsystem available. With this hardware and software, the author-trainer can introduce complex overlays into the training carried by the

51

videodisc. ITS markets a considerable number of generic training packages produced with this system, principally for data process training, and has developed company-specific interactive videodisc training for US companies such as IBM, Sears, Xerox, Eastman Kodak, JC Penney, NCR, Chrysler, Texas Instruments and the Bank of America.

CDS/Genesis

CDS/Genesis is a refinement of a high level authoring language, *CDS2*, developed in the United States by Electronic Information Systems. It can be used on either IBM PCs and their lookalikes or on a Macintosh. *Genesis* uses a mouse and icons with templates to make this fairly complex authoring language more easily accessible to non-programmer authors. The system can also use colour graphic overlays, and can drive a video player.

Course of Action

This US product is an example of an icon-driven system and runs on the Macintosh. It has a level for planning lesson structure, can capture text and diagrams from other files and offers animation. We have seen no examples yet of its use in company training.

CreationStation

A US company, Warren-Forthought, departed from the usual kind of authoring system in producing its *CreationStation*, first marketed in 1987. This runs on the company's MocKingbird hardware, at the heart of which is a specialised multiuser industrial graphics micr⁻ computer, supported by Macintosh Plus microcomputers. The vendor claims that its system is more powerful than any authoring language and easier to use than most authoring systems. To prepare a course, the trainer-author creates a set of hundreds of high quality graphics screens, including animations, linked if appropriate to each other and to videodisc players and digitised audio. Screens from other systems can be emulated in detail. Video is presented on a separate screen to avoid degrading the graphics image. Branching and other instructions are embedded in each computer graphics frame. A course is stored on floppy disk, and can be changed by the trainer even while it is being used for training. There is a trainee management program as well. Although we have not yet heard, at time of writing, of a company-specific CBT course produced on the system, the vendor's description convinces us that *CreationStation* and its associated hardware and software deserve careful consideration, since they offer trainers considerable freedom in creating courses.

Domino

Marketed by Compsoft, *Domino* is a British menu-based authoring system, according to a review by Beaumont (1985). A trainer-author using this plain language system, says Beech (1985), can design a string of 'pages', each with text and graphics, in colour, and a question to the trainees, and can compile his replies on other pages. It has a system for keeping track of trainees' responses. In 1987 Compsoft extended the package to include network capabilities, so that several microcomputers can use the same software and several trainees can work together on it. The program's ability to analyse trainees' answers was enhanced, and better graphics were added.

Mandarin

Marconi Instruments in Britain developed and sells the *Mandarin* authoring system, claiming it to be 'the first authoring system to address the whole range of computer based training needs, from course conception and planning to student assessment and management'. We agree that *Mandarin* incorporates some useful displays for use by the trainer-author who is planning a course, but it is not yet the ideal authoring system (see Chapter 4). It is menu-driven, and runs on the IBM PC with enhanced colour graphics, touch-sensitive screen, mouse and interface for a videodisc or videotape player, as required. *Mandarin* offers as complete a range of straightforward authoring facilities and trainee management records as any we have seen on a microcomputer. British Nuclear Fuels (see Chapter 13) used the system to develop CBT.

Mentor II

This is a flexible menu-driven British authoring system, with graphics and animation capabilities plus an interface to control an interactive videodisc player. It was developed by the Provident Financial Group and is now sold in Britain by Mentor Interactive Training and its agents. Trainer-authors need no programming knowledge, as they compile frames and chain them together in sequences. The system, which runs on the IBM PC (with limited graphics capabilities) and several other microcomputers, maintains trainees' performance records to assist in managing the training. It can control an interactive video player, as in the project at W.H. Smith (see Chapter 10).

MicroPLATO

Another integrated authoring system is the microbased version of *PLATO*, developed by Control Data Corporation. Authors can work on IBM personal computers and compatible computers, using the *TUTOR* authoring system complete with graphics. There is thus no need for authors to access the central *PLATO* system unless they wish to. The same company is now marketing the *Micro Authoring System (MAS)*, another dialect developed from *PLATO*, which also runs on IBM personal computers and compatible machines. *MAS* provides a wide range of editing features, including a character set editor, animations, five standard question types that allow for word or phrase matching in open-ended responses, and access to BASIC for additional routines if needed.

Microtext

An easy-to-learn British language is *Microtext* (in 1987, also available as *Microtext-Plus*, but only for the now obsolete BBC-B computer mainly used in education). It can be adapted to control interactive video, but lacks a trainee management system. Friend (1985) and Barker and Singh (1984) review *Microtext*, which was developed at the National Physical Laboratory, and Whiting (1986) makes some suggestions about its use. Rothwell (1983b) points out that early versions had limited graphics capabilities and no calculation was possible. Nevertheless, Jaguar Cars used *Microtext* to develop an early videodisc (see Chapter 8).

PILOT

One of the easiest microcomputer-based languages to learn is *PILOT*, which has only fourteen basic commands. Early versions lacked important features, however, such as a trainee management program to record individuals' progress. *SuperPILOT* is an upgrade and provides some of these missing facilities. Austin Rover used *GPILOT* in its CBT, and the Organics Division of the Imperial Chemical Company (see Chapter 8) used *PILOT*.

ProCAL2

ProCAL2, reviewed by Rhodes and Azbell (1986), and marketed by VPS Interactive, is a British example of an authoring system developed particularly for interactive video CBT. It runs on IBM, Apple and Acorn BBC microcomputers. The trainer-author uses *ProCAL2* to design sequences, each of which can incorporate up to 200 lines of text and control codes. A course is made from up to 90 sequences. There is a sequence, course, and an effects editor that includes a graphics, picture, tune, and a video editor. Each editor has a help menu and many options. Additional subroutines written in BASIC can be built into the overall program.

QUEST

Developed in the United States by Allen Communications, this is one of the new generation of flexible authoring systems, for use with the IBM PC range and Apple II machines. It accommodates a range of peripherals, including a touch-sensitive screen and a video player. It has good response matching, branching, graphics editing and templates for developing training frames.

TEL

Barker (1987) reports on the *Training and Education Language* (*TEL*) developed by Regency Systems in the United States for use on an IBM PC and says it offers good high resolution graphics, including animation techniques, but lacks audio or any means of controlling external devices such as videodisc players.

55

TenCORE

Marketed in Britain by STC Technology and Education Technology, and in the United States by Computer Teaching Corporation, *TenCORE* is a US product that provides facilities for text and graphics editing, with touch-sensitive screen, light-pen and mouse as appropriate. It can handle interactive video and has a trainee management system. It incorporates considerable flexibility and different levels of authoring, to allow for more sophisticated work as trainers gain experience. For example, at the lowest level authors use the menu-driven editor, and at the highest they use a 'language authoring environment' with 200 commands available. High resolution graphics are possible with additional hardware. The National Westminster Bank used *TenCORE* to develop basic procedural training (see Chapter 7), and Essochem used it for a pilot package on operational maintenance (see Chapter 8). The Automobile Association (see Chapter 11) tried *TenCORE* in a small pilot project.

Top Class

This frame-based authoring system is sold in Britain by Format PC. Among its special features is its ability to capture screens from another program, say a word-processing program. It can handle colour graphics, and some animation is possible. It can control interactive video and audio.

VW/I (VideoWorks/Interactive)

This was developed by MacroMind and is an animation program that allows both course developers and graphic artists to string graphics together and move images. Instead of simply having text interspersed with graphics, the user sees complete animation sequences, with appropriate text overlays, that serve as a guide to a 'how to operate' sequence on the computer. This type of tool is especially well adapted to the new Macintosh computers since it requires a large amount of memory (at least a megabyte, Mbyte) and uses the Macintosh graphics capabilities. Figures 6.1 and 6.2 show sample screens from this system.

56

Figure 6.1: Screen for designing animated graphics from the *VW//* authoring system (reprinted by courtesy of MacroMind Inc., copyright 1986). This shows how to enter and modify information and looks very different from the usual text-type of entries or even typical programming entries used for other authoring languages or systems. TOUR LIST Score is the graphic scoreboard completed by an author or graphic designer to show entry, duration and exit of each of the various elements in the graphic design. TOUR LIST Cast shows the cast of graphics available and the number designators for blocks of text.

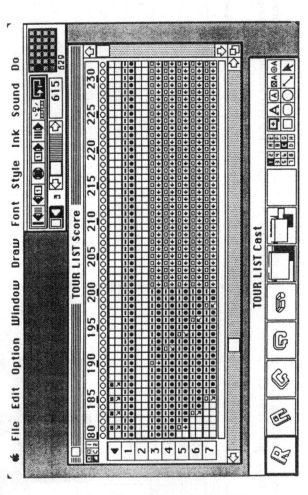

Figure 6.2: Screen for designing graphics and text from the *VW//* authoring system (reprinted by courtesy of MacroMind Inc., copyright 1986). CheapPaint and CheapEdit are the graphics and text editing functions built into this program.

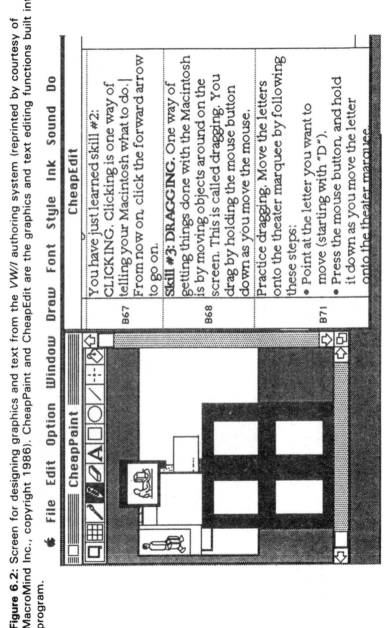

File Edit Option Window Draw Font Style Ink Sound Do

CheapEdit

B67 You have just learned skill #2: CLICKING. Clicking is one way of telling your Macintosh what to do. From now on, click the forward arrow to go on.

B68 **Skill #3: DRAGGING.** One way of getting things done with the Macintosh is by moving objects around on the screen. This is called dragging. You drag by holding the mouse button down as you move the mouse.

B71 Practice dragging. Move the letters onto the theater marquee by following these steps:
- Point at the letter you want to move (starting with "D").
- Press the mouse button, and hold it down as you move the letter onto the theater marquee.

SOME COMPARISONS

Comparisons date rapidly, because many providers are constantly improving their products. In our contacts with providers, we were frequently told that the version we had seen was being superseded. While improvement is desirable (by definition), these changes cause problems for client companies as well as providers, because later versions are seldom compatible with earlier ones.

Generally speaking, however, the simpler authoring languages, such as *PILOT* and *Top Class*, require the program to be built up line by line and are sometimes referred to as line-oriented. Other fairly simple languages are frame-oriented: for example, *COMBAT*, *Domino* and *MicroText* provide for and require the design of a screen-full of information at a time. Postings (1986) compares the *Domino* and *Top Class* systems and concludes that *Domino* is easier to use but *Top Class* offers greater flexibility.

COMBAT limits the trainer to using templates to develop instruction unless he or she knows the general programming language Pascal, in which case more variation is possible, including various training strategies (for example, tutoring) and a range of editing commands. Interactive video control is feasible and there is a management system to record trainees' progress.

Not everyone agrees that simple line-oriented systems are easier to learn than more complex frame-oriented systems. Johnson (1984, 1985) provides a detailed comparison of *PILOT* and *TenCORE* at the programming level, and concludes that *TenCORE* is easier to use and offers more options in display, answer judging, sequencing and data manipulation. He rejects the common criticism that *TenCORE* is harder to learn, saying that of the 200 commands only 50 are frequently used, and the others can be learned as required.

MICROCOMPUTER GRAPHICS

In many microcomputers, the hardware and software now available are powerful enough to handle sophisticated colour graphics, although the IBM PC standard does impose some limitations. Barker and Skipper (1986) identify three forms: icons, animation, and sketching. Icons are graphic symbols or pictures: a training example might be a circuit diagram presented on the screen. Animation, as in films, introduces movement: part of the circuit diagram might be made to operate a 'flashing' lamp. Sketching offers a trainee the opportunity to create or add to pictures on the screen, using a tablet.

Computer graphics are particularly useful in designing small-scale simulations. For example, trainees can rotate a three-dimensional plan in several axes to obtain different views. They can observe the effects on graphs of changing certain variables.

The authoring languages for several microcomputer-based systems (such as *CreationStation*, *Mentor II*) cater well for trainer-authors wanting to create graphics. The *VW/I* system we have already described. The better interfaces for interactive video (such as *MIC 3000*, see below) enable them to introduce high-quality moving pictures and to overlay the pictures with text.

MICROCOMPUTERS AND TRAINING WITH VIDEO

Video materials are widely used in training, but usually as 'linear' videotape, on cassette, which runs from start to finish, or is occasionally interrupted for group discussion. The sequence of pictures (and sound) is predetermined, and trainees usually watch passively.

With the arrival of microcomputers on the training scene, some forms of interactive video have become quite cheaply available, permitting trainers to produce materials that engage trainees actively, with the result that learning is often improved considerably.

INTERACTIVE VIDEOTAPE

It is relatively easy to create interactive videotape training materials. A videorecorder can be controlled by a microcomputer so that training presented in text and graphics on the computer's screen can be integrated with video sequences, as Laurillard (1982) and Duke (1983) explain, and the microcomputer can keep track of the trainee's progress. A fairly simple version is used by Zales (see Chapter 10), and British Airways (see Chapter 11) made good use of interactive videotape in training ground crew to de-ice aircraft.

Several systems on the market include authoring software and all the hardware. Among them in Britain are Scicon's *Computer Audio-Visual Instruction System* (*CAVIS*). According to Griffiths (1986), British Petroleum has been using *CAVIS* interactive videotape training packages for some years, mainly for refresher and safety courses for refinery operatives in Europe. The packages are valuable as reference sources, as well as for training, particularly for infrequently practised procedures such as shutting down or recommissioning a furnace. Singh (1985) reports that British Petroleum commissioned three *CAVIS* programs on control engineering from Blackrod. Norsk Hydro Fertilisers invested £85 million in a new chemical manufacturing and packaging plant in England. The company purchased a *CAVIS* system for training supervisory, operational and maintenance staff to use the new plant safely and at optimum productivity. The system was supplied by Scicon (*Training Digest*, July 1986).

Other systems include the *Video-MIT*, introduced by BMW to train dealers and automotive technicians (Griffith, 1986), and Dalroth's *Interactive Video Learning* (*IVL*), used by Du Pont in Northern Ireland and British Rail (see Chapter 11). Felix Interactive Learning System's *FELIX*, taken up by IBM and Citibank, is now marketed in Britain by Wirysystem. In the United States, Whitney Educational Services' *Insight* was designed specifically for videocassette systems (Haukom and Malone, 1986). Most of the authoring systems now available for microcomputers can drive videocassette and videodisc players.

Alternatively, a special interface can be obtained. No single interactive videotape interface dominates the scene in Britain, although the *Multi-media Interactive Control MIC 2000* and *3000*, marketed by Videologic, NCR's *Interac TV-2* and others are in use. Laurillard (1982) reminds us that although such systems require no programming expertise, they have educational limitations, and she prefers specially written software.

As a rule, however, existing 'linear' videotapes produced for training do not convert well to interactive videotape, even if copyright problems are resolved, because there is insufficient suitable footage in such tapes to provide for branching and multiple sequences used in interactive videotape (Further Education Unit, 1986).

INTERACTIVE VIDEODISC

As Barker and Skipper (1986) point out, it is technically feasible to bring older teaching media, such as films and slides, under computer control, although there are few such systems for industrial or commercial training.

61

Interactive videodisc is attracting far more attention, however, and companies need to understand what it is. There are two kinds. The laserdisc player, marketed by Philips, Pioneer and Sony, bounces a laser beam off minute indentations recorded as tracks on an aluminium layer within a 12 in (30 cm) plastic disc. The player detects changes in the reflected beams, and converts them into pictures and sound. The less widely used very high density (VHD) disc player is sold by Thorn-EMI Videodisc in Europe and by its developers, Japan Victor Company (JCV) elsewhere. It uses a 10 in (25 cm) disc on which are recorded differences in capacitance that are read by a sensor as the disc spins.

A laser-read videodisc can contain up to 54 000 'pages' or screens of training material. On the faster machines, any one of these can be found accurately in a maximum of five seconds. Pages can be displayed one at a time (as perfect stills) or in slow, normal or fast motion. A laser-read disc offers the equivalent of more than half an hour of film, and computer programs and two sound tracks can also be recorded on it.

Among interactive videodisc players, Philips (Pioneer in the United States) LaserVision equipment is dominating the market. In the United States, for example, Advanced Systems Inc. sells over 100 generic discs covering data processing topics such as micro-computer literacy, Unix and database design. The discs are used on LaserVision players, with Digital Equipment Corporation's *Inter-active Video Instruction System* (*IVIS*), based on an IBM micro-computer (PC, XT or AT). In Britain, IBM PCs and their lookalikes are linked to the players with *Videologic's MIC 2000* or the more versatile *3000*, whereas Acorn BBC-B (now obsolete) and BBC Master microcomputers are interfaced using *Soft Option* or Cox *Genlock* systems. Acorn Interactive Video, for instance, markets an interactive video system based on the BBC Master microcomputer with a *Genlock* interface to synchronise the microcomputer and disc player signals and ROM-based software for controlling the Philips LaserVision player. Cameron Communications sells two interactive video systems: one for the IBM PC/XT with a Philips Laservision player, and the other for the BBC-B and Thorn-EMI player. *Microtext* is one of the commonest British authoring languages for interactive video.

Thorn EMI's Videodisc Division, in partnership with Japan Victor Company (JVC), markets the VHD videodisc player and associated discs, which it claims are a low-cost alternative to laser disc and videotape. Thorn-EMI has worked with companies such as

British Telecom, British Steel, the Midland Bank, and Austin Rover to develop CBT using the player.

LEVELS OF INTERACTIVE VIDEO

Videodiscs and their players are commonly classified into five levels, according to the amount of interactivity they offer. Of course, videodiscs can only be played satisfactorily on players or systems at the level for which they were produced. Level 0 players, now obsolete, cannot offer freeze frames, slow motion or reverse.

Level 1 players, such as the Pioneer VP 1000 (for the United States) or LD 1100 (for Britain), are similar to those sold for entertainment, and offer freeze, slow and fast motion, reverse, and search more slowly than level 2 machines.

Level 2 players (such as Discovision PR 7820 or Sony LDP 1000, both for the United States), can find any particular frame in less than five seconds, can communicate with microcomputers and contain a limited, but increasing, intelligence of their own that enables them to accept batches of commands.

Level 3 players are more complex systems (for example, Discmaster 5000 and Omniscan, both for the United States, and Philips LaserVision and NCR InteracTV-2 for Britain), which always include a microcomputer as well as a player and are usually made up of separate components and suitable interfaces. At this level, the microcomputer carries training material as well as controlling the player, and pictures from the disc can be merged with text and graphics from the computer. The videodisc is permanently recorded, of course, but the computer programs can be changed and updated.

Level 4 systems may incorporate databases of information. WICAT markets a level 4 system for training, linked to WICAT computers and using the *WISE* authoring system. FlightSafety International developed a level 4 system incorporating a compact disc (CD-ROM) that stores 31 hours of audio (see Chapter 11).

SEARCHING AND BRANCHING CAPABILITIES

On videodisc players, why is fast and accurate searching for particular frames so important? Parsloe (1984b) suggests that 'branching' is the essence of interactivity. The term itself comes from the design of programmed instruction, in which linear programming took trainees on a single route through the content, but branching programming offered optional routes after trainees answered multiple-choice questions (one route per choice). In designing an interactive videodisc, authors provide trainees with different routes through the material, and need a quick way of jumping around to different parts of the disc. Thus a trainee selecting the wrong answer to a question posed by the disc may be taken to the start of a remedial sequence or even to a single frame.

While the rate at which searching takes place is important to maintain the pace of a program, rate is only one factor in its effectiveness. Trainees seem able to tolerate, and may even welcome, short pauses while the microcomputer commands the videotape or videodisc player to find the next sequence. Trainers may be more critical. Rate is certainly not as vital, in our judgement, as being able to present single frames clearly, which is possible with laser-read videodisc but not with videotape.

VIDEO PRODUCTION STANDARDS

Producing interactive videodisc training materials is more difficult than producing interactive videotape materials, because the system required is more complex. Austin Rover and British Steel are two companies in Britain that have experimented with making videodiscs using material shot with fairly cheap video equipment, but many training departments look for quality close to the broadcast standard. Trainees are accustomed to seeing broadcast quality television every night in their homes and are seldom content for long with poor quality video. Low quality can actually reduce the effectiveness of training videos because trainees pay more attention to its flaws than to its content.

A videodisc player can be controlled by a microcomputer in much the same way as a videorecorder, but integration can be more sophisticated because the disc can find individual frames, as well as moving images of broadcast quality. Planning production of a videodisc therefore requires considerable effort, often from a team that includes subject matter experts, trainers, video producers and computer programmers.

Almost all the newer authoring systems support interactive video, whether on cassette or disc. Older systems have in many cases been modified, making the same kind of interactivity possible.

EXAMPLES OF COMPANIES USING INTERACTIVE VIDEODISC

There are some very large-scale users of interactive videodiscs. In the United States, Ford and General Motors (see Chapter 8) have over 15 000 interactive videodisc players installed, for training and for updating and point-of-sale reference. Digital Equipment Corporation make very extensive use of them. IBM has more than 50 courses available on them. FlightSafety International uses a level 4 system to train hundreds of pilots. In Britain, Lloyds Bank (see Chapter 7) has interactive videodisc players in action to train more than 2000 cashiers each year in its many branches (Griffiths, 1986), and British Telecom plans to retrain 20 000 telephone operators. British Airways (see Chapter 11) uses interactive videodisc for training its 1500 ground supervisors.

INTERACTIVE VIDEOTAPE VERSUS INTERACTIVE VIDEODISC

Comparison of the two technologies is not straightforward, because of the various levels of players and systems. Origination of good quality video is not cheap for either. Production planning is usually simplified for videotape, with many training programmes being produced by in-house video units using cheap equipment. Production planning for videodisc is certainly more complicated, and production of the original video material is more likely to be done outside the company. Tape can be mastered cheaply, whereas videodisc is expensive to master. Copies cost about the same, provided that many are made. If only a few are made, tape is much cheaper. Videotape can be edited, of course, whereas videodisc, once mastered, cannot be, making the latter costly for training that must be modified frequently.

Technically, videodisc players have more to offer. It is a distinct advantage to be able to pick out individual frames accurately, and that is not possible with videotape. Two sound channels are available on some industrial videocassette players, but are standard on videodisc players. Videorecorders generally cannot handle program branching well and lack fully automatic controls or intelligence of any kind, whereas the higher levels of videodiscc players have these. There are more computer interfaces available for the latter, too.

So far as videocassette training materials are concerned, large

65

quantities exist in linear form, but not as many in interactive form, either generic or company specific. Converting linear tape materials into interactive training is difficult and 'the results are usually unsatisfactory. For videodisc players, the number of generic discs is growing steadily, and there are quite a few company-specific discs. Of course, tapes can be easily copied by other companies, whereas discs cannot be copied, as yet, except at the originating factory.

In this field, Parsloe (1984a) provides a straightforward account of what interactive videodiscs are, how they are produced and what they can do. Rothwell (1985) offers further practical advice on developing programs, and using authoring systems, and also reports case studies of early British work on interactive video in training at the National Westminster Bank and Jaguar Cars. Lambert and Sallis (1986) offer a technical guide to interactive video and CD/I (see Part Five).

INTERACTIVE AUDIO

Incorporating sound within CBT is possible using a variety of hardware and software. Barker (1986a) deals with speech synthesis based on ROMs (read-only memories on silicon chips) with fixed vocabulary, phoneme-driven synthesisers that compile words from phonemes and text-to-speech synthesisers that translate print into spoken words. He also discusses using sound stored on audiotapes (with conventional or rapid-access players), audiodiscs or laser-read discs. He does not describe any specific company-based CBT application of these techniques, but clearly interactive sound and speech can be valuable to trainees, whether they are learning engine maintenance or how to deal with customers on the telephone.

A few special-purpose authoring systems have been developed to make easier the task of integrating interactive audio. Barker (1986a) describes the British *AECAL (Audio-Enhanced Computer-Assisted Learning)*, *TES/T*, *MASTWRITER*'s *AudioEdit* and *AUDIOTEXT* systems, none of which appear to have been used so far in CBT. The *CreationStation* system, discussed in Chapter 6, integrates digitised audio.

As we mentioned earlier, FlightSafety International integrated interactive audio into their training by using a compact disc (see Chapter 11). This is actually one of the first uses of CD/I for training, developed by Philips jointly with FlightSafety International.

Since CD/I employs digital information it can also accommodate computer data and some video (see Chapter 19). Its capacity to carry audio separately from the video is very important when audio must play over still frames. On an interactive videodisc this is possible by using a different track to record the audio, but the more audio information is placed on this track, the less video is available on each disc, since both audio and video use up space on the disc. As videodiscs are more cost-effective when used for video rather than audio, separate audio will probably become a requirement for complex interactive training programs, especially for those which are long, technical or require multi-image video.

TOUCH-SENSITIVE SCREENS AND BARCODE READERS

When trainees respond to questions in the course of CBT, they often have to press specified keys on a normal or augmented keyboard. Many CBT systems, such as *PLATO* and *Mandarin*, offer as an alternative a touch-sensitive screen. Trainees simply touch the part of the screen corresponding to the answer they wish to give. In some contexts, touching does not provide a sufficiently accurate response, however, particularly if parallax is encountered. Trainees touch the wrong spot, sometimes with consequences, within the CBT program, from which they may not be able to recover. At Eastman Kodak, touch-sensitive screens and the 'mouse' that controls a pointer or cursor on the screen were evaluated as input devices, since Kodak's field engineers (the trainees) could not be assumed to have keyboard skills. The mouse was chosen because it allowed more precise positioning on the screen. It did not need to be calibrated periodically, as do the touch-sensitive screens, and obviated fatigue caused in some trainees by having to reach up frequently to touch the screen.

The *ActionCode* interactive video system has a touch-sensitive screen and the workbooks also contain barcodes, which trainees 'stroke' with a barcode reader to answer multiple-choice questions. *ActionCode*, marketed in Britain by Datasolve Education, is said to be in use by 100 large US companies, including IBM, General Motors, Eastman Kodak, Xerox, Texas Instruments, Shell and McDonnell Douglas (see *Interactive Learning International*, 2(3) February 1986). Cameron Communications sells *INTERACT M*, a touch-sensitive screen, that operates with the *MIC 2000* interface (see above) to 'break down the keyboard barrier'.

SIMULATIONS WITH MICROCOMPUTERS

Although large-scale training simulations, such as of the control room of a nuclear power station, require mainframe computers, smaller simulations can be controlled quite well by microcomputers. In process industries, such as nuclear power generation and petrochemical processing, training is needed at a very early stage in the development of a new plant, as Hatfield and Howard-Jones (1986) point out. Simulators can play an important role. When a plant is being designed, its designers begin to prepare manuals for operators. These manuals often become the basis for developing a training simulator that can bring operator's skills to a high level before the plant is actually commissioned. In the course of developing the simulator, the company carrying out the development may well discover gaps in the detailed information about how the plant will operate. This information is essential for developing the simulator and, of course, for training, and requests for this information can in turn influence the design of the plant. The company may even detect design faults which only show up when the simulator is running.

When such process plants are started up and brought to the designed rate of operation, trained operators work alongside the commissioning team. At this stage, the training simulator is often needed for checking, without risk, the consequences of certain actions.

Once one of these plants is operating normally, operators must undergo further training on the simulator, to maintain their high standard of knowledge about how to keep the plant running safely and efficiently. The commissioning team will have moved on, and the trained operators will be working in shifts. Typically, shift workers have few opportunities to practice techniques for dealing with abnormalities and emergencies, unless time is set aside for training on a simulator.

As trained operators leave the company, their places must be filled, immediately, by newly trained employees. This further need for training is again best met by CBT on a simulator.

Simulations are also used where microcomputers train employees to work on mainframe systems. For example, trainees may have to complete standard forms or reference information. American Express Travel Related Services uses simulation of this kind extensively in its microcomputer-plus-minicomputer-based training.

Simulation based on an interactive videodisc system seems

straightforward enough, to the extent that the video can present realistic scenarios for training purposes. An extension of this idea is described by Rushby *et al* (1987). In a project involving collaboration with Lucas CAV, Kodak and the Trustee Savings Bank, the Centre for Staff Development at London University explored the problems of simulating a 30 minute interview dialogue. The trainee interviews a simulated applicant, initially selecting questions from a menu but in later phases using a voice recognition system. The applicant is simulated by 300–400 short video sequences which are selected for display to provide responses to the questions.

By contrast, consider Kelly Services, the largest temporary employment company in the United States, with over 750 branches worldwide. Its British branch, Kelly Temporary Services, has about 20 branches, with more opening each year. Since the company aims to provide its customers with highly competent secretarial and clerical staff, it developed a simulator in conjunction with Kee Inc., a US company specialising in simulator training. The software, PC-Pro, runs on the Kee simulator, which is installed in every branch. The system was initially designed to simulate IBM, Wang, and AES dedicated word processors, which accounted then for nearly half the market. Xerox and DEC simulations were added later. No less than eleven word-processing packages can now be simulated by PC-Pro for this range of machines, and it can also simulate spreadsheets and data entry tasks.

Kelly commissioned development of the simulator, at a cost of $8 million, to solve the problem of how to test its recruits and provide them with training relevant to the particular hardware and software they were likely to work with. During testing and training, the simulator compares the operator's performance with that of an expert. When the work is carried out correctly, the machine responds on the screen in exactly the same way as the real word processor or microcomputer would. When a mistake is made, however, the simulator points it out and helps the operator to correct it. The simulator also keeps score (Figure 6.3 shows a score sheet for a Wang word-processor operator), and operators must obtain 85 per cent on all tests, within specified time limits, before being sent out to customers. Because operators may need to move from one word-processing system to another (perhaps from Wang to Xerox), the simulator does 'cross-training' too.

Kelly says that the end result of this embedded training is that customers get operators trained to use the right systems. In fact, the company offers a guarantee of satisfaction: if customers are not

Figure 6.3: Screen showing the test scores for a student using the Kelly Services' Kee simulator (reprinted by permission of Kelly Services)

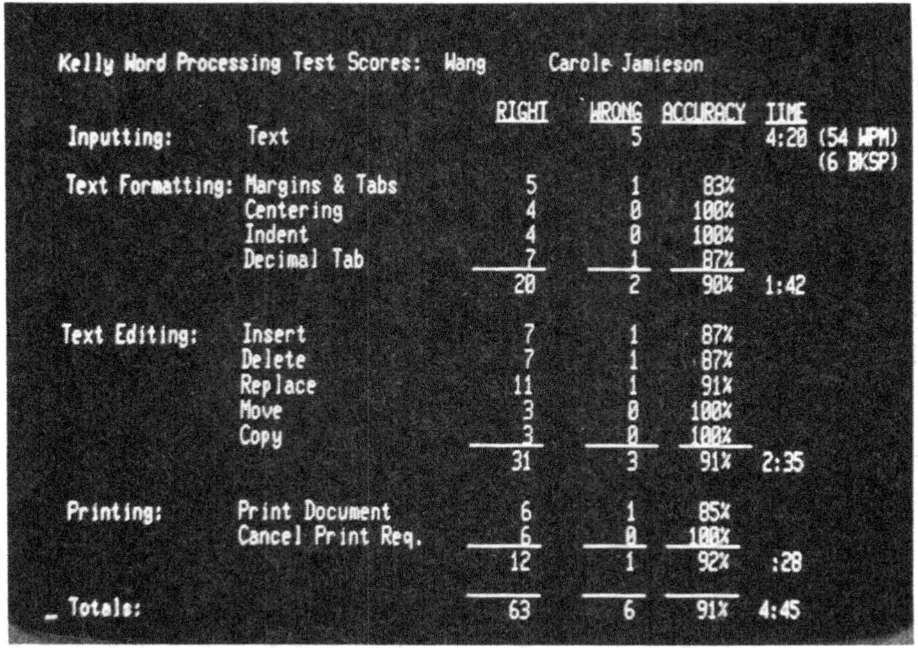

Kelly Word Processing Test Scores: Wang   Carole Jamieson

		RIGHT	WRONG	ACCURACY	TIME
Inputting:	Text	5	5	83%	4:20 (54 WPM) (6 BKSP)
Text Formatting:	Margins & Tabs	4	1	100%	
	Centering	4	0	100%	
	Indent	4	0	100%	
	Decimal Tab	7	1	87%	
		20	2	90%	1:42
Text Editing:	Insert	7	1	87%	
	Delete	7	1	87%	
	Replace	11	1	91%	
	Move	3	0	100%	
	Copy	3	0	100%	
		31	3	91%	2:35
Printing:	Print Document	6	1	85%	
	Cancel Print Req.	6	0	100%	:28
		12	1	92%	
Totals:		63	6	91%	4:45

happy with the standard of work provided, they do not pay for the services.

Simulations on interactive videodisc are employed extensively by Eastman Kodak in establishing typical customer situations for its field engineers, by Syntex in training sales representatives to converse intelligently with medical personnel and by FlightSafety International in training pilots. In the United States, company trainers clearly indicated to us that simulations are a major reason why management is interested in using CBT. Simulations are even replacing conventional CBT in some cases, because they add a dynamic element. Trainees become more actively involved and can practise by branching to options in ways not possible on other systems. This practice is non-threatening to the trainees.

Part Three

Company Experience

7

Banking, Finance and Insurance

TRAINING NEEDS

It is not surprising that banks, financial and insurance companies
have taken the lead in exploiting computers and communications for
training their employees. More or less as soon as mainframe
computers came onto the commercial market in the 1960s, they were
leased or purchased by some of these companies to gain efficiency
in carrying out financial transactions between very large numbers of
clients and often hundreds of branch offices. Smith and Wield
(1986) point out that banks, for example, had to embrace new
technology to reduce costs, generate and market new services and
respond to increased competition.

For more than a decade, however, companies with computers
used them for training one group only, their data processing
employees. This was because mainframes were not easily accessible
to other employees and CBT for them was simply not developed or
available. In the few cases where CBT was tried, it was of low
quality. Drinkall (1985) describes how the Provident Financial
Group, with 600 branch offices, began using its mainframe for training in 1975: the programs were 'embarrassingly poor', but worked.
The Group now has as a subsidiary one of the foremost CBT
providers in Britain, Mentor Interactive Training.

By the late 1970s, computers were becoming ubiquitous and data
processing departments less protective of them. Companies in the
financial sector were extending or considering the extension of their
networks. These changes required that many employees, at junior as
well as senior levels, would move from manual to computer-based
procedures, and require rapid retraining, as at American Express
and at Barclaycard, part of the VISA international credit card

consortium. Mainframe computers and networks of terminals appeared to offer opportunities for introducing videotex systems, with embedded CBT. These systems have not been without their problems, however, as the Abbey National and Barclays Bank case studies demonstrate, and the National Westminster and Lloyds are two examples of banks that have avoided embedded training.

A development in the 1970s was the close linking of clients' computers with those of banks and other financial institutions. Thus, for instance, a company could pay all its employees by means of electronic transfer of funds to individuals' accounts. At first, this meant the physical transport of tapes from the company's computer to the bank's. Today, telecommunications and appropriate software achieve the transfers. The Bank of America case study deals with CBT applied within such a system.

To the extent that mainframe systems require trainees to use software and real procedures and data, banks and other financial institutions faced a problem. They could not allow trainees to introduce errors into clients' accounts while training. The solution lay in simulation. The simulation could mirror all the systems trainees were expected to learn to operate, and it could even 'use' temporarily sets of real clients' data down-loaded (borrowed) from the real systems. The American Express, Bank of America and Stewart Wrightson case studies describe this kind of CBT. A British provider, Hanover Education Systems, is supplying CBT of this type to Fellesdata, the information processing service for Norway's banks, with 7000 terminals.

The arrival of microcomputers and the means to join them in networks provided another facility of value to financial institutions. Although for obvious reasons a large proportion of these companies' transactions must be dealt with at processing centres, the centres can be scattered over the nation, given sufficient distributed computing power and adequate data transmission links. With microcomputers in place, the companies began to consider using them for decentralised training. For example, the Standard Chartered Bank evaluated several microcomputer-based authoring systems with a view to standardising its training, before adopting *Mentor II* (Ward, 1986). The Provident Financial Group moved over to microcomputers and soon had 50 machines handling an estimated 3500 training sessions each month (Drinkall, 1985). Abbey National Building Society (see below) wanted to find out whether microcomputer-based training could raise training standards without adding to costs. Stewart (1986) reports that the Forward Trust

Group decided to use, within a wider training scheme, custom-made programs developed by a provider, Intra Systems, to train employees to deal with clients in difficulties.

The urgent needs of some financial institutions led them to choose generic microcomputer-based CBT software and/or interactive videodisc, rather than taking time to develop their own or have it developed for them. For example, National Westminster Bank, one of the largest British banks, introduced generic interactive videodiscs, such as *Smile — You're on the Telephone*, into their training (Rothwell, 1985). Some providers produce generic products specifically for banking and finance: for instance, Financial i sell *An Introduction to Foreign Exchange* and *The Gilt-Edged Market* level 1 interactive videodiscs, the latter to train middle management and operations staff following the 'Big Bang' restructuring of the London Stock Exchange. Similarly, Blackrod Interactive Services developed generic interactive videodiscs for Hambro Life and Allied Dunbar, both British insurance companies, for training life insurance sales employees (Singh, 1986).

In keeping with their conservative image, British financial institutions have approached CBT with caution. The National Westminster Bank, for instance, has progressed carefully through other training media before trying interactive video and CBT. According to Hitchcock (1986), Abbey National took until 1985 to become the first British building society to implement CBT. She says that at least three others are developing or piloting courseware for training branch employees. Other societies are formulating policy. They see well-trained efficient employees as necessary to maintain their competitive edge, and that CBT may help them in a cost-effective way. In 1986, new legislation widened the functions of building societies, obliging them to increase dramatically their training programmes to meet a variety of new needs for training and retraining.

In the United Kingdom the National Computing Centre (quoted by Hitchcock, 1986) published the results of a market survey that identified the financial sector as the major user of CBT, a user convinced of its effectiveness and committed to using it. Respondents said that CBT's benefits were more convenient training, less training administration, and an easier method of updating employees, with a significant reduction in training time. Its cost-effectiveness was apparently confirmed by one major bank which claimed a 48 per cent internal rate of return on investment in CBT, with cost savings of £1.7 million a year.

The rest of this chapter consists of case studies (arranged alphabetically) of CBT in several large financial institutions in the United States and Britain. From these a clear picture emerges of the financial sector's adoption and implementation of training through new technology. Evaluation details are difficult to obtain, as we show in Chapter 17, but there is certainly evidence of success, even a little of failure.

ABBEY NATIONAL BUILDING SOCIETY

Abbey National is the second largest building society in the United Kingdom. Its top managers made a commitment in 1985 to try new training technology, in parallel with a major investment in training at branch level. Changes in national legislation have brought entirely new business into building societies since 1987, such as the ability to offer personal loans (as well as mortgages on property) and other more diverse financial services. These changes require the large-scale retraining of employees.

Within the Society, a proposal from the Training Department in late 1985, for a CBT pilot project, aimed at finding out whether computer-based training could cost-effectively raise standards, improve consistency of training and whether the application of CBT in the organisation would fit within its culture (Wakeley, 1985).

There were two components in Abbey National's original strategy, which involved using two kinds of hardware with different operating and authoring systems. First, a short series of micro-computer-based CBT packages would be prepared. Second, a videotex (viewdata) system would present the same packages as those selected for the microcomputer.

Apart from the Society's action in recruiting specialist staff, the project's success was fostered by a considerable financial commitment. In addition to the courseware design costs incurred, the cost of the microcomputer authoring system (*TenCORE*) was over £6000 (including authoring hardware). Olivetti M24 microcomputers were supplied to thirteen branches for the pilot trial. For the videotex project, the McDonnell Douglas Sequoia minicomputer was rented with *Disc Tutor* CBT software from Disc International. The *Disc Tutor* authoring system, running on the Sequoia was linked by telephone lines to existing Philips HCS110 terminals (normally used for insurance quotations) in eleven branch offices. Regrettably, delays in the delivery of the complete *Disc Tutor* software meant that the videotex training package was only used for one month during the pilot trial.

Although the intention was to produce six short CBT packages, each on a topic in demand, time constraints allowed the production of only three, each providing one hour of training material. The topics chosen were *Property Insurance Claims*, *Health and Safety*, and *Product Knowledge*.

Property Insurance Claims was designed to train branch employees, of whom 97 per cent are women, to do this part of their job better. The program trains them to identify ineligible claims, so that customer service can be maintained at a high level through fewer misunderstandings. It teaches through highly interactive (in the case of *TenCORE*) on-screen text, linked to a set of printed brochures issued to customers. It tests application of knowledge through case studies. Experienced employees can go straight to the case studies and test themselves. The package runs on the Olivetti M24 and also ran on the videotex system.

Health and Safety was deliberately designed in black and white, because the Training Department needed to see whether cheaper monochrome screens could be purchased instead of colour without a loss of student acceptance of the courseware. The program was less interactive than the *Property Insurance Claims* but still gave students the opportunity to produce bar charts, answer questions, and, at the end, play a high-risk game from which they emerged 'dead or alive'! It ran only on the microcomputers.

Product Knowledge provided training for all branch employees who deal with customers. It covered the main product (services) offered by the Society, and helped staff to identify customers' needs before selecting the appropriate product.

To develop these packages, the CBT group used the *TenCORE* authoring system. They produced detailed screen designs, which were either coded internally or by external consultants. The Society decided, in the light of this experience, to expand the development team, because working with external resources did not always produce the desired results.

During the pilot, branches ranged from those that established a rota for employees to use the CBT packages to others where the packages were scarcely touched. Yet the general response was highly favourable, with 84 per cent of trainees who completed an evaluation questionnaire after using *Property Insurance Claims* saying they felt positive about CBT. The CBT software recorded the time employees were on the machines, their responses to questions

79

and whether they merely used the case studies or worked through the complete module. Staff were also interviewed afterwards. The results showed that employees found the system easy to use, stayed on the computer for quite long periods and felt they had learned something useful, particularly if they were new to property insurance.

Finding the right location for the equipment was a challenge. In the Society's high street offices, space is scarce. Counter positions and back office areas are public, busy and subject to interruption. In some cases the only private area is the manager's office.

For the videotex part of the pilot, the minicomputer was linked up, using standard telephone lines, to the existing Philips HCS 110 videotex terminals in eleven branches. This enabled the Training Department to use *Disc Tutor*, with a videotex package, *Viewbase*, to produce and deliver the *Property Insurance Claims* package over the system. Because control was centralised, updating of the package was easier. In theory at least, a system that could be installed fairly easily at over 700 branches seemed of great value to the Society.

These potential advantages of videotex, however, were offset by problems. Following delays in getting started, caused by late delivery of the *Disc Tutor* software, there were some difficulties in scheduling videotex training time because the terminals were being fully used for normal branch business. Staff felt that videotex was not a suitable training mode. They did not mind using it to access information from time to time, briefly, but objected to watching for very long the poor quality graphics and low resolution, characteristic of videotex systems. Since the videotex screens could carry only a small number of words, frequent page-turning was necessary.

The Training Department found the *Disc Tutor* authoring system much less flexible than *TenCORE* and wanted a faster response time. *Disc Tutor*, the trainers said, is best suited to producing text-based courses that need to be regularly updated and demand rigid central control. It is not suitable for developing courses with sophisticated layout and graphics. The Society saw the relatively high cost of the minicomputer, and the cost and unreliability of telephone lines, as additional factors against using videotex as a training system.

As a result of the pilot study, Abbey National has now installed over 200 Olivetti M24SP microcomputers in its branches to deliver courses covering clerical procedures, product training and management accounting, with further topics under development. Perhaps the main finding of the pilot project was that a new training needs analysis had to be carried out in the company before CBT is adopted as a company-wide 'training solution'. The technology must match the training need. By the time this book appears, the company will have moved all the way from its feasibility study to full implementation on microcomputers, rejecting videotex in the process.

AMERICAN EXPRESS

American Express is a large international group of companies, several of which use CBT. For example, in the United States, the parent company chose CBT for training new employees in Salt Lake City to clear and process millions of travellers' cheques moving between American Express and other companies. It wanted a method that could simulate what happened in the expensive real system, without using the system or running the risk of accounts being wrongly processed. After finishing the course, employees would understand the work flow in their department and be able to perform each task required. The simulation was developed by trainers who had never prepared CBT, using the *WISE* authoring system and WICAT's model 150 microcomputer. Some of the courses currently on offer are screen simulations of clerical systems used in various departments. On the screen, trainees see trays of work containing documents to be processed. They use American Express's procedures and see on-screen the same screens as they will see on the company's real system (Beech, 1983). Courses currently offered include:

(a) Alarm inquiries
(b) BARS
(c) Sales balancing
(d) Card data services
(e) TC data services
(f) Key entry
(g) PAS
(h) REPES phase II
(i) 3178 sign on/off

Following the success of this CBT simulation, the company invested in a larger WICAT system with 30 terminals and developed further courses. Developmental courses include a combination of informational lessons and practices/tests, including:

81

(a) Effecting writing for work
(b) Overview classes for SOSS, RSC, REPES, and new accounts
(c) TC settlement process
(d) Using your telephone
(e) World of TC and card

American Express's card division in the United States used IBM's *IIAS* to develop business procedures training, which was delivered on an IBM mainframe through *IIPS* (see Chapter 5), according to Heaford (1983), who also says that the company's insurance division, based in San Francisco, uses CBT developed with *IIAS* for an IBM mainframe and with *PASS* for Apple microcomputers.

American Express also uses the *PHOENIX* system to train their data processing staff on their IBM mainframes in eleven training centres across North America. Training programs are primarily generic ones purchased from Advanced Systems Inc. and Deltak. This type of training is not satisfactory, however, for the other 4000 employees who use the mainframe system each year. The reasons are much the same as those identified by other companies: the expense of mainframe time for training, the fact that *PHOENIX* offers only text, and the limits to interactivity imposed by such a system.

Thus in 1984 the Operations Training section of the American Express Travel Related Services Company, developed a more innovative approach, with the help of McGraw-Hill, which adapted its *MHIAS* authoring system for the purpose, and IBM. Operations Training successfully designed the interfaces and software to inter-connect IBM personal computers to an IBM System 36 mini-computer and to the mainframe IBM 3090s. The personal computers have their more user-friendly training advantages of colour, branch-ing and so on. The 3090s are available for straight simulation of jobs towards the end of training. The actual work of the system is divided. The personal computers, which are the development tools, run the programs and keep track of trainees. The System 36 is the file server, storing and delivering courses. It also acts as a database manager, collecting information, and as a communications channel between personal computers and the mainframe.

A pilot project proved to management that the concept was feasible, and funding was approved. Training staff developed the concepts and menu structures, and did the programming to allow the System 36 to serve as a central clearinghouse. Development of the software for the courses took eighteen months' work by four people, resulting in 20 weeks of training for four different types of correspondence representatives (see below). Course developers and trainees sign onto the PC, which allows full access to all programs and to the mainframe. Users are not aware which computers are in use at any one time: the system seems 'transparent' to them.

Program development and trainee use of the system is managed and continually updated on a training management system, which groups lessons into modules and modules into courses. A trainer can build a course to suit new employees or old, or can create an entire curriculum by combining appropriate lessons and modules. Trainees register on the personal computer and, depending on their needs and the nature of their job, are assigned a curriculum.

There are centres for CBT at Fort Lauderdale (Florida), Phoenix (Arizona), Greensboro (North Carolina) and New York. Programs were initially developed to train card-member correspondence representatives to carry out proper procedures in answering letters from American Express credit card customers. The trainees typically had at least one or two years of community college education. The CBT is set within comprehensive training for the job, and consists of five weeks on the computer, in classes of ten or twelve people. After learning about the company, trainees receive procedural training and learn the relevant federal Government rules and guidelines. Finally, they are trained to give good service to customers. The CBT is followed by two weeks of training on the job, monitored by the trainer, a day back in class to summarise the course, and five weeks doing actual work in the training centre under supervision. Only then are trainees allowed to operate on their own in 'production', that is, normal working conditions.

The CBT begins with tutorial information, after which drill and practice builds on the tutorials. Next come simulations on the system, starting with instructional simulations (responding to descriptions of situations, feedback and branching) and going on to testing simulations (task simulations of actual cases, with the trainees' performance being recorded). Once trainees can perform to a predetermined level they are allowed to go onto a production system using the mainframe computer directly, but not before.

American Express expects to expand its CBT in the United States to train telephone service representatives. Parts of the existing CBT will be combined with new modules that cover telephone technology and techniques of using it.

In Britain, American Express (Europe) also uses IBM main-frames, to which are linked several hundred terminals. Some embedded CBT has been developed for the company's procedural training, but the terminals also carry generic courseware prepared by other *IIS* users.

In an experimental project, interactive video training was initiated by American Express (Europe) using the *PASS* authoring system with Apple II microcomputers coupled to LaserVision videodisc players or U-matic video players (Heaford, 1983). Subsequently, the company began to develop CBT for its own trainers, using *SuperPilot* on its Apple computers. These projects were halted at the trials stage, however, because the company was moving to the IBM PC standard, and because its trainers found *PASS* and *Super-PILOT* very time-consuming to use. Limitations of speed and screen display eventually ruled out the Apple II as an interactive video controller. The company did not reject CBT, however, and in 1987 was awaiting delivery of several programs made with the help of external providers.

BANK OF AMERICA

The Bank of America is the largest US bank, with headquarters in San Francisco and branches in many states. Its training needs and methods are varied. For example, to reach its widely scattered employees who deal with corporate customers, it has used for some time an American Telephone and Telegraph (AT&T) Alliance telephone conferencing system, which links several offices at one time (see Chapter 12).

Experience with the Alliance system led the World Banking Division of the Bank to install a Telewriter network, using Optel voice-and-data modems (again, see Chapter 12). This network of microcomputers and telephones enables the trainers to standardise training. On the Telewriter screens, the visual information provides a series of 'anchors' for discussion over the loudspeaker telephones. As trainers get practice with drawing on the special tablet, there are more free-hand additions to the displays. As trainees become accustomed to the system, they gain the confidence to use the screen as a notepad, or to use the keyboard to enter values on a table drawn by the trainer.

There have been some criticisms, however, of this form of CBT. The users, particularly the trainees, say that the screens are too much like flipcharts, with few opportunities for proper interaction with the trainer. They find the screens too small, even when only three or four trainees try to use the same one. As of 1986, there were only two drawing tablets within the network, severely limiting the amount of drawing that could be done. Trainers and trainees feel the communication rate (300 bits per second) is too slow, leading to some frustration on their part, and, of course, high telephone line charges for the bank.

The Bank of America's Business Services Division took a different approach, to meet different training needs. For its own employees, a fairly small-scale project was the preparation of ten to fourteen hours of online training in human resource management. At first the company tried the *McGraw-Hill Interactive Authoring System* (*MHIAS*), but ended up using the prototype version of a new Spectrum product, *The Educator* authoring system. The initiative came from a senior vice-president (who had an Apple computer at home).

Paynet

A larger development, for employees of the Bank's client companies, was *Paynet*. This embedded CBT is intended to help these employees to learn how to use the automated payroll system that the Bank sells to clients as a service. The Bank saw CBT as potentially 'cheaper than sending out customer service representatives to live with the clients', following installation of *Paynet*.

Paynet was developed in consultation with potential users. The CBT portion is based on the *ADROIT* authoring system, which enables the trainers to 'capture' and simulate real portions of a company's payroll without putting that payroll at risk from trainees' mistakes. The real system has some online help and job aids built into it, as well. The CBT has reduced a five day training programme to three days, with immediate savings to the Bank. Corporations do not like releasing their employees from daily duties, particularly in payroll departments, because often these staff are difficult to replace temporarily. The client companies therefore appreciate not only the shorter training period but also the fact that trainees can do the training at the workplace, on the same computer terminal they normally use, and can if necessary be called away from it to attend to urgent other business.

Again, with *Paynet* the Bank has come to recognise some

problems. First, obsolescence is rapid. Frequent updates and upgrades occur in the two data processing systems that underlie *Paynet*, and then the CBT must usually be updated too. This is so despite the efforts of the trainers to stick to generic concepts only. Second, the CBT cannot replace classroom training completely. It helps to bring clients' employees to the same level before reaching the classroom stage, and if a client company wants to, it can use the CBT to train a fair number of its staff before selecting a few for classroom training, which focuses on updates. Third, development time for this type of CBT is greater than the Bank's trainers had anticipated.

Overall, the Bank's experience with CBT has been sufficiently satisfactory to make it likely that more programs will be developed.

BARCLAYCARD

According to Rothwell (1983a), Barclaycard was the first bank credit card outside North America, being started in 1966. Following extensive reorganisation in 1976, very speedy retraining was essential for about two-thirds of the clerical employees, who were scattered geographically in six centres.

Barclaycard, which already had IBM equipment, decided to use IBM's *Interactive Instructional System* (*IIS*), which was capable of simulating all the usual routines carried out by the clerks once trained. Graphics were not needed. The main simulation, which was created by Barclaycard's own programmers and trainers in six months with assistance from an IBM consultant, included a file of 600 cardholders' accounts that provided good teaching examples. This simulation, intended for keyboard operators, piggybacked on the IBM system, therefore trainees could use the same type of terminal for training as they used for their routine work. They simply switched to the training terminal.

The company found that training time was halved and trainees liked the CBT. Training expenses such as travel dropped dramatically because trainees could receive all their training at their home office. Development and installation costs were recovered within six months. Trainers had to spend less time away from their home offices; in fact, the number of trainers involved dropped by two-thirds.

Barclaycard subsequently streamlined its training still more by selecting certain common skills to be taught first. Once trained in these, a clerk gets further training, to build up a repertoire of skills, at the discretion of supervisors, but all job skill training is done by CBT. As an example of more effective training, one course on keyboard skills has led to higher standards (9000 key depressions per hour instead of 6000). In training data entry operators, CBT cut by two-thirds (from six months to two months) the training time needed to reach standards required. There is one training screen per 70 clerical employees, and it is used most of the working day. If necessary, sudden fluctuations in demand for training can easily be met by using extra terminals (Open University, 1985).

BARCLAYS BANK

In the United Kingdom, Barclays Bank has about 47 000 employees in nearly 3000 branches. About 10 000 employees receive some form of basic procedural training each year.

As well as using conventional training methods, the Bank uses new training technology of three kinds. It adapts existing computer terminals connected to a mainframe, it employs a videotex system, and it uses interactive videodiscs.

Barclays used to encounter problems in taking computer operator recruits, particularly young women aged 18–25, away from their branches for week-long training sessions. In-Branch Operator Training (IBOT) was introduced for these employees and is based on workbooks plus embedded CBT. For this training, the terminals are taken off-line and a training program is inserted (on cassette or disk). Staff thus use the same terminals on which they work, to learn, for example, to enter correctly debits and credits without disrupting customers' accounts.

The programs simulate real processes the trainees must master. The training packages are designed to be used with a supervisor on call, who controls the training and records trainees' progress and test results. Altogether sixteen hours are available, divided into 45 minute sessions, which trainees can repeat if they wish.

In 1980 Barclays decided to experiment with videotex, which links a mainframe computer to terminals using ordinary telephone lines. This system had the advantage, among others, of offering a simple authoring language that could be easily used by trainers and of not conflicting with the mainframe-based network used for the Bank's financial system.

First came a pilot project in 33 branches, extended later to 116, using Rediffusion R2800 mainframes at Teddington via British Telecom lines. To keep costs down, the Bank confined its videotex operations to two British Telecom regions, both heavily populated and with many Bank branches. Although the system has worked reasonably well, there are no plans to provide national coverage.

The programs are aimed at clerical employees and concentrate on basic procedural and product knowledge training: for example, *Balance Sheet Analysis*. About 80 were prepared, each providing 45–330 minutes of interactive training, the longer ones being subdivided into 60 minute segments. The programs can be easily and cheaply updated, since they are held centrally on the training mainframe. This can be important in a bank, where procedures may change slightly from time to time. Student progress can be monitored centrally, too. Diagnostic tests are built into the programs and the results are fed back to branches for each student.

Evaluation of the videotex project has shown that the number of hours each terminal is used per working week fluctuates greatly (1–40 hours/week), but a 1983 survey reflected satisfaction with the system on the part of trainees and their supervisors (Mortimer, 1984).

Siting of terminals for training proved to be a problem. The Bank wanted the terminals to be readily accessible for reference purposes, as part of the ongoing training, but this aim conflicted with the need for training to take place in a quiet part of the branch.

Scheduling regular training sessions also proved difficult. The pressure of daily work often prevented trainees from moving onto the terminals. This is reflected in the overall usage figures, which, at about 55 000 trainee/hours up to the end of 1986, are modest considering the number of trainees, programs and terminals. As an incentive, branches get a breakdown of hours of usage by neighbouring branches.

The Bank has found no way of relating videotex training performance to on-the-job performance or supervisors' reports, therefore it is difficult to establish precisely the cost-effectiveness of videotex training.

At general manager level, in 1984, interest stirred in interactive videodisc. The Bank planned a pilot project, with *Genesis* as the authoring language. The first topic chosen was *Uncleared Effects*, to be followed by a disc on lending. Opinions differ in the Bank on whether interactive videodiscs are cost-effective in interpersonal management skills training, but there may be a pilot disc in that field

too. The project, when completed, may lead to a very large investment in interactive videodisc technology for training, but frequent
changes in Bank procedures mean that the discs will have to be
supplemented by updating text (printed, or onscreen from microcomputers).

There may be a pause in developments, however, while the Bank
conducts a new training needs analysis, based on a model of market
segments it serves. Then the Bank may decide what to do next about
using new training technology on a company-wide basis.

DUNN AND BRADSTREET

This US company, a provider of business information services, was
one of the first companies in the country to have a national
computerised training system on mainframe for their marketing
representatives and credit personnel.

When interactive videodisc technology arrived Dunn and
Bradstreet took a close look at the possibility of using it with their
personal computers, which by then they were using to simulate the
mainframe system. They developed and tested a pilot interactive
videodisc training program. The results showed that it was unlikely
to be cost-effective. The company's primary training needs are
highly procedural, and simply do not require video to aid learning.

ERNST AND WHINNEY

As one of the largest accountant firms in the world, Ernst and
Whinney decided in the early 1980s that the company needed a CBT
course on basic electronic data processing concepts, for their
accountants and for the 1700 new recruits who enter training as
general auditors and computer auditors each year. Extensive
research showed that although developing CBT would be expensive
and time-consuming, it was capable of teaching the concepts faster
and at less cost than any other technique.

Over two years, Ernst and Whinney conducted an extensive survey
and interviewed 23 training companies before choosing Pinnacle
Courseware of San Jose. This company was contracted to develop two
courses of 20 hours each, using objectives developed by Ernst and
Whinney: *EDP Concepts for Accountants*, which was already available in 1987; and *Specific EDP Applications*, still being developed.

Pinnacle developed the first course for and on personal computers, using a specially designed authoring system (*Saber*), flexible enough to accommodate the program's needs. No video interface was required, since the trainees do not have videodisc equipment.

The course was completed and judged successful in training its target audience. The auditors like the graphics and colour presentation of the material, enjoy being able to train at their convenience and feel comfortable on a computer once they have completed the courses. Their success showed Ernst and Whinney that the course, with minor revisions, would be suitable for any business people working with computers. The name of the program was changed to *EDP Concepts for Business*, and it is being sold to other companies, banks and colleges.

HARTFORD INSURANCE GROUP

The Hartford Insurance Group is a US insurance company with a learning centre that was originally established to train data processing employees (Seaver, 1987). After using videotape for some years, trainers at Hartford looked at mainframe CBT for teaching technical skills, but found that it was not likely to be effective within the context of the company. Instead, interactive videodiscs were introduced for two courses. By 1987 there were sixteen courses, with some 90 discs, all generic materials used under licence. The discs are only one medium among many used in the centre, and complement classroom training. Trainees particularly like the discs, however, and finish the courses on them more often than they do the other courses. They spend 15–20 per cent less time taking the courses, too.

LLOYDS BANK

Lloyds Bank is one of the largest British clearing banks, with 46 000 employees nationwide. During the 1960s and 1970s, it invested heavily in programmed learning texts as a decentralised medium for procedural training, with no less than 27 courses in use. Next, it was a natural, but not simple, step for Lloyds Bank to move into interactive videodisc, and the introduction of conventional CBT is now being considered.

In 1985 Lloyds Bank invested £4 million in a training system based on Philips Professional LaserVision interactive videodisc equipment in 1473 branches (all with more than eight employees) and head office departments. The system is for use in three ways: for procedural training, for disseminating to employees important information about new products and services, and for skills training.

One of Lloyds Bank's early experiments consisted of sending out an interactive videodisc that contained a 'game' aimed at increasing employees' knowledge of and motivation to sell a credit card service. This was a great success, and employees wanted to play the game in any spare moment in the branch offices. The training was highly cost-effective: its average cost was £2 per trainee, and it resulted in many thousands of new credit card accounts.

New recruits take their first interactive videodisc course, in procedural training, during their first week in Lloyds Bank. The program expects them to make some 'real life' decisions as part of this training. The second course, *Am I Making Myself Clear*, is aimed at more experienced personnel and its use is decided by branch managers.

The training includes *Cashiering: Basic Procedures*, a course on cashiers' procedures, on six sides of videodisc, with associated floppy disks. The topics include form-filling and security procedures. Some 2000 cashiers a year are being trained by this means.

Because the training takes place when individuals need it and at their own branches, they can apply immediately what they have learned (Griffiths, 1986). The training contains alternative routes because not all branches have yet installed the newest technology.

By early 1987, Lloyds Bank (and the providers who contracted to provide production services) had produced 23 sides of interactive videodisc for training purposes. The policy is to choose training topics where updating is less likely to be needed, but Lloyds Bank had to update part of the cashiers' procedures course to take account of new technology in branches. When the £1 note disappeared, some parts of the cashiering course had to be eliminated: the computer program no longer accesses portions of the video in which the note appeared.

When evaluating the cashiering course, Lloyds Bank found that whereas the original face-to-face course had taken two weeks, a decentralised one using programmed texts and audiotape took twenty hours and interactive video only eight hours. The response of trainees and their managers to interactive videodisc training has

91

been very favourable, although a few employees commented on the lack of a person to turn to if they could not cope.

MASSACHUSETTS MUTUAL LIFE INSURANCE

This company has a unique CBT training project, according to Austin (1987). It has combined two systems to provide a remarkable form of standardised training for its agents. One is the standard interactive video system from Interactive Training Systems, and the other is the Performax Simulation Systems Trainer. Together they include touch-sensitive screen, video camera, keyboard, videodisc player, tape recorder and IBM AT microcomputer, linked by a controller.

Agents take the first portion of the selling skills course through other media, then individually conduct an eye-to-eye sales presentation with a simulated customer while the Performax Trainer videos their performance. Afterwards, they see and hear themselves and judge their own effectiveness before deciding whether to study the first part of the course further or to proceed. The agents are said to like the method. The company likes the standardisation of its training.

NATIONAL WESTMINSTER BANK

The National Westminster Bank (NatWest) is another large British clearing bank, with 92 000 employees in over 3000 branch offices. After early trials with text and video, the bank decided in 1983 to try interactive video, using a mixture of generic discs and others prepared specifically for NatWest. For example, there were discs on telephone techniques and customer relations over-the-counter. The initial NatWest telephone techniques trial is described by Rothwell (1985), who comments that the interactive disc was developed from the earlier text and videotape material, which proved exceptionally easy to convert. Trainees reported very few problems, and liked being able to work at their own pace.

With some of the videodiscs, however, the updating problem was soon encountered, because NatWest's procedures change rapidly. Merely updating the computer side of the interactive video was not enough, and issuing updated discs was expensive.

By contrast, conventional CBT could be more easily and cheaply updated. In the first six months of trying CBT, NatWest had to issue no fewer than 20 updates. The bank, however, chose CBT principally to decentralise a large part of its training. It wanted to make training more accessible to its employees and to take advantage of the interactive training CBT can offer. CBT's trainee management system, with its record of training, seemed to be an additional benefit.

The bank conducted a limited trial of CBT with 50 trainees and compared their results with another 50 trained by conventional means. The results of the CBT group were at least as good as those of the control group. Trainers, managers and employees, cautious at first, were enthusiastic about CBT.

Following this experiment, NatWest decided to implement CBT, plus text, for basic procedural training in about 220 locations, which were equipped with microcomputers. Every year the bank needs to train large numbers of recruits in procedures such as setting up accounts and processing applications for loans. Thus procedural training was an appropriate field to start in, where large savings might be made because of the high cost of releasing staff for centralised procedural training.

After considering a variety of authoring systems, the bank selected *TenCORE*, because it wanted a system usable by trainers who were not programmers. Its CBT production teams consisted of a subject matter expert, an instructional designer and an authoring system specialist, although in practice their roles often overlapped. Among the packages they produced was *Out of Order*, which won a gold award in 1986.

Few employees have to travel more than 20 miles (32 km) to reach one of the microcomputers now installed for training, and most have one in their own branch. They can train on days that suit their branches. They can usually train in private, away from the gaze of customers or other staff, and work at their own speed. They can test themselves, knowing that performance on the job will be what counts, because the scores are not passed back to the managers. But managers like the new system because they can decide when and where any particular employee should receive the training, and what its topic should be. Trainers and managers have a record of which topics each trainee has completed successfully.

STEWART WRIGHTSON

Stewart Wrightson is a very large international insurance broking group, based in London, with over 2500 staff worldwide (Siomiak, 1987). It has a network of Wang minicomputers to which are linked several hundred terminals and microcomputers, in Britain and America.

The group introduced a new computerised insurance broking accountancy system, for which CBT was developed. It decided to use embedded CBT, delivering the training direct to its employees through its already existing terminals. The group regards the new accountancy system as a tool to be used by employees to achieve their business objectives. Understanding the role of the system is more important even than knowing how to operate it. Thus the trainers have to explain the business before they train employees in correct procedures.

A provider, CNJ Systems, undertook the development work, which was subsidised by the Manpower Services Commission as part of its promotion of new training technology, to demonstrate CBT's effectiveness. The training and support required by trainees is embedded in the operational system they use to deal with claims.

Trainees using the operational system can initiate a request for training simply by pressing a particular function key. The system will tell them what is available and transfer them to the training modules they ask for. The training software, which incorporates full interactive help menus, calls on the operational system for 'live' examples as necessary but protects it. Employees have many opportunities to practise complex procedures and test their knowledge.

During development, Stewart Wrightson and CNJ Systems found that more printed training guides were needed than originally anticipated, to give trainees instant access to checklists while being trained on the screen. Windows or split screens might have obviated this. They also found that over 2000 screens of 'help', more than they had expected, were needed to support some 350 operational screens (Bentley, 1986).

Stewart Wrightson's computerised systems are extremely complex, and Siomiak reports that the group's ultimate aim is to use a knowledge-based or expert system that will help employees to identify weaknesses in their knowledge of the systems. Such a system could well become an advisor to employees. If individual job performance can be assessed and related to job requirements by the expert system, then that system should be able to specify individuals' training needs. Development work of this kind demands that employees' personal attribute profiles can be matched against job demand profiles. With CNJ Systems, Stewart Wrightson is attempting this ambitious project, supported by funds from the Manpower Services Commission.

UNUM LIFE INSURANCE (FORMERLY UNION MUTUAL)

UNUM is a large US life insurance company. Its primary training need is to enable employees to use the mainframe computer system in ways required by the majority of jobs in the company. Five years ago the training and development manager suggested looking at options, including CBT, for delivering training. A project team of twelve people took a year to decide that CBT would be best, choosing the *PHOENIX* authoring system. Its decision was based primarily on a comparison of the long-range costs of CBT versus training in classrooms, with CBT coming out a clear winner despite the high developmental costs.

The trainers developed simulations to train UNUM's own employees, including a *Long Term Disability Claim* simulation aimed at training them to process certain forms, and a *Human Anatomy* course for staff dealing with claims.

The *Human Anatomy* included graphics produced on the mainframe with *PHOENIX* which only offers the standard keyboard characters. Developers used photos of sections of the body which were reduced before being pasted to the screen and drawn with dots and other keyboard characters (Figure 7.1). Despite these difficulties the course produced excellent results, possibly due to its innovative use of visuals in what had previously been a text-only system.

In 1985 changes in the company and cutbacks reduced the size of the training section, almost eliminating CBT. Late in 1986 UNUM decided on a massive change in computer systems, and reconsidered CBT because of its capacity to train large numbers of people in a fairly short time.

Currently computers are being integrated into a variety of training courses, wherever it is most effective. They provide testing and exercises for clients and sales representatives at the end of training modules, and manage training by keeping track of trainees and their progress. Case studies are provided in workbooks, and trainees use the computer to look up answer and options, thus using it cost-effectively.

Figure 7.1: Example of simple *PHOENIX* mainframe graphics used by UNUM Life Insurance (reprinted by courtesy of UNUM Life Insurance)

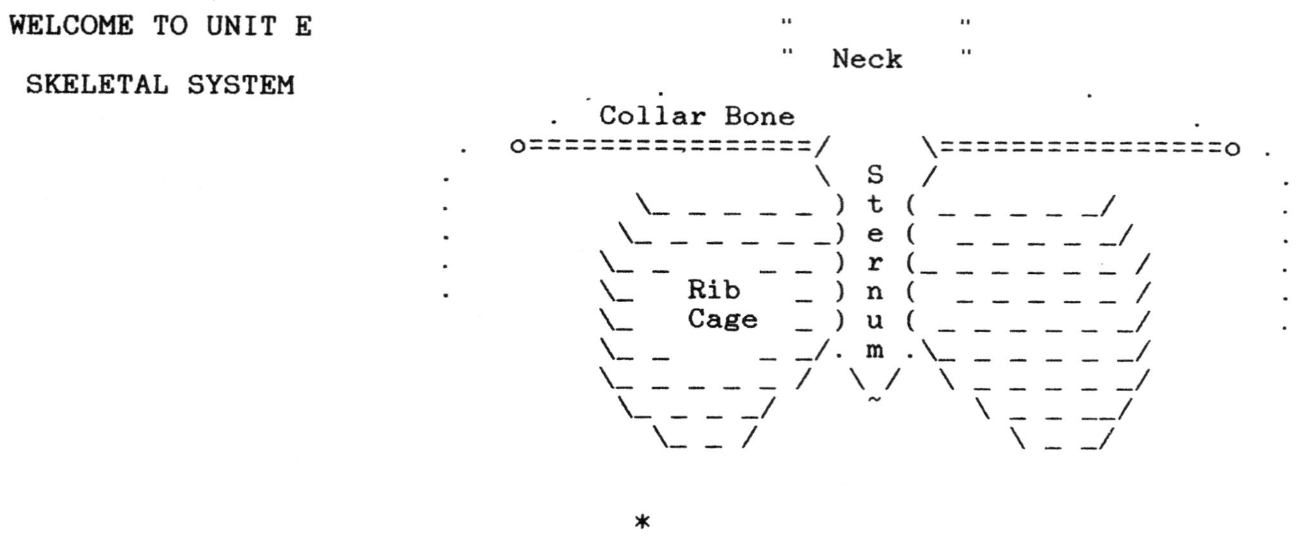

WELCOME TO UNIT E

SKELETAL SYSTEM

```
                                              : :
                                   : :   Neck
                    : : Collar Bone
                    o==================\      /=================o
                          .         |   )S(   |              . .
                              .     |   )t(   |           .
                                    |   )e(   |
                          Rib       |   )r(   |
                          Cage      |   )n(   |
                                    |   )u(   |
                                    |   )m(   |
                    \               |   ) ~ (  |              /
                     \              |   |     |             /
                      \             |   |     |            /
                       \            \   |     /           /
                        \               \___/            /

                                        *
```

Along with this new wave of interest in aspects of CBT has come the use of personal computers with boards that enable them to act as mainframe terminals, thus eliminating the use of the mainframe system for training. Users and managers now see CBT benefits in saving time and efficiency.

USLIFE

USLIFE is another large US insurance company. Traditionally, USLIFE used seminars, with videotape and print, to introduce new products to its representatives, who are independent agents. Cutbacks in personnel have made seminars no longer cost-effective. Since 1982 all USLIFE sales personnel have had microcomputers to input client information and benefits, and to use in preparing product proposals for determining the products to present to clients. The company has standardised on IBM personal computers, and it was logical to consider training through them both the agents and internal service employees.

Personal computer CBT tutorials are now being developed for new products, services and policies. Colour graphics and interactive video is not being considered because the agents do not have the hardware. The CBT developed so far is mainly text, with box-line graphics to simulate forms.

8

General Manufacturing

TRAINING NEEDS

The general manufacturing section of US and British economic activity has not approached new training technology from the same angle as the financial institutions discussed in the last chapter, and its experience of CBT has been different. Companies in this sector particularly needed mainframe computers to control manufacturing processes, through automation and, later, robotics (see Chapter 1). They also needed computers to control inventories, place orders, collect debts, pay bills, keep accounts, operate payrolls and to assist in marketing their products through distributors and salespeople. At first, they seldom installed mainframes with hundreds of terminals to meet these needs.

Manufacturing companies first used CBT to train employees in their data processing departments. For example, British Aerospace, according to Rothwell (1983a), is a large company with considerable training needs among its employees who use computers. CBT was adopted because it offered training on demand to employees who could not easily be released for conventional training. The company first purchased *IIS* generic training packages from IBM to teach such skills as keyboarding. The company's Computer Education Department modified these, using the *IIAS* authoring system, to conform to the company's standards, and, building on this experience, developed a new package on report writing. The case study below of Chevron Information Technology, part of the Chevron group of petrochemical companies, is a more recent US example.

The second application of CBT in manufacturing was to train employees to operate new manufacturing processes and systems. For instance, in the Austin Rover case study it is clear that this company used videotex to train engineers to use a new components specification system. Elsewhere, Jaguar Cars commissioned an interactive videodisc to provide an introduction to industrial robotics. British Shipbuilders worked with Training Advancement to produce CBT on statistical process control, for employees at various levels. Mobil Chemical Company developed a microcomputer-based simulation to train employees to operate plant making polypropylene film. Essochem asked a provider to produce microcomputer-based CBT, including a simulation, to train technical employees in the operation of the lubricating system for the company's new ethylene manufacturing plant in Britain.

Quality control training has become another field for CBT. At the Ford Motor Company in Britain, for example, interactive videodiscs are used to train employees in quality control techniques such as statistical process control, for Ford's manufacturing and supply sections. The discs use extensive simulation to provide individualised training for most grades. Austin Rover has a *Quality* videodisc.

Safe operation of the plant is important for manufacturers. Employees at a new chemical manufacturing and packaging plant built for Norsk Hydro Fertilisers in Britain receive training through an interactive videotape system. Imperial Chemical Industries (ICI) developed microcomputer-based packages to train employees in the safe operation of a nitric acid plant and refrigeration equipment. Austin Rover has developed a *Health and Safety at Work* interactive videodisc. Jaguar Car's videodisc on industrial robotics, through computer graphics, trains employees to recognise the 'operational envelope' of a robot, within which they must not venture. Kellogg's uses microcomputer-based simulations to train employees to operate safely an ammonia production plant.

Many new manufacturing systems include one or more microprocessors, computer-like devices installed to control processes. Thus in these industries 'PC' may mean 'programmable controller' rather than the usual 'personal computer'. Employees who operate systems that are controlled at least in part by these devices need to understand the new mode of operation, which is often dramatically different from earlier modes. For example, these controllers are reprogrammed when an operation changes, rather than the equipment being changed. Emulating controllers on a microcomputer, or connecting them to a microcomputer, are two ways of providing CBT in their use.

Beyond actual manufacturing, some companies in this sector need to train dealers and salespeople to sell new products, and technicians to maintain and repair them. BMW (the Bavarian Motor Works), for example, now use Video-MIT computers for providing dealer and technical training in their 150 United Kingdom dealerships (Griffiths, 1986). Jaguar commissioned from Blackrod a series of interactive videodiscs for dealers, engineers and mechanics handling the new Jaguar XJ-6.

Finally, manufacturing companies have recently turned to CBT to train managerial, administrative and secretarial staff. Again, Austin Rover has decided to use interactive videodisc to train managers in interviewing. Remploy developed for its 9000 disabled employees a CBT package on statutory sick pay. Volkswagen Audi turned to CBT to deal with the problem of training its British employees to use a complex new telephone system, and commissioned an interactive videodisc.

Some of the case studies that follow are full, others are short. Together, they give an impression of diversity in the CBT experience of the general manufacturing sector.

ALLEN BRADLEY

Allen Bradley manufactures and sells software and hardware for production control, and supplies the training for users of these products. Since 1983 the company has developed training for its own products as well as evaluating and remarketing courses developed by other companies in the field of industrial control technology and manufacturing automation. CBT is one component in a multimedia approach taken by Allen Bradley in its efforts to supply training to customers as far as possible on their own premises.

Most of Allen Bradley's courses are on basic concepts of industrial technology and are marketed directly to customers to ensure that they have the basic training required for operating the company's products. These courses are followed by product-specific training at Allen Bradley.

The first courses to be developed in-house by Allen Bradley's programmers and training designers were on *PLATO* with *TUTOR*, and on an IBM personal computer. The company is now moving towards using microcomputer-based interactive video. Video (with text) is seen as another important component in the company's multimedia approach.

Senior management in the company supports this kind of training because they see it as necessary as the complexity of the products increases, and because they have perceived a direct link between the training they offer and the value of Allen Bradley equipment purchases by customers.

AUSTIN ROVER

Austin Rover, now the largest British car manufacturer with an annual turnover of over £2000 million is widely acknowledged as being among the leaders in developing CBT. The spur to development of a progressive training policy has been the need to remain competitive through the installation of high technology, including robots, large scale automation and sophisticated flexible manufacturing systems. These changes brought needs for training and retraining.

Computer managed learning was an essential component of the company's open learning network, to which a major commitment was made in 1982, later backed by resources from the Open Tech Unit of the Manpower Services Commission. The network represented the largest single investment in training ever made by the company (Stretch, 1984), but Austin Rover wanted to increase its training effort without significantly increasing the overall resources required to do the training. It was also aware that any training it offered might have to be updated at very short notice, and would have to cater for widely varying trainee needs.

Being early in the field, Austin Rover encountered special problems, such as the need to train its trainers, as well as having to decide on the best modes of training. First, ten trainers were trained to produce CBT courses using *PILOT* on Apple II microcomputers. They developed about 100 hours of training, through which about 1000 employees were trained in aspects of electronics, robotics, value engineering, network analysis, keyboard skills, BASIC programming, statistics and time management. Next, a further 20 trainers were trained to prepare CBT courses, and another 150 hours of training were developed, covering topics such as semiconductors, logic gates, alternative current theory and instrumentation. Some topics run on DEC Rainbow microcomputers, which provide colour, high resolution graphics and better response times than the Apple II computers. Within a multimedia training strategy CBT has become very important and integral to the company's extensive network of open learning centres that deliver training at the right time, place and pace.

101

These developments enabled Austin Rover to train, in a mere six weeks, no less than 600 engineers in a new specification system for vehicle components (Hutt, 1986). The system required the engineers to learn how to use fourteen-digit code numbers instead of plain English, which had been found to be too ambiguous. Using a mainframe-based videotex system, supported by printed workbooks and job aids, the company's trainers met the deadline, spending only £35 000, about half the cost of traditional methods (Open University, 1985).

Since 1985, Austin Rover has produced, with the help of a Manpower Services Commission grant-in-aid, three generic interactive videodisc courses entitled *Health and Safety at Work*, *Selection Interviewing*, and *Disciplinary Interviewing*. These were developed using the *GPILOT* authoring system, and inexpensive low-band Sony U-matic videorecording equipment, to run on IBM-compatible computers with *MIC 2000* interfaces to Philips VP-831 videodisc players. The discs are for sale, together with nearly 20 of the earlier CBT packages, developed for Apple II, BBC or DEC microcomputers, and Austin Rover's own authoring language, *GPILOT*. Receipts will be offset against development costs.

According to Perryman and Freshwater (1987), Austin Rover analyses the cost-effectiveness of its open learning, within which is the CBT described above, while recognising the problems of definition. Each plant provides figures for student throughput. Fixed and variable costs, hours of study and student throughput figures are kept for each course, too. The company found that the initial fixed costs of open learning were high (at £800/hour) but running costs were about half those for conventional training. It calculates the breakeven point for particular courses: that for an electronics course was 113 trainees, but for 300 trainees the savings would be about £20 000.

In a separate project, Austin Rover developed interactive videodiscs for use in training dealers in product knowledge (*Audio Visual*, November 1985). The company has supported its dealers with programmed learning and audiovisual materials at the time of product launches, and has moved from filmstrip to slides to videocassette. In 1984, a videodisc for use on Thorn-EMI VHD players accompanied the launch of the Rover 200. This limited experiment was followed by a regional project in which 'View-centres', consisting of players and discs, were placed in 25 dealers' offices. In 1985, ten more were added, being units made up of the players plus BBC-B microcomputers. The company's dealers have

35 000 employees, however, based in 1300 premises owned by the dealers, not Austin Rover. These facts constrain dealer training policy. Innovations must be sold to the dealers. Conformity cannot be enforced, and a variety of delivery systems and formats must be provided.

Throughout its development work, Austin Rover has managed its own program design, on the grounds that the company has the subject knowledge and the training expertise. It has gone elsewhere for specialist skills in video production and computer graphics. Probably interactive videodisc will be used widely in the company to supplement face-to-face training, refresh basic skills and to bring employees up to the same entry level before they begin more advanced courses.

BRITISH STEEL

British Steel is a very large nationalised steel-making company, with many plants. Its hot strip mill at Ravenscraig in Scotland makes strip steel products by a continuous process that can be stopped only at considerable expense. In 1984, the mill had about 3500 employees, most of whom were operators, according to Bayard-White (1985). Most training is done on-the-job, being the responsibility of shift supervisors.

The need to use new training technology arose partly from managers' concern over high energy consumption in the plant. Consultants who studied the plant's use of energy advised that better trained operators would result in savings, and suggested interactive video. A pilot videotape on hot mill operations convinced managers and trainers that the technology was worth trying further. The consultants studied whether such training could improve efficiency of the cold rolling tandem mill, and a production company belonging to the consultancy group made an interactive videodisc about the tandem mill, at considerable expense (about £50 000).

Evaluation of this second video showed it was effective, says Bayard-White, and resulted in improved quality and quantity of steel products. The training manager decided to produce an interactive videodisc, in-house and at lower cost, for training operatives on the pickle line (where the strip is dipped in hot hydrochloric acid).

Bayard-White says that nobody in the company knew how to produce an interactive videodisc. The training manager assembled a small team of himself, a trainer who had worked on the pickle line,

103

a pickle line supervisor, two staff from the British Steel video production unit at Scunthorpe and an instrument mechanic who could programme a computer. The team made cheaply a 46 minute videotape ('lowband', therefore of relatively low quality) which was transferred by Thorn-EMI to videodisc for use on a Thorn-EMI VHD disc player, with an Apple II microcomputer controlling the interaction. The total cost of *The Pickle Line* was about £15 000.

The video is in eight segments, corresponding to the eight types of operators in the pickle line. Trainees view first the segments appropriate to their own job and then those about the next two jobs up the promotion ladder. This usually takes less than an hour, including answering the questions asked about each segment.

Following the success of the tandem mill video, the trainers did not test the pickle line disc during development, and the first trainees to use it performed satisfactorily. Shift supervisors arrange for employees to leave the pickle line for training, until all were trained. At British Steel, the new technology results in cost-effective and consistent training, in a shorter time, than the old technology.

British Steel's Central Training Unit has since made a 20 hour *Basic Electrical Knowledge* generic CBT course with interactive videodisc support (British Steel Corporation, 1986), marketed for use by trainees in any company.

CINCINNATI MILACRON

This US company produces equipment for moulding plastics. With the aid of a provider, Scientific Systems, it has been developing CBT since 1985. Cincinnati Milacron calls its interactive video programs *Computer Expert Training (CET)*. These programs train customers how to maintain, troubleshoot and operate their production equipment. The company's trainers decide on the technical content, which Scientific Systems puts into interactive video format.

Cincinnati Milacron's customers include companies such as General Motors, Electrolux and other automotive and domestic appliance companies. Technical personnel in these companies know about plastics moulding but not necessarily about how to deal with new computer-controlled moulding equipment, which operates very differently from the old 'button-and-switch' type of machinery, with different features and benefits.

The company decided to use CBT because new moulding technology was being developed faster than they could train their customers' technical personnel, and classroom training was becoming less and less effective in training these personnel to retain the 'how-to' procedural knowledge. Since use of a computer was inherent in the new technology, the company also felt that it would benefit its own image if training was done through computers too. Previously Cincinnati Milacron had used films, videotape, and classroom instruction, which could not provide the benefits of interactive training.

The training is run on a microcomputer, with an added card that emulates the control equipment. One of the first programs covered the basics of controllers, troubleshooting and maintenance. Others deal with operational procedures and control software program language.

Several divisions in the company are developing such programs, including the plastic machinery and machine tool division and the robot division. Management support has been strong because this type of training is equated directly with the company's ability to sell its products.

COCA-COLA USA

Coca-Cola USA manufactures and distributes syrups and concentrates, bottles and cans, for soft drink beverages. The company's main production centre in Atlanta, Georgia, has a large training department divided into three units: bottler training, specifically for management, sales and operational personnel in their bottling plants; employee training, for on-the-job needs and career advancement; and corporate training, for management skills needed by their professional staff and managers.

As in many large companies today, one of Coca-Cola's primary needs is to train employees how to use appropriate software (word-processing packages, spreadsheets, etc.) on microcomputers. Although the trainers use microcomputers increasingly in their classes, they have not yet developed or used self-paced training programs. Instead, they use consultant-developed seminars, lasting from one day to two weeks, which include practice on the systems, backed up by print and video. One of the largest courses, called the Production Management Development Program, trains managers and technical staff to use company-specific production management software on microcomputers.

This training approach seems to work, but the increasing expense

105

of using consultants and seminars is becoming more of a problem. There is no shortage of machines in the training department, as the tremendous increase in demand for training in use of micro-computers enabled the department to purchase a large number (mainly Compaqs), all with IBM boards to enable them to function as mainframe terminals. In-house development and use of self-paced CBT is being discussed.

EASTMAN KODAK

Eastman Kodak Corporation is a US company, manufacturing photographic sensitised materials and equipment, chemicals, plastics and manmade fibres. All seventeen lines of Kodak's business function separately, and have their own training. Within the company, the Training and Communications Technology Group is a shared resource, with a mandate to develop more innovative and cost-effective training.

In the United States, Eastman Kodak developed early CBT for its mainframe IBM computers, using *IIS*. Heaford (1983) mentions a course, *Job Control Language*, and describes a careful but small-scale evaluation which showed some evidence of time savings. He criticises the course, however, because little simulation was included.

In 1984, the Training and Communications Technology Group introduced CBT with interactive videodisc to train field engineers, who are responsible for repairing customers' equipment on the spot. The group began with an Apple IIE computer, and now has a unique system that uses Sony PVM monitors with a VDX 1000 videotex unit and a Pioneer LDV-6000 videodisc player, plus the Apple keyboard and Apple mouse for input.

The system is used for course development and delivery, and for administrative record-keeping, allowing trainees and managers to keep track of progress. Even training modules not delivered via videodisc are tested and tracked by the course manager program. Training programs are sent to approximately 60 district offices around the country, each of which has at least one interactive train-ing system.

Copy Products is the largest group trained via videodisc. Training includes how to carry out preventive and corrective maintenance, with very realistic situations being depicted. As during an actual customer repair call, the field engineer does not get constant reinforcement: he either solves the problem or not. In one innovative application the system simulates diagnosis and repair of a copier product with print quality problems, and the trainee sees copies of printed sheets, with errors, from the videodisc. To pass the training test, the field engineer must solve the problem by using the most cost-effective solution.

Another innovation is a Parts Locator on videodisc, as part of the Help information. With the video locator, trainees can request and see a closeup of any area of the equipment, down to a single component. An index of Adjustments and Removals is included to enable field engineers to review procedures before going on a customer repair call. The videodisc can be updated, in some cases, using a graphics package to create an overlay to superimpose on the video image.

To expedite production, Kodak has developed a coordination tool, called the Interactive Storyboarding System, which uses coloured sheets to identify content and status information so that all involved can track progress. This has substantially reduced development time by cutting the error rate and debugging by authors. In this system, authors are publications support people who use EIS's authoring language *CDS/Genesis* to enter into the computer the courseware developed by the instructional staff.

At the end of 1986, Business Imaging Systems introduced equipment training for which no equipment is provided, only simulations on videodisc. The first time the field engineers see the actual equipment is on their first service call. The project took 30 weeks to develop and fills four videodisc sides, which have been extremely successful in overcoming engineer's initial fears, with good results in the field.

Senior management support for this CBT has been good, based primarily on projected cost savings. The Customer Equipment Services Division spent $13 million in 1985 for travel-related training expenses alone. It was this high cost that motivated management to search for alternative training methods. The search was accelerated when Kodak stopped regional training, closing down the facilities so that all training would have to be handled either at the Rochester headquarters or in the district offices.

Eastman Kodak has found that interactive courses shorten training time, and that appeals to both management and trainees. For example, a week-long course may take half the time in interactive mode, depending on the complexity of the subject.

In Britain, the company has tried CBT, too, using courses

developed for the IBM mainframe. Heaford says, however, that training received low priority on the computer, resulting in slow responses when trainees were in the CBT programs. Kodak decided to introduce a Commodore PET microcomputer, for which the training department wrote simple CBT programs in BASIC. This led to the introduction of Apple microcomputers for CBT developed speedily with *PILOT* and *PASS* (see Chapter 6), and trials of interactive videotape based on Dalroth's *Interactive Video Learning*.

ESSOCHEM

Essochem decided to explore the potential of CBT in their new ethylene manufacturing plant at Fife in Scotland. In collaboration with Intra Systems, they produced CBT software for a four to five hour course, *The Lube and Seal Oil System*, for technical employees. The course includes a simulation, using high quality graphics, of the oil flow through the system, and is enhanced by animation of such detail as a bearing rotating in its housing.

The course has 'shown significant benefits in providing consistent and quality training', say Intra Systems, and is expected to yield major savings.

A pilot operational maintenance training package, based on the *TenCORE* authoring system, was supplied by Education Technology. At the time of writing, the pilot was being evaluated to determine the effectiveness of this kind of CBT course in the company.

FORD MOTOR COMPANY

The Ford Motor Company is a very large international company manufacturing cars and other vehicles. In the United States, the company's Management and Technical Training Department acts as a training consultancy to all the plants, developing training courses for managers and technical personnel throughout Ford's. It offers courses at its training facility in Dearborn, Michigan, as well as courses at individual plants.

Within this department, the Management Training section offers primarily traditional classroom instruction in management skills. The Technical Training section uses a wide range of media in their courses, however, as appropriate to the subject and audience

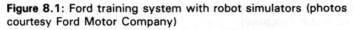

Figure 8.1: Ford training system with robot simulators (photos courtesy Ford Motor Company)

(Figure 8.1 shows a robotics simulator). The 55 courses for manufacturing technology include a videodisc course on mathematics and six CBT courses covering troubleshooting, how to use an oscilloscope (Figure 8.2) and advanced relay logic. The computer technology courses include several generic CBT courses purchased off-the-shelf and adapted by the trainers to suit Ford's needs.

Again within the Department, the Apprenticeship and Launch Center offers a large range of apprentice training courses and makes available teams of trainers to work at plants on developing training needed for new Ford products. For example, the AXOD Launch Training Team at the Livonia Transmission Plant in Michigan trained employees when new production equipment was installed to produce a new type of automatic transmission. This team was the first to try interactive videodisc. An IBM PC-XT is linked to a Sony monitor, an RGB touch-sensitive screen, a Sony or Pioneer videodisc player and a graphics board from Video Applied Lab. An

109

Figure 8.2: Ford oscilloscope training program (photos courtesy Ford Motor Company)

external provider, Allen Communications, handled the interactive development, but the trainers shot the video.

The first course produced by the team was *Troubleshooting Strategy*. Trainees respond to typical problem conditions shown on the screen, diagnosing them by using the keyboard to enter a suspect list of problems. The program gives appropriate feedback to wrong answers.

Other courses followed: *Laser Welding*, *Allen Bradley Controllers*, *Geometric Dimensioning and Tolerancing*, and *Vibration Analysis*. The team also makes use of other courses from their Department and from outside Ford's.

The group has found the courses cost-effective because small numbers of employees scattered throughout the plant can be trained without instructors. These employees can train during their off-shift or at work, and they can practise in a non-threatening context.

Management has been very supportive, up through the hierarchy. CBT for technical training is now part of the training mandate, and other plants are asking for more interactive training, using the programs developed for Lavonia.

GENERAL ELECTRIC

The division of General Electric at Charlottesville, Virginia, produces programmable controllers and numerical controllers, for manufacturing systems. The division's technical trainers produce tutorials using a microcomputer board that plugs into a controller, providing trainees with hands-on training in using such a device. The microcomputer board is accessed through an IBM personal computer modified by IBM to meet the company's requirements.

The microcomputer board can be programmed with a BASIC tutorial, independent of the controller. The tutorial uses typical BASIC statements such as 'if, then, go', which the controller reads through the microcomputer board. The trainees are users of the equipment, sales personnel and distributors. They progress from easier to more complex routines. If they make mistakes, error messages appear.

The company's trainers are looking into other ways of using the IBM personal computer for training. With qualified support from management, they are considering interactive videodiscs for maintenance and troubleshooting courses for employees in General Electric's client companies. These companies find it very difficult to send their employees to classes at General Electric.

Elsewhere in General Electric, at its Aircraft Engine Business Group's new plant in Massachusetts, a decision was taken, after careful analysis, not to use CBT or interactive video, according to Zani (1987). *ActionCode* and *PLATO* both came under scrutiny because they are used by General Electric's Major Appliance Business Group, to very good effect. They were rejected for the Aircraft group, however, bearing in mind the training needs at the new plant. What were these needs? The 100 trainees were of three different kinds. First, there were machine operators, who would be maintaining fully automated and highly advanced equipment. They lacked training in troubleshooting and hydraulics. Second, there were unskilled workers who had to learn how to use computer terminals from which they obtained information. The third group were to be highly trained electronic repair specialists who did not yet have all the specific knowledge they required. Zani says that the main reasons for not using CBT or videodisc in this situation were high cost per trainee and the likelihood that programs would have to be updated frequently to keep pace with changes in the plant.

111

GENERAL MOTORS

General Motors is another very large international company manufacturing cars and other vehicles. In the United States, the company has used interactive video courses since the early 1980s, from the time when it was informed that it was obliged to train all plant personnel in the handling of hazardous materials. The first, developed by Interactive Medical Communications for General Motors, was on this topic, which, as Austin (1987) points out, is ideal in that the subject matter remains more or less constant and many employees must be trained. The company now has about 1000 sets of training hardware located at more than 140 manufacturing sites across the country.

General Motors commissioned from the Digital Equipment Corporation an interactive video course for its Buick, Oldsmobile and Cadillac Division, to be used as aid in establishing a new flexible island assembly system similar to the team assembly made famous by Volvo. On each island stands an interactive video workstation with touch-sensitive screen, upon which each assembly process is demonstrated, including what parts and tools are needed, with on-line job aids. If a trainee needs further help, he or she can turn to video sequences that show an expert performing the specific operation. The system will also send a message to the stockroom about any faulty components for which replacements are required, therefore it not only trains but helps trainees to recover from errors caused by such components. New video sequences can be added to the system whenever new parts or processes are introduced.

IMPERIAL CHEMICAL INDUSTRIES

In the Imperial Chemical Industries (ICI), one of Britain's largest companies, there has been very considerable interest in CBT. Foggo (1986) reports that computer-based training is one component within an overall training strategy that fits the needs of trainees and ICI. This strategy fits in turn within company policy that calls for analyses of all performance problems, 80 per cent of which may not have training solutions (Treadgold, 1987). The trainers wished to explore CBT and interactive videodisc applications in the company, not merely to acquaint themselves with the technology but also to meet perceived needs such as training in safe operation of new plant and providing this training to small numbers in separate locations.

For the Organics Division the trainers selected Apple II hardware and the *Apple PILOT* authoring language, and prepared a pilot training module on certain aspects of chemical hazards. Using BASIC, they produced another module to simulate the operation of a commercial refrigeration unit. Beech (1983) describes this module. ICI's Huddersfield plant needs 100 tonnes of ice a day, made by refrigeration. The CBT is aimed at increasing trainees' understanding of the principles of refrigeration and at helping them to diagnose faults in the equipment. A trainee sees realistic and animated diagrams of this equipment on the screen, and has to decide what to do as certain conditions develop, such as loss of oil pressure in the lubrication system. The computer tells the trainee whether his or her actions are correct or not, and records the number of incorrect actions and the time taken to correct the fault.

ICI's Severnside works produce 1.5 million tonnes of nitrogen fertiliser and 0.6 million tonnes of compound fertiliser each year. The works, which are potentially very dangerous if something serious goes wrong, run continuously for a year or more without being closed down. If a plant closes down automatically because the control computers have sensed a serious problem they cannot correct, the cost to the company can be very large indeed, as the very cold winter of 1981–82 showed (Treadgold, 1987). Conventional training methods could not train workers well to manage the plant in extraordinary circumstances, such as extremely cold winter weather or an emergency. Because ICI managers and supervisors had had some experience of CBT when taking *PLATO* management courses, they recognised that only through CBT, complete with simulated dials and controls, could trainee operators discover the limits of the processing system and see the simulated consequences (even the destruction of the plant), if these limits were exceeded. Through CBT, they could learn how and when to correct errors.

CBT also offered a solution to another specific training problem at the works. Workers there are organised in shift teams of three or four, and withdrawing team members for training is particularly difficult. Since during much of their shift time they have to do little more than monitor the operation of the plant, they can use the CBT on the spot during shifts until they reach the required standard. This standard is indicated by the absence of processing problems.

Development of the CBT programs was undertaken, with the help of a grant from the Manpower Services Commission, by ICI's own team, which at first used a *PLATO* terminal linked to CDC mainframe. By 1984, however, the company had switched to Regency

113

microcomputers, one being placed in a learning centre in each part of the works. The latter have proved very reliable, and Treadgold says that their capabilities outweigh the lower cost advantage of IBM personal computer hardware, which is also used within the company. Training of the team was carried out by CDC and later by a consultant.

Two ammonia plants, both badly affected by the winter of 1981–82, were chosen for simulation for the first CBT. Because the design programs were available, a mathematical model could be produced for the two plants and for parts of their operations. Before any simulations had been prepared, however, it became clear that these two plants were to be replaced.

CBT for the nitric acid plant was developed and came into use in 1984. The company found that training time was roughly halved by using it (Open University, 1985). ICI's Severnside works produced 101 hours of CBT courseware over three years, at a cost of about £75 000 in hardware and £168 000 in author salaries. The costs were recovered in the first two years of training (Treadgold, 1987).

Overall, for its ten sites, ICI had by 1987 committed £2 250 000 to CBT and had developed no less than 700 hours of programs, a significant accomplishment by any standards. In general, the company is saving one-third of the training time previously required, says Treadgold.

Elsewhere in ICI, a computer-based simulation, *CAR-100*, has been used for management training. The simulation is of the car manufacturing industry, and the 'game' is played by teams that compete to run the business successfully.

ICI was one of the companies chosen for the first set of case studies of open learning prepared for the Manpower Services Commission.

JAGUAR CARS

Jaguar Cars is a British company making cars in the luxury range. In 1986, its expenditure on training was 1.25 per cent of the firm's annual turnover, compared with a reported average figure for British company training of 0.15 per cent of sales revenue (*Training Digest*, September 1986). As part of its modernisation in the early 1980s, Jaguar decided in 1984 to set up an open learning centre where employees could train on a variety of minicomputers, using software for computer literacy, keyboard skills, word processing, spreadsheets,

114

statistics, electronics and so on. When the company installed a new telephone system, Jaguar commissioned production, using the *Procal Interactive Video System*, of a short interactive videotape course on how to operate it correctly (Rothwell, 1985).

The company then commissioned from the National Computing Centre a Laservision interactive videodisc, *An Introduction to Industrial Robotics*. *MicrotextPlus* was the authoring system employed. This disc is generic and can be purchased by other companies. It makes good use of video footage to show, for example, the shape and extent of a robot's operational 'envelope', that is, the exact space it needs to do its work. Computer graphics provide statistical information in pie-chart form. Trainees can move through the material in sequences of their own choosing. The text, as in most interactive videodisc systems, seems somewhat slow to appear on the screen.

This was followed in 1986 by six interactive videodiscs for dealer and mechanic training on the new model of the Jaguar XJ-6. These provide excellent support. For example, the gearbox of this car is an excellently made piece of machinery that is unlikely to break down, therefore mechanics seldom have opportunities to repair one. When they do, they need special tools and must follow procedures very carefully. The disc about the gearbox demonstrates exactly which tools must be selected and how they should be used. There is no need for mechanics to receive frequent refresher courses. Instead, they can turn to the discs whenever they are uncertain about how to deal with the XJ-6.

KELLOGG

Among its many international activities, the M.W. Kellogg Company trains petrochemical plant operators. Computer-based simulations are used, since training operators for such processing plants often cannot be carried out on the plants themselves. As Madhavan (1984) says, these simulations can meet a variety of training needs:

(a) When plants are being built so quickly that training cannot keep up.
(b) When employee turnover is high and new employees must be quickly trained.
(c) When employees need frequent retraining because plants are being modified to save energy or improved yield.

115

(d) When employees need frequent practice in handling emergencies without these emergencies actually happening.

(e) When employees need to control plants within tight limits, through a sound understanding of the relationships between production factors and yield.

In the case of Kellogg's ammonia process simulation, trainees learn to control the ammonia plant. The trainees' screen displays, for example, process flowsheets with continuously updated process variables. Trainees learn to start up and shut down the plant, and to carry out safely a range of dangerous operations. Trainers can intervene. They set the 'plant' in a particular condition, they can create equipment faults or emergencies, or they can freeze the trainees' screens to give time for discussion.

LUCAS INDUSTRIES

Lucas Industries manufactures electrical car components in Britain. When the company's Research Centre decided to invest in CBT as part of its open learning scheme, its trainers looked at no less than eleven systems then on sale, narrowed these down to four and eventually chose the WICAT system. WICAT offered a good trainee management system and its equipment could interface with IBM personal computers already in the company. The trainers had to be trained to use the *WISE* authoring system so that they could prepare training software specific to the company's needs, since no suitable generic software could be found (Open University, 1985).

Some programs have been converted for delivery on cheaper IBM personal computers in several of Lucas' learning centres, but the number of WICAT terminals has been increased to take full advantage of the system's graphics capabilities. The company has recognised that the additional hardware cost is small in comparison with development costs and justified by improved quality. The WICAT *SMART* system records trainees' progress, for their information and for their training manager to act upon (Perryman and Freshwater, 1987). The signs are that Lucas will increase rapidly its use of CBT.

MOBIL CHEMICAL COMPANY

The Films Division of this international company uses a simulation of the procedures involved in making polypropylene film, for training shop-floor operatives, according to Beech (1983). It was developed with the *USE* authoring language, and for a Regency Systems RC-1 microcomputer with touch-sensitive screen. The company wanted a training method that would provide standardised training for all employees working on the equipment for making polypropylene film. To make high quality film requires precise control of the manufacturing processes.

The CBT program starts by teaching the basics of the equipment and of fluid flow of molten material. Trainees then take a test about problems that occur in the plant. Lastly, they are given responsibility for a simulated plant and asked to produce film to certain standards. Nine different faults can occur, all requiring action from the trainees to correct them quickly. Conditions, such as temperature of the environment, can change too and trainees must know when to respond and how.

Beech (1983) says that after a thorough evaluation the company was certain it had recovered the CBT development costs in one year, taking into account savings on normal training costs alone. In addition, wastage was reduced and productivity increased.

NISSAN MOTOR

Nissan conducted a US survey in 1984–85 to find out what other car manufacturers were doing with CBT on microcomputers for sales personnel. Results indicated that CBT would probably not be as cost-effective as Nissan's existing use of videocassettes. For example, Nissan found that Toyota's US sales personnel did not use interactive programs, although they would improve their product knowledge by viewing a videotape. Nissan has nearly 1100 US dealers, 99 per cent of whom already own video equipment but would not be prepared to buy the extra hardware and software required for interactive training. Instead, the company sends them about nine videocassettes each year. Sales-related material goes out of date fairly quickly in the car industry.

PLESSEY MICROSYSTEMS

Plessey Microsystems manufactures electronic equipment in Britain. The company required a system for training its testing engineers in fault-finding on the System X microelectric memory board, being manufactured for British Telecom. Conventional training of these engineers at Plessey had consisted of about two recruits a month being trained by a senior supervisor. This was costly and inefficient. Plessey's trainers decided to turn to CBT and after enquiries adopted the American *PLATO* system. Control Data Corporation trained them to use the *TUTOR* authoring system, and they developed their own training package, which includes circuit diagrams on the touch-sensitive screen and use of an actual memory board (Open University, 1985).

PRATT AND WHITNEY

Pratt and Whitney, a manufacturer of aeroengines and industrial and marine gas turbine engines, has developed sophisticated technical interactive videodiscs to train their engineering staff. Programs cover such areas as engine testing and troubleshooting techniques. Several were adapted from existing training material which was transferred to videodisc, with a computer integrating data with the video.

These programs simulate real-time situations as far as possible with the computer. One program allows the trainee to choose which data points to plot while looking at an engine under test in the simulation. Others propose hypothetical problem situations to which the trainee must respond, and provide feedback by evaluating these responses.

REMPLOY

Remploy was established in 1945 by Act of Parliament to provide sheltered employment for severely disabled people. It has 94 operational units in the United Kingdom, with nearly 9000 employees working in over 40 industries and trades.

Changes in sick pay legislation led Remploy to use CBT for training its (able-bodied) clerks. The company developed a two to three hour course, *Statutory Sick Pay*, in collaboration with PMSL

118

Mentor, now Mentor Interactive Training. The computers and software were moved every few days to another unit. In this way, at least two people in each unit could be trained during the crucial four week period before the legislation came into effect.

Remploy estimates that by using CBT it had saved at least £12 000 over conventional training, and intends to prepare further CBT courses (*Mentor Interactive News*). The pack is now marketed as generic training to other companies by Eurotech.

VOLKSWAGEN AUDI GROUP

Problems encountered by the Volkswagen Audi Group (VAG) in Britain after acquiring a new multifunction telephone system in 1984 led to the development of an interactive videodisc to train employees to use the system well. Initial training by conventional methods was inadequate, and employees were not getting the best out of the new system. New employees did not know what the system could do. Now any employee needing to learn how to use the system can turn to the videodisc training. The disc, produced by Interactive Information Systems, covers all the systems functions. It is generic, since it can be used by any company purchasing the same system.

9

Computers

TRAINING NEEDS

Of all types of manufacturing companies, those that produce computers would seem to have most reason to use computers in training. Mainframe computer companies have had access to CBT systems since the 1960s, including IBM's *Interactive Instructional System*, Goal Systems' *PHOENIX*, CDC's *PLATO* and Boeing's *Scholar/Teach*. These systems were to some extent aimed at serving the training needs of data processing professionals, whether engineers on the hardware side or programmers of the software. They were also used to develop CBT to meet needs in areas such as management, supervision, and financial control, for sales training, and for training in equipment maintenance and troubleshooting.

From the 1960s, companies like IBM and CDC that sold mainframe computers always took the line that their own employees needed comprehensive training, and that it was sound policy to train, where appropriate, the employees of client companies as well. To train the latter, it seemed logical and cost-effective to use the same system that they later operated.

New training needs arose with the advent of the microcomputer and, through it, the creation of a large pool of computer users who were not data processing professionals (or computer scientists). It was no longer the case that only these professionals could find their way into a computer to use it to train themselves. For example, Honeywell Information Systems is an international company manufacturing and selling mainframe computers and information systems. In Britain, it offers many computer-related courses to customers, including CBT courses on COBOL programming and computer operations.

Microcomputers also increased the CBT options. The older main-frame CBT systems were text-oriented, with little or no provision for graphics or animation. New authoring systems, new hardware and new CBT software for interactive training that included graphics and animation were developed by computer manufacturing companies and by a growing number of other commercial agencies, many of them staffed by trainers as well as computer specialists.

Among the microcomputer manufacturers, Apple was the first to recognise the need and offer customer training included in the purchase price. The company sold Apple II machines with *Apple Presents Apple* software. These early training disks had virtually no graphics or animation, largely because of the limited capacity (143K) of the disks. Other computer companies, such as Hewlett-Packard and Digital Equipment Corporation, produced similar CBT for their customers. Where necessary, their own programmers developed the software, using authoring languages written for the purpose, after checking that none of the published authoring systems for microcomputers was suitable.

A significant problem for computer manufacturers as they try to meet such needs is that they have to develop training in parallel with development of their computers. Engineers are developing the hardware and applications software right up to the last moment, but the training software must be available the day the new model is launched. This software must also be updated as frequently as the systems it relates to are updated.

A further constraint is that computer companies cannot assume that their dealers will always possess, or want to possess, in suitable numbers, the hardware required to run the training being sold on floppy disk, videodisc, or any other non-print medium.

Like other companies, those manufacturing computers had training needs in the field of management, finance, sales and so on, some or all of which might be met by CBT provided on the companies' own hardware. The experience of computer companies in training their own employees through CBT and offering CBT to employees in dealerships and client companies has been mixed, as illustrated by the examples, arranged alphabetically, that follow.

APPLE COMPUTER

Apple Computer, the largest US company manufacturing solely microcomputers, has developed and used CBT for two very different

121

groups: technicians within its own dealer network, and customers.

In the early 1980s, Apple experimented with interactive programs for training technicians who worked on repairing and maintaining Apple computers throughout the dealer network. The course was implemented in 1983 by Apple's Technical Training Group. Throughout use of the course it was demonstrated that most technicians required good visual job aids even more than detailed initial job training. The group therefore proposed a videodisc-based job aids program, combining all technical procedures on one videodisc. The disc would function as a Video Reference Manual, accessible by technicians as needed when carrying out repairs. This proposal was not accepted by the company, however, primarily because of cost but also because it came at a time when Apple was in a transition period from one set of products to another. It also became clear that some dealers would be unwilling to purchase the disc player required to use the Manual.

Since that time, the technical training group has found other methods of training more likely to be cost-effective. The group concluded that, for product training, good CBT takes so much time to develop that by the time it is completed the product or need has changed and the training is obsolete.

The User Education Group in Apple took a different approach, and has delivered piggybacked training to its customers, as a matter of policy, with each of its microcomputers ever since they came onto the market. *Apple Presents Apple*, the first 'guided tour' program, lacked graphics or animation because of the limited capacity of the disks. *SuperPILOT*, the authoring system used to prepare the packages for the Apple II, was not really sophisticated enough for Apple's needs because it could not simulate a piece of software nor support high quality graphics. *Apple at Play*, *Apple at Work*, *Inside Story*, *Exploring Logo* and *Getting Down to BASIC* were along similar lines, each providing CBT to supplement the printed manuals.

For the Macintosh, the Guided Tours were prepared, involving the computer, an audiocassette and a manual. Again, disk space was somewhat a constraint, although not in the case of the Macintosh Plus.

CBT for customers has had strong support from management, as demonstrated through funding and the fact that trainers are encouraged to work closely with engineers developing new products, something which is not common in companies. Apple management recognises the marketing value of having training available when a product is sold (a vastly different attitude from that of many high technology companies, in which product training is considered only after the new product is on the shelves).

Now that greater capacity disks and disk drives are available with the Macintosh SE and Macintosh II, much more is possible with CBT for customers. Apple has taken advantage of this capability with a new highly graphic authoring program, *VW/I* (see Chapter 6), developed by MacroMind of Chicago and customised for Apple to use in customer training on the new Macintosh products. Figure 9.1 shows what this program can do. *VW/I* is typical of the new creative and flexible authoring systems now being marketed.

DATA GENERAL

Data General is a US company, with international operations, manufacturing and selling mainframe computers. The company decided to computerise its own human resources information system, according to Rosenberg, Smith and Hoffman (1987), and to do so meant training 1700 employees, ranging from secretaries to the company president, at 100 locations in the United States. CBT was selected to do the job, and the training was successfully completed in only 2 months.

The content of the training was of two kinds: employees were informed of the benefits of the new system and they were taught how to complete three kinds of forms on the computer.

Data General used its own frame-based authoring system, *The Educator*, which can be easily learned by trainers with no computing background. In fact, the CBT was developed by a team made up of an instructional technologist, a subject matter expert, an editor and a 'quality assurance specialist' who evaluated the initial design and tested the programs. The programs were delivered through Data General's own network.

The company estimated that the CBT cost some $25 000 to develop, whereas conventional training would have cost about $200 000. Employees were able to fit their training into their normal schedules, and the CBT was available afterwards as an online job-aid if needed. Rosenberg, Smith and Hoffman suggested that CBT is particularly well-suited to training tasks that require, as this one did, intensive self-paced practice of routines. Whether or not this is so, Data General's experience shows how effective decentralised CBT can be, delivered through an existing network.

123

Figure 9.1: An example from *Your Tour of the SE*, the Macintosh animated tour for new users of the SE (reprinted by courtesy of Apple Computer Inc.). The user practises using the mouse to identify and drag each letter onto the theatre marquee. The program ensures that letters are placed correctly by beeping if a letter is chosen out of order and positions them correctly as soon as they have been put reasonably close to their designated place

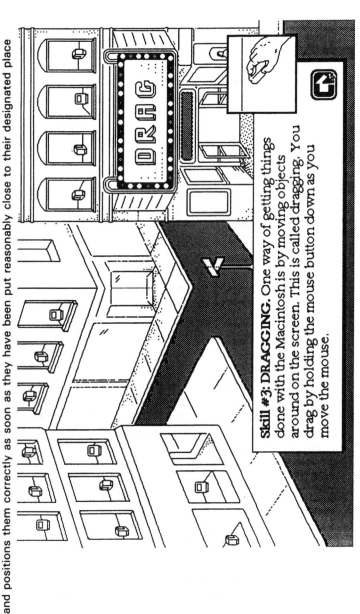

Skill #3: DRAGGING. One way of getting things done with the Macintosh is by moving objects around on the screen. This is called dragging. You drag by holding the mouse button down as you move the mouse.

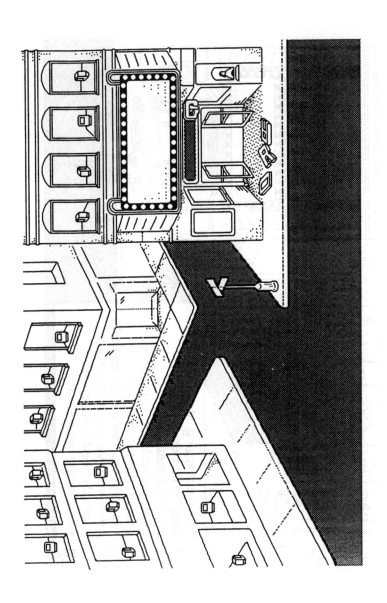

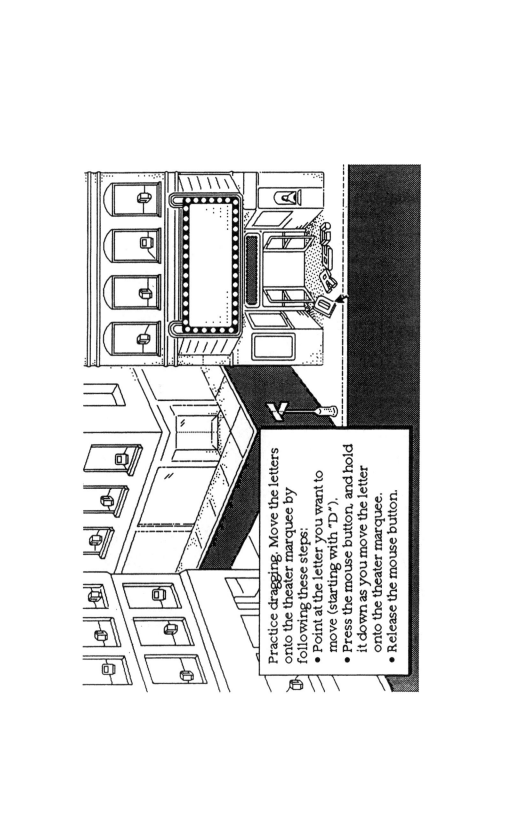

Practice dragging. Move the letters onto the theater marquee by following these steps:

- Point at the letter you want to move (starting with "D").
- Press the mouse button, and hold it down as you move the letter onto the theater marquee.
- Release the mouse button.

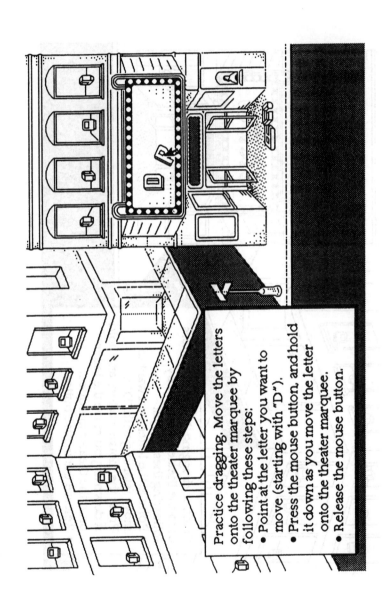

Practice dragging. Move the letters onto the theater marquee by following these steps:

- Point at the letter you want to move (starting with "D").
- Press the mouse button, and hold it down as you move the letter onto the theater marquee.
- Release the mouse button.

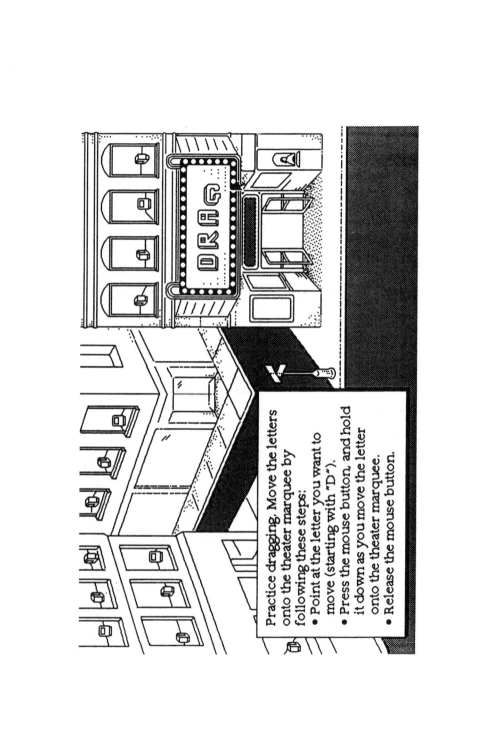

Practice dragging. Move the letters onto the theater marquee by following these steps:

- Point at the letter you want to move (starting with "D").
- Press the mouse button, and hold it down as you move the letter onto the theater marquee.
- Release the mouse button.

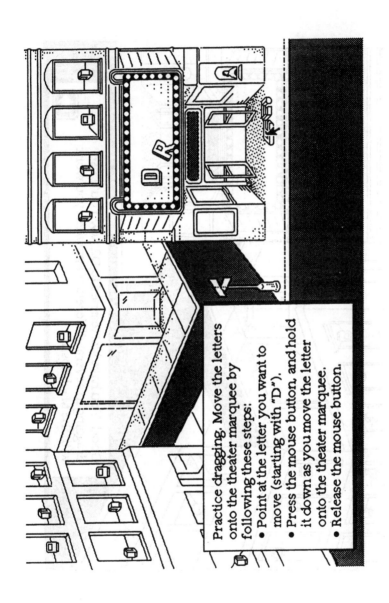

Practice dragging. Move the letters onto the theater marquee by following these steps:

- Point at the letter you want to move (starting with "D").
- Press the mouse button, and hold it down as you move the letter onto the theater marquee.
- Release the mouse button.

Good. You have just learned to DRAG. You'll use dragging in several different ways when you work with the Macintosh.

DIGITAL EQUIPMENT CORPORATION

The Digital Equipment Corporation (DEC), second only to IBM in size, is a US company that manufactures and distributes mini-computers and microcomputers throughout the world. Like many companies in its field, it suffers from a high turnover of engineers, and rapid product obsolescence. These two factors are behind a considerable demand in DEC itself for training and retraining. It is also important that this training is well standardised in all countries in which DEC operates.

DEC considers that it has proved that CBT results in improved training, cost savings and increased sales. In fact, the company has established that it is the single largest user of CBT apart from the United States government. CBT has eliminated the need for employees to travel to expensively established training centres. Every DEC office building has an individualised learning centre shared by all employees working in that building.

Piggybacking CBT on the company's VAX minicomputers seemed an obvious step, and dependence on the VAX's in this way has increased steadily. In addition, interactive videodisc CBT has been introduced, using DEC's *Interactive Video Information System* (*IVIS*), which combines a videodisc player with DEC's micro-computer, the Professional 300, which was derived from the PDP 11 minicomputer.

Development of *IVIS*-based training is handled entirely by DEC's Educational Technologies Group (Adaptive Learning Systems), which includes instructional designers, software engineers, graphic artists and video production specialists. The group came into existence to develop CBT courses for employee and customer train-ing. These courses had to present situations vividly and encourage trainees to grapple with them. *IVIS* provides the technology required and is the primary medium, but it is accompanied by other media, including print, as appropriate.

In the field service area, an *IVIS* course is created for all new products. Course development begins when the product is in the design stage, and continues in parallel with development of the product. The content includes concepts and theory, product applica-tions and equipment preparation, and finishes with a troubleshooting section. Questions require trainees to make decisions, which the program allows them to follow through, to simulate real life as closely as possible. Built-in safeguards prevent trainees from stray-ing too far in the 'wrong' direction. The system provides appropriate

131

feedback, including hints and advice. When a trainee finishes a module, the program evaluates his or her performance.

In management training, *IVIS* courses cover how to manage employee performance, using scenarios to which managers in training must react as they might to employees under their supervision.

To make these courses available to a wider audience, the Group is trying out a new approach. Proper 'front-end' (predevelopment) design can isolate concepts applicable to all trainees on a particular course, says the Group. These concepts may constitute 25–99 per cent of the course. For example, although salary policies may vary from company to company, many procedures are common or generic. Similarly, trainees in manufacturing must often learn common procedures, with variations for different models of the same kind of product, say, a Ford car. In other words, the Group is looking for ways to separate the generic and specific aspects of training in particular sectors, and may then base its development of CBT on this analysis.

DEC has prepared many CBT courses for customers in the United States. For example, General Motors uses a DEC network job aid (see Chapter 8). McDonnell Douglas has a computer-assisted design (CAD) course developed by DEC, during which the $100 000 CAD system is emulated on a touch-sensitive screen to allow practice without tying up the system when it is needed for routine work. Metcalf and Eddy use a DEC course on systems and processes for waste water treatment. Alcoa, the US aluminium manufacturer, uses a DEC simulation, which looks like a game, to train operators of a smelting plant. The operators learn, in particular, about the interdependence of the jobs they do. American Telephone and Telegraph trains its managers on a DEC-developed simulation to perform effectively at meetings concerned with regulation of telecommunications. Citibank trains managers and controllers through DEC's CBT that emulates new financial control processes. Other CBT courses and *IVIS* videodiscs have been developed in the United States and Britain (Open University, 1985).

HEWLETT-PACKARD

Hewlett-Packard is a very large US manufacturer of computers, calculators, solid state components and electronic instruments for medical and analytical purposes. The company, which has traditionally had a decentralised structure, with many divisions that have created diversity, serves as an excellent example of the range of CBT being developed by computer companies for employees and customers. We deal here with four separate Hewlett-Packard CBT projects.

First, in the Personal Software Division is the Learning Products Centre, within which is the Interactive Learning Products group. This group has developed CBT products for customers buying software for the HP 3000 minicomputer, and for the HP 150 and Vectra microcomputers. The group, which consists of CBT developers, a programmer and instructional designers, identified the need for CBT when results of trials showed that users had problems learning the more difficult procedures from documentation provided with the new products.

Prototype CBT programs for the HP 3000 were developed in the early 1980s. These include *Report Writer*, a word processing program, and a program on the use of electronic mail. In 1985, *Access* was prepared, a database management training program that runs on both the HP 3000 and with simulated screens on the HP 150.

The group now uses an authoring language, *Shelley*, developed by ComTrain. Part of it, *Showman*, simulates screens and can create graphics. The other part, *Monitor*, 'wraps round' the main software program, using the actual software with an added window for instructions to the trainee. The 'wrapping' ensures that trainees use the correct instructional sequence by disabling other program-related keys.

The two CBT programs produced for the Vectra software include one that incorporates a graphics program, *Drawing Gallery*. This has an introductory overview of capabilities, with examples, to encourage trainees to try some of the techniques. The other is a word-processing program, *Executive MemoMaker*. *Monitor* wraps the training round the program. The group plans to increase its use of graphics, particularly for the Vectra software.

The group's CBT programs can be used by themselves or integrated into classroom training. Feedback from telephone surveys indicates that many users want the interactions of classroom training as well as being able to learn on their own from CBT.

Second, in another part of Hewlett-Packard, the Customer Engineering group has developed CBT with interactive video to train its own employees and those of customers. System concepts, maintenance and troubleshooting are the topics, since this group is responsible for responding to the majority of customer calls for assistance once a Hewlett-Packard system is installed. The courses

133

include an introduction to data communications, Vectra service training, an introduction to UNIX and RS232 protocols, and a course is being developed on testing and repairing the HP 3000.

In developing each course, the group's designers determine the best media and methodology to deliver the content. In courses on fundamentals, they decided video was the logical and cost-effective medium. This material does not change as frequently as product information, and trainees must see examples of situations that are not always available or easily replicated at their usual site. Videodisc was chosen for its fast and random access capabilities. For the group, as with any CBT course, standardisation and replicability of training for widely scattered trainees were important considerations, and trainee performance could be recorded properly.

Techniques developed by the group during the making of earlier courses were valuable in raising the quality of later ones. The first course, on data communications and networking, was developed for internal training and has been used since 1985. The group benefited from this experience, and that gained from other CBT programs, and modified the course for training software engineers and sales representatives elsewhere in the company, and for the company's customers.

The next course covered product training for customer engineers and dealers, on how to install, maintain and troubleshoot the Vectra. Before deciding to turn to interactive video, the group prepared the course in print, to accommodate trainees who did not have suitable hardware. Then an interactive videodisc was developed as the hardware became more generally available. Subsequent evaluation showed that the course in print took five days to complete, whereas the interactive video course took only three days, primarily because a process often takes longer to describe than to show.

The UNIX course developed in 1986 employed more sophisticated presentation techniques that enabled the course to be produced in much less time. Trainees need five days to study the fifteen videodisc sides, which were produced in four months, whereas the data communications course, which takes only half a day to study, took seven months to produce. Study time for the UNIX course had to be as short as possible, since its runs on a timesharing basis on a minicomputer system. Graphic techniques also save training time as trainees move from one section to another.

Time is of the essence, says the company. In all these courses, cost has not been nearly so important as time — time to produce the courses and time saved in training. Customer engineers require basic and updating training as quickly as possible to be effective in responding to customers' needs.

Third, the Marketing and Educational Media group was established in Worldwide Customer Support Operations to respond to a variety of customer training needs. This group works directly with customers to develop or help customers to develop an agreed program. For example, the group selected appropriate off-the-shelf packages and developed a CBT course for them, for use with the Vectra. The group has also developed simulated minicomputer and microcomputer applications in interactive sales that run on the Vectra.

Fourth, Hewlett-Packard's Corporate Video group is becoming involved in producing interactive management training. Its first product presents techniques for dealing with employee problems, using typical scenarios to which managers are expected to respond by saying what they would do next. The programs branch to enable managers to follow the implications of their choices.

IBM

IBM (International Business Machines), the largest manufacturer of computers in the world, with over 400 000 employees in the United States alone, has major international CBT networks, based on its mainframe computers, for training service engineers and others (Gange, 1986). The company also has considerable experience in offering CBT to its customers who wish to learn how to use IBM hardware and software. Pritchard (1986) says that increases in IBM's business and in applications for computers led to an explosion in the demand for training in the company, to such an extent that traditional methods could not cope.

In the United States, IBM has guided learning centres in Atlanta, Georgia, and in four other cities. The centres were established primarily for customer training, but have expanded to train primarily IBM marketing representatives and installers (systems engineers). They are equipped with microcomputers and level 3 interactive videodisc systems, which are used intensively. Over 50 of the courses available include videodisc material.

In Atlanta, IBM personnel are trained on System 36 and 38 mainframes, and use IBM PC-based generic courses developed by IBM's subsidiary, Science Research Associates (SRA), and covering topics such as how to use the PC, the disk operating system (PC-DOS)

135

and BASIC programming. A training course for PC technical coordinators is offered, as are courses about new IBM PC software such as *Vision* and *InfoWindow*. The latter is IBM's computer-based interactive system (see Chapter 6), which IBM used internally for over a year to train new employees in data processing, management and sales skills. The results were very good, with training time cut by 25–40 per cent compared with live training (Austin, 1987).

In Britain in the late 1970s, IBM customer education was provided through some 200 courses, almost all in classrooms, covering the IBM product range. By 1986, there were 450 courses but only 35 per cent of them were in classrooms. Whereas before the trainees were mainly data processing professionals, now they are employees of all kinds, ranging from chief executives to production workers and secretaries. IBM has also changed its marketing strategy in recent years. Previously IBM had only its own sales force to train. Now agents and dealers must be trained too.

From 1978, IBM (United Kingdom) used CBT to train IBM system console operators. The system was simulated so that critical conditions could be included in exercises without endangering the system itself. The courses were subsequently offered to customers as well as IBM employees. In 1982, a guided learning centre, on similar lines to IBM's US ones, was established in Manchester using US materials. There are now twelve such centres in Britain, between them handling several thousand trainees each year, without instructors. Interactive videodiscs, such as *Business Skills*, and CBT feature prominently among a range of training media. It is significant that IBM decided to use its personal computers rather than terminals linked to one of its mainframes. Pritchard (1986) says that with personal computers no control units or telephone lines were needed and the machines could be moved and added to more easily. For IBM employees only there are five additional learning centres that offer more than 80 SRA-published courses (some of which include generic CBT), several interactive courses about personal computer applications and six computer product knowledge courses that use interactive videodisc (Dowsey, 1987).

IBM (United Kingdom) International Products is the IBM subsidiary responsible for the introduction of the IBM PC into Europe, the Middle East and Africa, according to Jay (1985). The company decided to offer its 2000 dealers and agents interactive videodiscs as the training medium for their employees and for customers purchasing IBM PCs. Dealers purchase a touch-sensitive screen and videodisc player and connect these to an IBM PC–XT from their own stock, while IBM supplies free the discs in *The IBM Personal Computer Family Course*, which takes three hours to view straight through. These discs were produced centrally, says Pritchard, with textual or country-specific information shown on the monitor in the relevant language (eight languages cover the 20 countries concerned).

NCR CORPORATION

NCR is a large US company that manufactures and sells computer systems. Within NCR, a group called New Instructional Technologies was established in 1984, as part of NCR's Marketing Services, to develop interactive videodiscs for field engineers on equipment maintenance, as a step beyond 'traditional' CBT previously produced for NCR's mainframe systems. The training need arose from a desire to decentralise training of field engineers, for which travel and accommodation costs had become very expensive. By sending out videodiscs for all basic concepts training, NCR hoped to be able to bring employees to training centres much less often, only for specialised and updating training. Development costs would be offset against future savings on trainers' salaries, since few would be needed.

To maximise the efficiency of using interactive videodisc, NCR decided to develop more generic courses, including those for well-established NCR equipment that was unlikely to become obsolete quickly. The company also decided to design its CBT for use by customers and trade schools, and chose to open up its market by making its CBT products available on several manufacturers' equipment.

NCR developed an authoring system, *InteracTV-2*, which is combined with the NCR PC 6 (or any other IBM PC-compatible) microcomputer, a laser videodisc player and a colour monitor or a monitor with touch-sensitive screen. Embedded within the system is a trainee management program which records trainees' progress. *InteracTV-2* is now available commercially.

The company's first course was an interactive videodisc completed in 1986, *Data Communications Concepts*. This was followed by *Data Communication Fault Analysis*, dealing with problems with modems and other data communication components. Together, these two courses occupy thirteen sides of videodisc, equal to several days of training time.

In early 1987, the group was working on a curriculum that may include 36 courses by 1989, with titles such as *Video Display Terminal Concepts and Fault Analysis*, *Personal Computer Concepts and Fault Analysis*, *PC-DOS* and *Retail Environment Concepts*. The last will deal with how computers and optical code readers are used in banking, retail stores and elsewhere.

RANK XEROX

Rank Xerox, which markets Xerox (see below) products in Britain, possesses embedded help menus for use with the versatile Documenter Workstation. An icon in the top right-hand corner of the screen 'contains' a series of small help windows by which users can quickly look up a feature and obtain instructions for using it. The company runs courses for its own employees, and introduces the workstation by means of this software, which was prepared by Xerox in America. Further programs in the US series, seldom used in Britain, teach advanced applications of the station, such as typing in Japanese or using spreadsheets, databases or graphics.

Rank Xerox also markets the Xerox 6060 microcomputer series, with CBT for customers on how to use these machines well. The embedded training software takes advantage of the 6060s good graphics to present concise text instructions supplemented a few seconds later by illustrations. Thus employees of companies buying machines in this series can learn quickly how to use a network of 6060s.

For training its own employees, Rank Xerox is experimenting with interactive videotape developed in-house using a *Take-Five* authoring system based on a BBC micro and a Betamax videotape recorder. The company has a video studio, and its own employees appear in the training tapes, which are generic, aimed at administrative trainees and covering topics like telephone techniques and verbal communication skills.

The company is installing interactive videodisc training equipment for use with discs prepared by Xerox Corporation in the United States. With these, company engineers will update their product knowledge.

XEROX CORPORATION

Xerox Corporation (not to be confused with Rank Xerox, its British partner) manufactures and markets copiers and duplicators, office systems equipment, facsimile devices and information, word-processing and publishing equipment.

In training its service personnel, the company has developed a model called the Training Continuum, a building-block concept which requires trainees to learn only the technologies relevant to the equipment they service. As the need to service other equipment arises, students have only to learn the incremental technologies associated with the new product. The field service training staff have used this concept to develop generic training for a range of technology, such as reprographics, personal computers, peripherals and office systems. Training is prescribed as required, based on job needs and measurements from previous training programs.

The New Hire Service Rep training programme includes interactive video on Customer Relation Skills, Tools and Safety. The ten-disc *Exploring Computer Systems* course covers microcomputer basics and a variety of topics, including processors, software, networks, mass storage, and communication devices and networks. A reprographics program was being developed when this was written (1987). Xerox also has an active continuing education programme that includes interactive video courses.

Other interactive videodisc training programs at Xerox include Leadership Through Quality training for managers, a New-Hire course for dispatchers to teach customer relations skills and a course for all dispatchers on how to do telephone diagnosis of customer problems. They also have developed a course on how to use and program their dispatch telephone switching system.

Many of the Xerox interactive video training projects were developed in-house. The training group supplies the curriculum outline and technical training expertise for each program. Development has generally taken three months for one half-hour videodisc side, which equates to 2.0–2.5 hours of instruction. This assumes that one designer has developed the instruction, working with a team composed of a video producer, interactive video author and co-designer.

Management support has been enthusiastic because interactive video is intuitively efficient, effective training. Large interactive video projects require approval of Service's Investment Review Board, however, ensuring that they conform to Service Training

139

strategies and that they are produced economically. The Review Board has also required and funded an interactive videodisc validity study to ensure that interactive video is relevant to Xerox training needs.

At the time of writing, the Service organisation is the only group actively using interactive video at Xerox. Its mission is to spread the interactive message, while working with the other training groups in a multinational and multifunctional interactive video training council.

10

Retail Trade

TRAINING NEEDS

The retail trade sector includes many companies selling goods to the general public. We have excluded from it those manufacturing companies that licence or give franchises to chains of retail outlets, such as most car manufacturers, but we have included companies that manufacture and sell through their own retail stores, such as Sainsbury's, or through retail representatives, such as Syntex. Naturally, we have included companies that distribute and retail to the public goods they do not themselves produce: B&Q DIY Retail Supercentres is a British company of this type, and Zales is a US example. We have also put into this chapter two examples of retail services. For travel retailing, the Association of British Travel Agents has a Training Board coordinating training in the majority of British retail travel outlets. For temporary office employee recruitment services, we discussed briefly the Kelly Girl agencies (Chapter 6). We deal in other chapters with other forms of service outlet, such as banks, in cases where they use new training technology.

According to Seabright (1987), British retailers have only recently adopted management training, with few exceptions, and management training institutions have neglected the retail trade. Retail managers need training that takes them away from their stores as little as possible, and which trains them to be very flexible and capable of undertaking a wide variety of tasks. Unipart, which retails car spares through a large network of Austin Rover car dealers, recognised these constraints and prepared an interactive videodisc to train managers of spares departments.

Among other grades, there tend to be high percentages of women and part-timers. There is also a high annual turnover of these employees, although this is not true for those in managerial and administrative grades. Retail trade is a six or seven day a week business, and time for training is particularly hard to secure. Trainees are frequently scattered in small numbers among many branches of a single company. It is fair to generalise by saying that training for the retail trade must be accessible, quick and effective, to a greater degree than in perhaps any other economic sector.

Companies in the retail trade have turned to new training technology comparatively slowly, in contrast to their use of technology for sales. In-store videotapes have been used for nearly a decade to promote products, as a supplement to television advertising. Sears Roebuck, the US retail and mail-order chain, introduced videodiscs some years ago as a sales medium. Similarly, the Cooperative Society in Britain introduced videodisc selling of microwave ovens, and, unusually, included on the same disc some training for sales personnel. Despite the presence of computers in large retail companies for inventory control and accounting, we found no examples of early (1970s) use of mainframes for CBT in the retail trade, not counting the retail side of the travel industry. It was suggested to us that the chief reason for this was the unwillingness of data processing departments to cope with training, but we cannot confirm or refute this opinion.

This situation is now changing as retail companies discover the training potential of microcomputers and interactive videodisc. Perhaps these smaller and cheaper machines offer the flexibility needed by such companies, whose employees can be trained for an hour or two at a time, one or two at a time, probably in a corner of the manager's office, when business is slack. Simpler technology is already deployed. Zales Corporation (see below) has more than 40 videotapes delivering training on many topics to its employees. Now microcomputer-based generic materials are readily available, such as *Selling Products and Services*, marketed in Britain by Macmillan, and numerous others sold in the United States by Advanced Systems Inc. Other company-specific programs are appearing, as in the case of B&Q (below) and Target Stores (see Chapter 17). Dixon's, a British chain of stores selling electrical goods, decided to commission CBT for its new sales employees, to run on the Amstrad microcomputers it sells.

The case studies that follow (arranged alphabetically) illustrate well the range of CBT applications in this sector.

ASSOCIATION OF BRITISH TRAVEL AGENTS

Computer-based reservation systems are not exactly new in the retail end of the travel industry, and a 1984 estimate suggested that about 80 per cent of British travel agents already had videotex terminals in their offices (Goodwin, 1984). It may not seem surprising therefore that new training technology is gaining a foothold in training travel agents.

The Association of British Travel Agents, which represents 90 per cent of the industry in Britain, has had some difficulties in standardising its computers and communications, however, as Prestel and rival videotex systems have proffered their services. These systems, including Photovideotex, which was developed by British Telecom and offers a high resolution picture ('a computerised colour holiday brochure'), compete with videodiscs, which are less easily updated for a trade in products that change very rapidly. Shaw (1984) reported that agents may have as many as five screens at selling positions, and finding space for more in their crowded high street offices is a problem, whether for selling, administration or training.

The Association has a National Training Board, which develops training to bring travel agency employees to one of two levels: counter clerk, dealing with the public, or office manager, running the agency. A permanent team of trainers is responsible for preparing training material, and, with funds from the Manpower Services Commission and the help of the Council for Educational Technology, they were trained to prepare interactive videotex training for the workplace as well as conventional printed manuals. A provider, Information Technology and Marketing, developed micro-viewdata software which allows travel industry trainers to simulate a viewdata gateway on a microcomputer and access different booking systems, set exercises and monitor trainees' progress. The Board commissioned a study at the Open University of the feasibility of using artificial intelligence to enhance training in telephone techniques via interactive videodisc.

B&Q RETAIL DIY SUPERCENTRES

B&Q Retail is a large and rapidly expanding British company in the highly competitive market of do-it-yourself and gardening supplies. With its 1986 turnover of £515 million it claims to be the largest firm

143

of its type in the world. Training is regarded as integral to the business and there is considerable awareness of the need for it throughout the company. Training strategy was debated by the main board in 1985, and a very substantial commitment was made, of the order of three times the national average. The board recognised that several characteristics of the company gave rise to special training needs. B&Q's 200 retail stores are scattered all over the country. There is a high turnover of retail employees, who include many part-timers and weekenders required for B&Q's six or seven days a week opening hours. New employees, recruited at the rate of 2000 a year, must be quickly trained in the safe operation of each store (Dobson, 1986, 1987).

The still-developing strategy demands that training should be located at or near each store, where the store manager manages training in the form of on-the-job instruction by supervisors. This is supplemented by other methods and printed training materials. Videobased training has become a crucial part of the strategy. A move to invest in a VHS videocassette system was superseded by a decision to buy the Philips LaserVision system. The advantages of the latter were that high production quality was assured over a long life, the equipment was less likely to be stolen or used as a source of entertainment, and the technology could be enhanced by adding microcomputers later, thus giving trainers more flexibility. B&Q initially purchased £80 000 worth of Philips videodisc hardware in the form of 70 players and monitors, which were installed in stores and at the head office by early 1986. By the end of 1986, all 200 stores had videodisc players installed, at a cost of about £220 000, and fifteen training courses were on disc, representing six hours of training. The players are accessible whenever the stores are open, up to 84 hours per week.

The first disc to be commissioned entailed transferring sequences from an existing VHS videotape, together with material already being used elsewhere in the Woolworth Group, to which B&Q belongs. Entitled *Health and Safety*, it contains three hours of training.

Store employees make up 95 per cent of B&Q's staff. New ones receive videodisc training on their first or second day of work. *Safety — It's Down to You* makes clear their responsibility to themselves and the company. *Take a Deep Breath* shows graphically the effects of solvent abuse, outlines the legal position and instructs employees on what action to take. Another disc, *DARTS — Do It Yourself Accounting Retail Trading System*, follows, on the totally integrated accounting system, providing training for dealing with all

144

in-store financial transactions, including an electronic point of sale (EPOS) system that provides automatic stock replacement and eliminates manual pricing. *In Case of Fire* is compulsory for all new employees. The disc has an introduction for store managers, then a variety of sequences for trainees.

Just the Little Things is a customer service training disc which has a trainers' introduction tagged onto the trainee training material. The aim is to get staff to identify with people who appear in the video, and to reappraise their own approach to customers. Employees were used rather than actors, and the title and the script came from short interviews with employees. This topic was formerly dealt with on tape/slide (and later on videocassette), but with only one set of equipment for every eight or nine stores.

All four of these discs were developed specially for B&Q by outside providers rather than in-house because the company saw the need to achieve high production standards (even the packaging of the discs is of high quality). Relations with these providers during production were very good and no problems were encountered. B&Q recently commissioned in-house videodisc development, however, with the first title being *Customer Service*. The company plans to make this available first in a linear form, and then to adapt it when microcomputers are added. Other titles being planned are *Gardening, Credit Cards* and *A Portrait of B&Q*, the last for induction purposes.

In addition, B&Q is experimenting with generic interactive videodiscs produced by Interactive Information Systems. These include topics such as *Making the Telephone Work for You* and *Writing for Results*. At first, demand for these was very high, and employees were signed up for five to six weeks ahead. The cost worked out at £4 per head per program in the first year and will drop in later years as more trainees find them.

Dobson (1987) says that the company had little difficulty in deciding which microcomputer to install. Three factors influenced the decision: the workstation needed to be capable of running generic CBT programs and the company was interested mainly in those running on the IBM standard; it was vital that the microcomputer could be used for other applications, if necessary, besides training; and the workstation had to be suitable for generic videodiscs, and may be designed for players linked to IBM machines. Videologic MIC 3000 is going into the workstations.

B&Q has found evaluation problematic. There was a keen awareness of the need to justify the system for financial reasons, yet

145

a feeling that any test results might be spurious. Possibly evaluation would become easier and more valid after the microcomputers had been added to the players, because then fuller records of progress could be held. Some evaluation was attempted, however, through monthly returns to the training department, based on the logging-on system employees used in the stores when they viewed a disc. In the long term, B&Q would like to gauge trainees' views on every disc, but criteria have not yet been established. Meantime, the 70 store managers first involved have completed a questionnaire, results of which show their desire for a larger training disc library, a favourable response from staff and the view that the system is easy to use.

B&Q did encounter some logistical problems. Since there is limited space for training hardware in the stores, and portable equipment may be stolen, the company commissioned design of £450 cabinets at first, but these proved too expensive and inappropriate. Instead, later installations are mounted on trolleys and kept in the store manager's office. Trainees use headphones to cut out office noise. There were technical difficulties with the headphones being linked to the disc players, therefore they were linked to the monitors.

Besides the videodisc packages, B&Q is introducing CBT on IBM personal computers. The programs under test include *Safety in the Office* (being modified for B&Q from an existing program) and *Equal Opportunities Legislation* and *Appraisal Interviewing and Recruitment* (both from Mast Learning Systems and being tested by head office managers). The introductory *Computerised Inventory Management* was commissioned from a provider, Datasolve Education. The more advanced *Stock Management* is being developed as an expert system in collaboration with Datasolve Education, with funding from the Manpower Services Commission, and should be widely available when completed in 1988.

B&Q, according to Dobson (1987), expects to upgrade its training technology by adding IBM personal computers to the videodisc players and monitors already installed. This will enable the company to introduce full-scale CBT into all its stores, using both generic and commissioned programs.

B&Q was one of the companies chosen for the first set of case studies of open learning prepared for the Manpower Services Commission.

146

FOODMAKER

Foodmaker, Inc., is the company that operates and franchises about 850 Jack-in-the-Box fast food outlets, mainly in the western and southwestern United States (Wall, 1987). Following a careful evaluation of new training technology, Foodmaker supplements its technical, managerial and operational training with level 2 interactive video. Seven discs have been produced to date, all in the company's own studio and editing suite, with the aim of standardising training throughout Foodmaker.

Wall stresses that the videos are not 'videotised manuals', but employ many images, storylines and vignettes rather than words. Topics are chosen very carefully, bearing in mind the trainees, the objectives and the environment in which training is delivered. Often videodisc is not the solution, once needs are analysed.

MERVYN'S

Mervyn's is a rapidly growing US retail chain specialising in soft goods. There are 180 stores in 12 states and the company plans to continue to expand into the eastern United States.

Mervyn's is currently using the *PHOENIX* authoring language on their IBM mainframe computer to train selected employees at their corporate headquarters in California. Programs were developed primarily for the internal buying staff, to teach the basics of the company's item processing system and how to complete the appropriate forms.

When the company wanted to train store sales personnel to use a new reference system for prices and point-of-sale equipment, it found that mainframe training would not suffice because it could not handle video, colour or the complex graphics needed. Since store needs also change rapidly, the cost of developing CBT for these new systems was judged to be too high. Current training of sales personnel relies on tried and tested methods such as manuals and demonstrations.

In 1986, Goal Systems, the main company marketing *PHOENIX*, launched Version 6.0 of the authoring language. This version enables trainers to use microcomputers as well as a mainframe. Although trainers at Mervyn's have made themselves fully aware of this version's capabilities, they have not advocated that the company should turn to microcomputers, mainly because of the expense and

147

staffing required to develop new programs and to install the necessary hardware in all the stores. Those in training recognise that 'plain vanilla' CBT on the mainframe is past its prime, given what else is now readily available — that is, colour, graphics and interactive video. A move to microcomputer-based CBT seems inevitable sooner or later. In fact, there has recently been an upsurge in interest at Mervyn's in CBT and for new program development.

SAINSBURY'S

Sainsbury's, founded in 1869 as a small dairy in Drury Lane, London, is today the leading food retailer in the United Kingdom, with sales in the financial year ending March 1987 of over £4 billion. By April 1987, Sainsbury's had 271 supermarkets, served over 6.5 million customers each week, and was the largest butcher, the largest wine retailer and the largest retailer of fresh fruit and vegetables in the United Kingdom. In the year to March 1987 the company was planning to continue its expansion with the opening of fifteen new stores.

Sophisticated computer-based systems permit Sainsbury's supermarkets to transmit orders via central computers and depôts for next day delivery. The company employs 64 000 staff, of whom more than 38 000 work part-time and the workforce is expanding with the creation of, on average, 75 new jobs a week. A commitment to training is regarded as integral to its activities. Staff training needs have expanded in recent years with the rapid expansion of retail outlets and the introduction of computer-based systems. Increasingly this training need is being addressed through the medium of computer-based training designed and implemented by the company's Open Learning Unit.

By June 1987, the Open Learning Unit had been investigating CBT for three years, staff trained in authoring, and eight courses produced, with four being worked upon. Target audiences were computer clerks in stores and head office buyers. There was also a project incorporating interactive video (IV) at the proposal stage. The development was taking place in-house using the *IIS* authoring system.

The first CBT project was completed in winter 1984 and has since been used for the training of Head Office Buyers. POM, a purchase order management system provides a forecasting, maintenance and modelling function. POM was designed to provide buyers with reliable order quantities for the branches, reduce depot stock levels, and guarantee high service levels to the branches.

The training program represents simulations of the procedures a buyer has to carry out through the week. Buyers based at head office can train at their own desk using their familiar keyboard and terminal. They have flexibility in training and can fit it in when convenient before they get into the live system, and can also use it as a refresher.

We looked at the course on maintenance. This comprises three training modules and matching test modules. The subject matter covers maintenance by commodity, supplier and call over of orders to suppliers. The three test modules can be used for revision but a new user can work through the programme in sequence. The user receives appropriate feedback on the screen for correct and incorrect answers.

CFM, Corporate File Management, is a central database. It stores information on commodities sold in Sainsbury's branches, like commodity number, price, supplier, and which depôt it is stored at. CBT is used to train buyers in initially setting up and also updating these details.

In early 1985 the CBT team started to explore the feasibility of a course in *Branch Computing and Scanning (BCAS)*, which by the autumn was tested by potential users in several branches. The big training problem that had to be addressed was for training in the use of the ICL System 25. System 25 is a minicomputer system which has been installed into branches to help control ordering systems and stock control. This involves the barcode on the product package, which lists product and price, being read by laser beam at the super-market checkout. These projects meant that by mid-1986 approxi-mately 180 branches had computers, and 45 had scanning. The introduction of these systems created a huge training need as all affected branch staff had to be trained. This large training workload would need extra trainers and training centres to provide extensive training for large numbers of people if delivered by face-to-face training and hands-on experience. It was decided this would prove both expensive and disruptive to the branches. CBT would allow training on location, and its potential for flexibility gave the capacity to fit training into the working day without taking people away from work for courses. In addition CBT was felt to be the right medium because of its capacity to transmit uniform information to trainees who would consequently be trained to a better corporate standard, the key features required being accuracy and speed of the systems operation. CBT would train more quickly, more cheaply and at the individual trainees pace. So in summer 1986 BCAS was first used intensively to meet the training need posed by the introduction of computers into 42 branches.

The package enables branch staff to train themselves to run an existing branch computer. The course is workbook driven in that the trainee first reads the book then uses the computer. Branches use the ICL computer system, but the same computers could not be used for training due to insufficient space. So although the course was originally written on IAS for ICL database, it was later rewritten using IBM's *IIS* authoring language *Coursewriter*. This authoring language offered SEF, a simulation exercise facility, as well as a free-flowing authoring facility. The author controls the program by filling out a series of forms in a framework set up by the system, which also includes elements of testing and branching. In this latter respect it was regarded as resembling micro-authoring systems, although more computer skill is required than for micro-systems. A disadvantage was seen that there was no graphics package to interface, so the end result has little graphics.

Mainframe-based CBT using IBM was seen as providing the advantage of the facility of intensive feedback through detailed reports on student progress. The trainers can check which branch or head office trainee is using the training, know at which stage each trainee is and where the trainees have left off, as well as monitoring student records which enables trainers to pinpoint on areas where students find difficulty.

All Sainsbury's supermarkets will have CBT installed for use in branch training by September 1987, covering a large geographical area from Halifax in the north to Bexhill in the south. It would be used by all levels of management and staff, from the inexperienced, with no knowledge of computer keyboards or terminology, to experienced branch computer users. BCAS CBT will be used for ongoing, refresher and system update training. New CBT and CAL courses are planned covering a large range of topics, both procedural and managerial.

For the future, Sainsbury's open learning unit was looking at the use of micro-based CBT, as well as expanding its repertoire of mainframe courses. There is ongoing evaluation of existing training packages available 'off the shelf'. Some micro-based CBT packages were already available at the head office training centre; most were very general, covering subject areas such as finance, managing time, and marketing, but one had been tailormade for Sainsburys. This

150

micro-based program on IBM PC was introduced in July 1986. The *Supermarket Simulator* takes the branch manager through a typical day in the branch, simulating problems that would typically arise. No micro-packages were available that would do the systems training Sainsbury's are already doing on the mainframe. However use of the *IIS* authoring language for other purposes was unlikely as it was regarded as too restrictive.

A firm commitment appears to have been made to CBT, with a board-level decision to spend half a million pounds on CBT equipment within the company.

W.H. SMITH

W.H. Smith is a large company operating stores throughout Britain and a few elsewhere. It sells newspapers, magazines, stationery and books, and, recently, travel. It has a high turnover of employees and a fairly large proportion of part-time staff. With the introduction of travel desks in 1986 in its larger stores, a new training need arose. The company developed an interactive videodisc package as a pilot project, testing it with travel sales assistants in three locations in late 1986.

The package, *Transact Travel*, was developed in-house, using the *Mentor II* authoring system (see Chapter 6). It consists of text integrated with an interactive videodisc. The system runs on an IBM-compatible personal computer interfaced to a Philips Professional laserdisc player.

The content of *Transact Travel* is based on a training strategy, transaction selling, developed by W.H.Smith's training manager. It introduces trainees to the idea that selling involves management of a sales transaction, during which the sales assistant has to discover his or her own personality type and that of the client, before adapting selling behaviour to the client. The training takes about three hours (in six 30 minute sections), including reading the printed matter, and ends with a computer-based quiz covering the whole package.

Based on experience gained in the pilot project, W.H. Smith is considering further CBT. The introduction of electronic point of sale (EPOS) technology is imminent and will require a large training effort.

SYNTEX LABORATORIES

Syntex is one of the largest US companies making and distributing pharmaceutical products, among which was the original birth control pill. In 1983, the company commissioned Picodyne Corporation to develop CBT programs to teach physicians about Syntex products.

In 1984, Picodyne prepared natural language software in PROLOG to enable Syntex sales representatives to query a large database of client (doctor) profiles. As Miranker (1984) reports, Syntex faced the problem of how to give its sales force access to this large database. The company also wanted to encourage accurate and speedy reports from the force, and sought a way to enliven the independent study at home that representatives must do to keep up to date with changes in Syntex product lines. When Picodyne had developed the software, Montana was chosen as the site for a pilot. In this state, each representative deals with 200 doctors, geographically scattered. The software enables a representative to ask the database, in plain English, such things as which doctors are in a particular town, which one prescribes most of a specified drug, and what is the best time to visit each. Needless to say, the answers are only as good as the information put into the computer in the first place by that representative or a colleague.

This development, more in the nature of a job-aid than strictly CBT, led in 1985 to a commission from Syntex for Picodyne to develop CBT modules, on IBM personal computers, for over 600 sales representatives who are scattered across the nation. This development was undertaken by employees of the two companies working closely together. Mace (1986) says that CBT at home was expected to reduce by a third the centralised face-to-face training given in ten regional centres and at the Californian headquarters, and that Syntex expects the CBT development costs to be recouped over three or four years.

There are 12 CBT modules for use by the representatives, some dealing with the nature of diseases and conditions for which certain Syntex products are recommended. One module provides a simulation of the selling process between a Syntex representative and a doctor.

ZALES

Zales is a retail jewellery chain, with headquarters in Texas and stores across the southwestern United States. The company has interactive videotape training programs for employees in its four credit centres, and for managers and sales personnel in its widespread network of stores.

When Zales decided in 1980 to go into interactive training, the company's training department chose interactive videotape, the most advanced technology that Zales felt was compatible with its needs, to place in each centre and each store. With videotape there was also the advantage of being able to change or reuse the tapes, whereas at that time videodiscs were mastered in Japan.

For hardware, Zales chose a level 2 (see Chapter 6) videotape system made by Sony, the SLP 305 controlled by a small handheld microprocessor. This microprocessor can be used for programming and for responding. It has only 63 addresses on each channel, meaning that up to 63 locations can be signalled on a tape, for starting and stopping the video, and 126 branching options.

The system was first used to train credit representatives at the four credit centres, because the centres had an environment in which the results could be easily measured. Each one had its own trainer who could monitor progress. It turned out that the time required to reach established productivity standards (such as the number of calls made per day) was halved, from three months to six weeks.

The system uses videotape to carry the content, with questions in a workbook. When they have studied a sequence, trainees enter a multidigit code on their responders to access the appropriate video frame that shows whether their answers were correct or not. For a wrong answer, they receive a further code with which to access the training sequences before trying the question again. For right answers, they get another code that takes them on to further instruction. When trainees finish a section, they go to other exercises, either in the workbook or job simulations. Interactive simulations are used particularly for sales situations, to train store sales personnel. A freeze frame of video requests a response, then videofeedback shows why the response is right or wrong. This type of simulation has also been used to teach managers how to conduct performance appraisals.

Over 40 hours of interactive videotape training courses have been produced, covering topics such as collection techniques, product knowledge, sales training and management training. There is a hands-on computer training course that teaches the credit system by simulating it on videotape, with practice provided on microcomputers in employees' home stores.

In developing the courses, the training department works closely with the credit centres and with senior executives of the company's various divisions. These divisions pay the department, through a charge-back system, for the training they receive. The department has its own video studio, which produces good quality tapes for about one-third of the cost were the tapes to be produced by a video production company.

Since there is now less control of training in stores than there used to be, evaluation of the interactive videotape training has been informal, but shows good results.

A key to Zales' success in interactive videotape training has been strong management support. A recent company takeover has cut back development of new programs. The general opinion at Zales is that more creative training has been done with a relatively simple system than is often done in other companies with videodisc systems that offer many more interactive options.

11

Transport

In the transport sector are airlines, rail networks, companies hauling passengers and freight by road and sea, and training agencies that serve them. We have also included here a case study of CBT in a motoring organisation that provides support to road users.

In this sector, the larger companies operate far-flung systems, with thousands of employees scattered in many places, sometimes even in other countries. Standardising and decentralising their training, which occurs in many locations, often with small groups, are important considerations.

Airlines need to train a wide range of employees, from aircrew to maintenance engineers and sales personnel. For some the training must be in the safe and correct operation of aircraft; for others it must be in dealing with passengers and customers. The new technology attracted airlines in the 1970s and they are no strangers to CBT. For instance, WICAT developed a training package for TransWorld Airlines to assist in training pilots of McDonnell Douglas DC-9 aircraft. The package covers operating procedures for flying by autopilot. The CBT system is used after two hours classroom training and before flight simulator training, thus reducing the cost of simulated cockpit training time (*Training Digest*, May 1986). American Airlines use *PLATO* to train DC-10 aircrew and maintenance staff. In particular, aircrew receive training in using the inertial navigation system through a *PLATO*-based simulation. British Aerospace trainers produce CBT with the *Regency* system for 34 terminals with touch-sensitive screens and full graphics, providing training for flight crews and engineers (*Training Digest*, May 1987). The variety of training needs being met in the British

Airways and British Caledonian case studies shows how essential computers are in airlines' training.

Rail networks, despite computerisation of many of their operations, have been slow to introduce the technology for training. Yet their training needs are similar in many respects to those of the airlines, as the British Rail case study shows.

Training needs in the thousands of small companies that exist in the British road transport industry are still being identified, according to the brief Road Transport Industry Training Board case study. The Automobile Association (AA) has piloted CBT to train its patrolmen. The patrolmen are geographically scattered, like airline and rail network staff, but need standardised training.

Finally, shipping companies find that training crew by conventional means is very difficult and expensive. As Texaco Tankerships found, CBT offers a means of training on board that is timely and relevant.

BRITISH AIRWAYS

British Airways is one of the world's largest airlines, with about 37 000 employees. It was the first to use a mainframe for reservations and ticket sales, and now has many computerised operations (Thirkettle, 1986). Although it does most of its training in the United Kingdom, it has 5000 employees at its bases in many countries of the world. Its training needs are immense and varied, and are served by several autonomous departments. The company has a decentralised training policy, with only 20 per cent being done centrally. Line managers at employees' workplace do much training, using materials developed centrally.

The airline uses CBT in flight simulation, flight management systems, reservations and checking, engineering and maintenance, operations, and management systems (Heaford, 1983). Thirkettle (1986) says that the company used embedded CBT for some years, but the programs consisted almost entirely of text and numbers, with no graphics. When British Airways was forced to cut its workforce by 52 000 in only eighteen months, the company's needs for training and retraining were very heavy indeed, particularly because many employees were being expected to become multifunctional. The new technology was needed to train manual workers in skills such as aircraft cabin cleaning, toilet servicing, water servicing, baggage loading, freight loading, aircraft towing and winter operations.

156

British Airways staff receive training for using the reservations system (British Airways Booking System, or BABS) through embedded CBT. The system has more than 3000 terminals worldwide linked to mainframe computers (Heaford, 1983). Learning to use them well entails being able, in particular, to decode the screen displays to the customer wanting to book a seat or change a reservation. Among the 15 000 employees who use the terminals, only a few need to know everything BABS can do, but all need basic training. Installing CBT has cut this training time from fourteen to nine days (35 hours of CBT). Employees completing basic training can deal with 90 per cent of requests. Training continues as employees need it. Advanced training is also available: the complete course takes 75 hours to complete.

For reservations, the airline uses stand-alone and embedded CBT. The stand-alone system is called the Universal Training Simulator, and looks like the BABS system. Trainees find that whatever answer they choose to the questions posed on the terminal, they get a prewritten teaching response. They use this simulator before they move onto BABS itself.

The embedded CBT used for BABS training is particularly interesting because it takes a trainee into the real booking system and then shows what would happen if the trainee's actions actually brought about changes in the bookings in that system (of course, they do not, lest mayhem result). The trainee sees the changes on the BABS screen, but the computer keeps no record of these. If he or she makes a mistake, the BABS system responds as it would in everyday use. Transfer from training to being an operator of the real system is thus very smooth, and trainees have plenty of opportunities to build up their confidence.

Flight simulation is probably the best known form of computer-based training. It is also the most expensive to develop (with the possible exception of nuclear power station simulation), yet is cost-effective. British Airways has cockpit simulators for each of the types of aircraft it flies. Pilots receive initial training and regular retraining on these simulators, which simulate flight conditions, including emergencies, extremely closely. A trainer, sitting at a console, causes a range of faults and conditions and the pilot must deal with each satisfactorily. The computer keeps a record of the trainee's actions and the consequences, for discussion with the trainer.

Reed (1986) notes that a Canadian-built simulator, used to train Boeing 747 pilots, is only the latest of eleven simulators at

Heathrow, with more being added. The visual system, Novoview SP-X, was provided by Rediffusion and gives a very realistic picture of each of a large number of international airports, in different weather conditions and at different times of the day or night. On the screen, trainee pilots see moving traffic on airport approach roads, neon signs near the airport, runway lighting and tyre marks. The hydraulic jacks under the simulated cockpit move it around, simulating runway and landing bumps and the effects of turbulence, as well as the normal maneouvres of the aircraft. Engine noise fluctuates correspondingly.

The advantages of this type of simulator, used by many airlines, are that pilots can practise routine and emergency procedures as often as required, without risking themselves or an aircraft, let alone passengers. They can do so at far lower cost to the airline. Reed says the cost of training on an actual aircraft would be ten to 30 times as much. Training can continue throughout the day and night, in all weathers. Simulator-based training of aircrews is now of such high quality that pilots in Britain and the United States can convert, entirely on simulators, to flying another similar type of aircraft. Much recurrent training and testing (every six months) is also done on simulators.

British Airways' latest Boeing 737 simulator provides training for pilots from Pan American, Continental, CAAC (the national Chinese airline) and others. Its three new Boeing 747-400 simulators train maintenance crews as well as pilots.

As Beech (1983) says, however, quite a lot of training can be done with part-task simulators that train aircrew to carry out particular parts of their jobs. In British Airways, the *PLATO* system is used. It can present a high resolution picture of what the pilot, say, will see on certain of his instruments in the cockpit. The pilot is expected to respond, through a touch-sensitive screen, to correct the condition shown by the instruments. The computer monitors, interprets, and responds to the pilot's actions.

Flight management is the process of programming a computer to carry out a range of tasks formerly undertaken throughout the flight by aircrew, such as determining optimum engine settings for the chosen cruising altitude, weight of aircraft and so on. Beech (1983) describes a flight management system that is simulated for British Airways' Boeing 747 aircrew on a *PLATO* terminal. The airline chose *PLATO* partly because the terminal in this case can run by itself with a disc drive, or be connected to the *PLATO* mainframe for editing the lessons.

158

Pilots must be trained to reprogram the flight management computer during flight, as there may be a change of routeing due to altered weather conditions. The *PLATO* terminal offers a part-task simulation by presenting on a touch-sensitive screen a realistic picture of the flight management computer. A trainee simply touches the screen just as he or she would touch the computer's keys. Training consists of entering and/or checking sets of data for passengers, freight, route, fuel, engine type and so on. Unlike the real system, the *PLATO* simulation corrects wrong entries and helps trainees.

In engineering and maintenance, which is aimed at keeping British Airways' fleet up to a high operational standard, there are about 3000 trainees a year, Heaford (1983) says. The demand for training is high, particularly for retraining as aircraft technology changes. Ground simulators are used extensively. For example, one simulates the cockpit of the Boeing 757. Trainees are taken through sequences by a trainer sitting at a special console, just as in the flight simulators. They have to deal with various faults and each one's performance is recorded by the simulator's computer for later analysis and discussion.

Bayard-White (1985) and Thirkettle (1986) describe the development and use of a highly cost-effective interactive videotape. The tape is part of British Airways' operations training, which covers all work by ground crew in servicing aircraft and includes many manual skills, for which videotape can present telling visuals. *Winterwise*, about aircraft de-icing, was produced at low cost (about £6000), with the help of an outside production house, Audio Visual Enlightenment.

Aircraft de-icing is not easy to teach by conventional methods. The trainee is high in the air on the end of a 'fruit-picker'. If he or she makes mistakes, they can be dangerous, and not easily stopped by a trainer elsewhere. Trainees cannot properly practise the correct procedures except on real aircraft under real icing conditions, yet 360–500 of them must complete their training each year in a period of six to eight weeks before winter sets in.

Although the interactive videotape cannot simulate precisely the tasks involved, trainees learn in about 1.5 days to de-ice an aircraft within safety limits and using only the amount of fluid needed, says Thirkettle. Within half a day of conventional training by onsite supervisors, trainees use the interactive video for about 35 minutes. The tape is divided into nine sections, each ending in a short multiple-choice test. Trainees who fail key questions receive further instruction. A whole day of practical training follows.

159

The videotape was tested using twelve employees, including a few trainers. Their responses were positive, and so were those of 120 employees who completed evaluation questionnaires once the tape was in regular use. As a step in raising awareness, however, and to create a demand for this kind of training, line managers had a chance to try out the system before it was used routinely. In the event, says Bayard-White, each asked for the system to be installed, and it became the responsibility of each to decide exactly how to use it.

Because de-icing training was urgently needed at the time of year when the interactive videotape system was introduced, as many as eight trainees worked on it at one time. This was not satisfactory, and the company found that, ideally, employees should train individually. No more than four should work through the training together.

Bayard-White reports that evaluation of the videotape's cost-effectiveness showed that there were considerable savings. According to Thirkettle, training takes 1.5 days, instead of five days required for conventional training. Trainees no longer have to travel to Heathrow. Performance on-the-job has improved, with costly delays due to de-icing reduced by 85 per cent. De-icing recalls by engineers or aircraft captains are fewer. Less fluid is being used, resulting in further savings. The employees feel well-trained: the trainees 'had a better understanding of the task, so their attitude and pride of achievement manifested itself in the confidence and approach to the task' (Thirkettle, 1986). Trainees found the videotape system (a Sony Responder) easy and non-threatening to use. Trainers obtained job satisfaction from developing the materials.

On the basis of this successful experience, British Airways developed further videotapes and invested in interactive videodisc for operations training. For certain training tasks, interactive videodisc brings down the cost of simulation. *Who Owns the Problem?* is aimed at improving safety standards and changing attitudes among some 1500 supervisors at London Heathrow. It portrays, very realistically, scenes on the 'ramp' at the airport prior to take-off. Two particular incidents are linked by a series of apparently unconnected events (Thirkettle, 1986), and trainees are never told whether they are right or not. In each scene, a complex problem arises, for which there is no simple solution. Trainees are offered three options and select what they think is the best solution, often only to discover from further scenes what complications then ensue. The interactive videodisc is ideally suited to the training task, as it can branch quickly to alternative scenes. At the end, trainees are told the costs of some typical accidents. Trainees are encouraged to discuss the problems with others, and thus learn to balance conflicting responsibilities and demands on-the-job.

The disc, which was developed with a production company and designed for a Philips LaserVision player with an Apricot F-2 microcomputer, was tested on about 30 line managers and a group of supervisors, whose reactions were entirely favourable. It has since been in regular use by the airline and has won national awards.

BRITISH CALEDONIAN AIRWAYS

British Caledonian Airways, a British owned and operated airline, has a large training centre and training occurs within several sections of the company. In 1985, it set up a new open learning centre, funded initially by the Manpower Services Commission, within the training centre. The new centre offers training at any time, at employees' own pace, related to career development, interests or hobbies. The courses range from foreign languages to keyboard skills and new technology. Six workstations in the centre provide media in various combinations, including a very limited amount of CBT. Some is embedded, for example, Apple's *Introduction to Apple II*. Other programs available are: Austin Rover's *30 hour BASIC* and *Introduction to Micros* and the BBC's *Structured BASIC*.

The Maintenance Engineer Training section is also part of the training centre. The engineering instructors have considerable reservations about the effectiveness of CBT for basic engineering training partly as a result of experience in 1983 when the Company started to prepare for the operation of the Airbus A-310. Aeroformation in Toulouse provided a series of CBT courses using touch screen *PLATO*. It was in black and white only, had no spoken commentary and the response time was extremely slow. Furthermore the programs were written by computer programmers, not technical instructors, and they did not go to the depth required by both British Caledonian and the Civil Aviation Authority. There were also problems resulting from the substitution of a Sony for a Thomson video disc interface.

Nevertheless because this was the only A-310 series of training programs that Aeroformation had available, the engineering instructors and certain senior engineering staff had no alternative but to use

161

the system. Without the addition of detailed training manuals supplemented with traditional 'chalk and talk' the training would not have reached the standard required by the CAA.

In 1986–87 the introduction of the A-320 Airbus raised the need for more training. In the interval of time since the A-310 training, Aeroformation had radically changed their CBT system. Called VACBI — Video Assisted Computer Based Instruction — it consists of a stand-alone computer with a colour monitor, using a mouse for access to the various menus, a related CD audio commentary and also interfaces with a video disc machine. In addition instructors were involved in the course structure, logic sequence and programming, and the response time greatly improved.

Evaluation of this system has shown it to be far superior to the earlier touch screen *PLATO*, but it still needs to be supplemented by 'chalk and talk' and good detailed training manuals. While British Caledonian consider that this is acceptable for some aspects of pilot training, they still have reservations about it for basic and detailed engineering training.

British Caledonian trainers feel more positively, however, about a British Airways program, developed with *PLATO*, to teach basic skills to employees seeking to update engineering qualifications. The program is seen as much better than the Toulouse *PLATO* program, partly because it has colour.

In Ground Services Training a new method of training is being tested for the new system of checking in and closing flights. The teaching strategy involves initial theory from a tutor, followed by a question and answer session, then by embedded exercises on the computer. The hardware is a *TELEX* microcomputer, compatible with and linked by satellite to Continental Computer Services' mainframe in the United States, which provides worldwide reservations of flights, hotels and car rental, and which can calculate fares, checking passengers and issue boarding cards. The systems were operational by 1987, and this special training program simulates the real process. The course lasts six days, and trainees learn as a group, rather than as individuals, with the tutor setting the pace for the group. Faster learners have to wait for slower trainees to catch up.

BCAL Flight Training operates as a separate Company and is jointly owned by BCAL and Rediffusion Simulation; 70 per cent of its income comes from outside training for other airlines world wide. The Civil Aviation Authority monitors training, sets the technical examinations and controls the number of flight simulator hours to bring flight crew to proficiency.

162

BCAL Flight Training uses CBT for some of its needs, although to teach theory its trainers use a tape/slide programme and workbook. For systems training a console, which replicates part of the cockpit, including switches and dials, is interfaced with a schematic display linked to a TV screen. Cockpit procedures training is carried out in a fixed base simulator. Using an exact facsimile of the cockpit, all systems work as in real life and the instructor can put in faults and monitor the trainees reaction. The hardware consists of a microcomputer supplied by Applied Digital Systems, using Regent software.

Rediffusion's Full Flight Simulators are used for pilot and flight engineer training. Rediffusion are building two more simulators onsite, one the A-320 Airbus, and the other the Boeing 737-300. Costing in excess of £4 million, each simulator realistically replicates noise, aircraft motion and realistic night/day visual displays of various selectable airports. Failures, for example, engine failure on takeoff, or smoke in the cockpit, can be effected by the flick of a switch. The trainee then goes through the appropriate drills under supervision. Simulators are used for converting aircrew from one type of plane to another when the student spends sixteen to eighteen hours on a simulator in four hour stints. They are also used for regular refresher training. To be fully cost-effective these simulators have a highly concentrated usage of 20 hours a day, seven days a week. The advantages of simulators are that they provide realistic training situations without having to put the trainee pilot in an actual plane. This minimises costs and avoids putting the aircraft in a hazardous condition.

The STA TM 150 system with a computer controlled tape/slide presentation was adopted at British Caledonian as its AVT medium. It is interesting to consider the process that led the company to adopt this medium. Some years ago various CBT systems such as *PLATO*, *REGENCY* and WICAT *WISE* were evaluated. At the time these were available mainly as mainframe systems with small screens, with no colour or sound, and the programs were difficult for British Caledonian trainers to author and amend. These limitations resulted in the decision that CBT was not right for BCAL at that time. The company already had experience of the *PLATO* system through Aeroformation, and the pilots' reaction to this system was not very enthusiastic. The Airbus A-310 introduced many new systems and combined with a new training technology could easily add stress to the students unless carefully handled. The Company decided to produce an 'overview' course using the STA TM 150 system which had the desired effect of taking the edge off the radical new systems.

There are frequent modifications to new aircraft such as the A-320, especially in the first years of an aircraft's life, and consequently these produce a need for quick training material updates. At one time British Caledonian considered the use of interactive videodisc, but the problems posed by the need for frequent amendments coupled with the high cost of a new master disc ruled out this technology.

Hence the attractiveness of the Swiss STA system. The STA, made by Simulation Teaching Aids of Zurich, uses a microcomputer to operate twin 35 mm projectors giving random access to slides which combined with a special audio tape gives synchronised sound and pictures. These features together with the advantage of branched learning techniques, gave British Caledonian what it wanted. The system has proved easy to handle, to compile and amend training materials. It has the advantage of being 'totally within our (the trainers') control'. A factor crucial to successful introduction of a training technology is its 'instructor/trainees friendliness'.

A further development came in September 1985 when British Caledonian took over the American Airlines training centre in England and undertook another survey of what was available on the market. The trainers again looked at the *PLATO* system and found that although refinements had been made, there were still problems especially with sound. They selected instead a new system, the STA TM 2000. This can interface with video and microfiche which gives the capacity for presenting dynamic subjects. The trainers have prepared programs for it. Again a major advantage is that the authors do not need to be computer programmers. The programs are easy to construct for it and easy and flexible for trainees to use.

Thus training within the company has been needs-led, with demands for pilot, technical, safety, and customer-services training viewed as essential to the industry. How trainers went about this training varied between sections, with attitudes to CBT ranging from total acceptance to suspicion and scepticism. Trainers at British Caledonian have pertinent questions to ask about CBT. Is it suitable for staff working in people/customer orientated environments? Can CBT build teams? Does CBT allow people to bounce ideas off one another? Isn't CBT an isolating experience? The trainers are dubious about the quality of generic CBT programs and feel these are probably too general for the airline's purposes. They see that therefore they have to author their own material. But they do not envisage CBT replacing all conventional training courses. British

Caledonian trainers work within an industry with rapidly changing requirements. They feel that they can quickly issue printed matter for updating needs, whereas to update CBT or an interactive videodisc is at present a lengthy and costly process.

CIVIL AVIATION AUTHORITY

The British Civil Aviation Authority, which is responsible for civil aviation training, operates the College of Telecommunications Engineering and the College of Air Traffic Control.

At the former, a CBT package was developed in the 1960s for an Elliott 803 mainframe computer, but the project was dropped because it was too difficult to program training courses using the system. Much more recently, new courses have been developed using the *MicroTICCIT* authoring system on a Data General Eclipse minicomputer. The authoring system was chosen after a lengthy search and supplied by a British provider, STC IDEC (new STC Technology). Other hardware and software systems were rejected on grounds of poor graphics, slowness and expense. The *Micro-TICCIT* system offered sophisticated colour graphics plus animated simulations, and an authoring system that permitted trainers to write into their programs the simulation of major equipment faults. The College first installed a pilot scheme, however, with only four terminals linked to the mainframe, which can accommodate up to 40. Other terminals and interactive videodisc players are to be added by 1988.

For the pilot, the College purchased *Computer Fundamentals* and *Digital Logic* courses off-the-shelf from STC IDEC, with a one-year licence that was not renewed. Its staff then selected, for development at the College, a short equipment course for technicians, *Modems*, which was already well-established on traditional training lines and was 'neat' and manageable for such a project, having bench-mounted equipment. The College developed a CBT version of this course.

In its conventional form, the course is normally taken by six students at a time, and lasts one week. For the CBT, the course was rewritten in modular form, an advantage should it need updating due to the introduction of new equipment. Interactivity was built in: students not only interacted with the computer but also completed assignments at a workbench, and watched a video. An unusual feature of the course was that it contained several variations on

165

symbols used in representing circuits, so that a trainee could choose the most familiar one to work with. Each trainee was given a workbook or file, and a study guide to the course. The College trainers felt it was crucial that students should 'have some hard copy to take away at the end of the course'.

Any trainee who already knew parts of a module of the course could skip to the test at the end of that module. On failing a test, however, he or she was sent back through the module and given another test, with different questions. At the end of the each module there were also practice questions, providing remedial help and making additional teaching points. If a trainee failed one of these he or she had to talk to the trainer before going on. Thus the program checked trainees' understanding and recall. It is worth noting that the College felt strongly that a trainer should be on call to support the course, and CBT was not seen as an opportunity to dispense with the trainer, even if the training role had changed.

For evaluation, a student questionnaire provided feedback. The six students on the pilot all supported CBT, although there were some practical difficulties. For example, using the light-pen accurately on the screen was not easy because of parallax: the simulation image was very detailed and touching the wrong part by mistake produced results, from which the trainee could not always recover, in the simulation itself. On the job, trainees must use probes accurately, but of course have no problem of parallax.

Building on the success of the pilot, the College is expanding the system and has already authored more courses, making good use of graphics and simulation techniques (Ashworth, 1987, personal communication).

Professional training for air traffic controllers and assistants is located at the other College, which provides courses for overseas nationals as well as employees of the British Air Traffic Services. These courses are based on the International Civil Aviation Organisation syllabus and include much practical training on simulators. The air traffic controllers are trained to very high standards and subsequently control some of the world's busiest airports. Accuracy is absolutely necessary in their job, therefore the training must replicate in every respect the situations they will encounter. The risk factor is very considerable, so trainees cannot be taken onto the job until they have reached a high level of operational competence.

Each trainee has to be qualified in and able to switch between three functions: airport, approach and area control. After a period of theoretical training, trainees learn the techniques of control of aircraft on the airport, including the movement of circuit traffic, of arriving and departing aircraft and of aircraft and vehicles on the ground. At this stage, trainees use a simple electromechanical simulator, to develop visual skills. An electrically lit wall display represents the air and ground ways, in two dimensions only. Trainees work on a desk-mounted flight progress board on which information on all air and ground movements can be displayed and updated. Simulated radio and telephone messages are controlled by the trainer, giving trainees practice in appropriate radio-telephone and telephone phraseology while learning the procedures for traffic control within the airport traffic zone. Trainees must simultaneously maintain an accurate record on flight progress strips. Although no electronics are involved, the simulation is an effective training system.

Trainees then move on to learn the principles of approach control. An approach controller is responsible for aircraft movements in the vicinity of the airport. There are two forms of approach control. In procedural control, aircraft separation is based on information supplied by pilots and flight data manually recorded on flight-data strips. In radar control, separation is based on data presented on radar screens. Computer-based simulators come into their own for radar approach training, enabling the real operational environment to be reproduced as closely as possible. Radio-telephone and telephone messages are included, so that trainees can practise all procedures, including those for emergencies. The screen shows the airport zone, airways and height so that trainees learn to think three-dimensionally. Each trainee has to sequence planes, taking them from the airways to safe landing, and the reverse process when they take off. The simulation programs can be changed to display different airports and airways, in various countries, as required by different trainees. The trainers can intervene in a simulation, feeding in information as if they were pilots. Typically, trainees bring an aircraft out of the planned flight path by talking to the pilot, who responds to trainees' instructions. In a series of 60 structured half-hour lessons, trainees must master radar approach control.

For instruction in area control, which is the handling of aircraft on journeys within a given geographical area between airports, another computer-driven simulator is used. Trainees have to learn to control the sequencing and separation of up to 20 aircraft of fifteen different types with different flying characteristics.

Trainees work on the simulators for about half an hour at a time. They are expected to reach the standard required within the number of hours allocated to them for CBT. The College's simulators are a good example of computer-based simulation providing highly individualised training, immediately relevant to the air traffic controllers' jobs, in a disciplined occupation where at any moment an error could cost hundreds of lives.

FLIGHTSAFETY INTERNATIONAL

FlightSafety International is the world's largest non-governmental aviation training organisation, in business since 1951. It is the official training agency for nineteen airlines, with 27 training centres in the United States and Canada. The bulk of its training is in corporate aircraft, but it is moving into more and more commercial airline training. The company's primary training methods have been classroom teaching and on simulators.

In 1982, in response to self-paced training offered by the company's main competitor, FlightSafety established an Interactive Systems Division to develop pilot training on videodisc. The company decided that such training would supplement rather than replace all other training, to allow trainees to review material at their own pace and to prepare for examinations. Experience had shown that in pilot training human influence was essential, and that automated training by itself was inadequate.

The Division evaluated various levels of videodisc systems and found that neither a level 2 nor a level 3 system would be able to cope with the specialised training needs of pilot training. For a single program, up to 15 000 scenes of video were needed, with each scene requiring branching in up to four directions. Over ten hours of audio were also needed, although audio and video were not always directly connected. Computer graphics had to be overlaid on freeze frames from the video, sometimes with voice over, therefore separate audio and video capabilities were required.

It was clear that the Division would have to develop a level 4 system with four components: an IBM XT microcomputer, with computer-generated graphics, a Sony video monitor with touch-sensitive screen, a Philips, Hitachi or Panasonic laser videodisc player, for random access video and audio, and a Philips compact disc player (CD ROM) for random access audio.

The vital addition was the CD ROM audio, on which standard

audio could be compressed to store 31 hours of audio at 5000 cycles, for playing when needed, independently of the videodisc. Fortunately, Philips was prepared to work with FlightSafety on developing the audio component even while the compact disc system was not yet on the market.

The Division spent most of the funds for the project on developing the software and instruction, and on integrating the video and audio. The program was written in a version of the programming language Forth, which is extremely fast and dynamic, enabling easier updating as well as totally graphic sections. A special camera was developed with a metal mask that allowed up to twelve shots at once to appear on a single frame of video. With the mask, much of the editing could be done within the camera, by shooting an image in its correct location for final production.

The current generation of programs was completed in 1984, covering seven different types of aircraft. A further thirteen programs were under production in 1987. Besides trainees using them, trainers can introduce the programs into classroom work, without the audio narration. They can also create files on floppy disks from the programs, and use them in any order they want to in class. Most of the programs have 400 learning units or segments, each of which can be called up as required.

The Division has grown and has acquired two full-time video crews. It is now in the business of marketing the FlightSafety approach to other companies with complex systems. Power safety and marine safety offer opportunities through two subsidiaries of FlightSafety, and medicine may be another field.

BRITISH RAIL

British Rail is a nationalised company running virtually all the railways in Britain. It was reorganised in the early 1980s into accountable Sectors and Functions. Sector directors became responsible for profitability, budgets and identification of training needs. At headquarters, the main tasks of Personnel Development with regard to training were to evolve a corporate policy, develop a training network and send information to profit sectors. Personnel Development also provides an advisory service for both regions and functions, which are autonomous, but subject to British Rail Board national policy decisions. The South West Regional Director, for example, has responsibility for training within the region, but the

South West Regional Director of Operations determines training policy within the national policy.

CBT, at various stages of development, is being used in several sectors and functions. The personnel department has recently reviewed authoring and other software with the aim of giving advice to the functions and regions. The need to develop authoring skills within British Rail is being recognised. There has been a natural progression, but as yet no national company policy on CBT has emerged.

We looked particularly at developments in the Western Region, where the Regional Training Officer has evaluated authoring systems such as *PLATO*, *Mentor II*, *Domino*, *TenCORE* and *Interactive Learning*, with the help of programmers in the information systems and technology function. He found that some systems were not very user-friendly, being difficult for trainers to use and needing a programmer. He considered *PLATO* a very complex authoring system. He recognised that different authoring systems meet differing needs, however, and did not recommend any single system.

In the Western Region, drivers and guards are learning new routes with a pilot interactive videotape, *The Route-Learning Package*. From the management's point of view, CBT in this case will provide cost savings. In the Region, 60–90 additional posts are retained specifically for training drivers and guards. At present an eighteen year-old becomes a traction trainee, is the second person in the cab and is not allowed to become a driver until aged 23. With new technology, the need for a second person in the cab is being questioned. Currently a trainee driver is taken down the route several times before driving in the cab alone. A traction inspector tests trainee drivers for knowledge of the route after a variable number of weeks with a driver. Implementation of CBT could therefore release drivers and cut training time and costs. A 50 per cent saving on training costs would amount to about £750 000.

The Western Region's Director of Operations took up the initiative and stimulated interest, negotiating via the Senior Training Officer. Initial funding amounting to around £10 000 for equipment came from within the Western Region for an IBM personal computer, monitor, Sony videocassette player and Dalroth's *Interactive Learning* interface from video to monitor. The development cost of the project was regarded as low at £60 000, with 49 per cent of the funds coming from the Manpower Services Commission.

First, a videotape of the route was made for British Rail by a commercial film-maker. Videotape is cheap and can be changed easily if details change, such as the configuration of the route and signalling. The videotape soundtrack provides a commentary, drawing attention to features of the route. It is of broadcast quality, spoken with a natural regional accent as well as incorporating the background noise of the engine. A microcomputer controls the player, via an adaptation of the *Interactive Learning* authoring system, and the program presents a linear learning task with branching, with frequent tests.

Trainees have code numbers to use in logging onto the system and are directed to segments they are entitled to study. Trainees use the keyboard to halt the video, take a test or go to the next point on the video. The program is linked to documents such as the Route Document, giving positions of signal boxes, junctions, etc. These details are not constant, but change if, for example, there are speed restrictions because of engineering work. Multiple choice questions test knowledge of, for example, speeds on certain parts of the route. Signal numbers and speed restrictions are superimposed onto the video recording of the line. If changes occur in speed limits then the computer input can be changed to flash onto the screen. The program gives several minutes of video, then branches according to the option chosen by the trainee, who may view the video again, see the video again using the stop/start control, or try the test. The trainee gets positive responses even if he or she gives the wrong answer. Trainees have to fill in answers in a workbook which accompanies the video.

Several questions cropped up during development and testing: Should the video realistically simulate the train's movement or should the camera be held rigid? Of the drivers questioned on this, half preferred each option. How much additional information, such as telephone line crossings, should appear on the screen? The trainers learned from feedback comments from drivers that engine noise was important.

By early 1987, the video had been demonstrated to various groups of managers, staff representatives, drivers, Trade Unions, The Industrial Society. Initial reactions were reported as very good. The programme was evaluated at four locations in the Western Region, with one set of hardware in each location. To avoid damage and theft, the hardware was boxed in so that only the keyboard and monitor would be visible. Train crew supervisors were placed in charge of the trials and asked to keep full records of students' progress.

Plans were laid to video the Region's 'spine route' from London

Paddington to Bristol and South Wales at an envisaged cost of £60 000. At the time of writing, this work was nearly finished. If this pilot proves successful in the Western Region, savings in training costs are likely to be about £400 000 each year. It may become Board policy to use similar CBT in other parts of British Rail.

The Passenger Marketing function in the Western Region is testing Apple microcomputers plus ordinary video (not interactive) in major travel centres, to provide flexibility in training of staff who need to update their knowledge of tickets at special rates and of railway geography. A review of the *Training for Trainers* course led to a proposal to use the course for testing software development. Building in a one hour CBT session within the course would provide an introduction to CBT as well as trainers actually learning from it. Separately a module was planned as a one or two hour CBT unit on an existing residential course, *How People Learn*.

Nationally, the Traction Sector is responsible for driver training and, with the backing of the Director of Operations, asked the Manpower Services Commission for funds to develop simulators similar to those used in aircraft training. Simulators are in use in Australia to train drivers of high-speed trains in New South Wales. Queensland Railways introduced simulation for training staff on a new railway for transporting coal to the docks. On this line several locomotives pull trains of hundreds of tonnes.

The British Rail simulator would probably be commissioned from a provider company. First, Rediffusion Simulation is carrying out a study to see whether simulation would be of practical and financial benefit. On the basis of recommendations stemming from the study, British Rail will decide internally what is the best course of action. The next five years are crucial in terms of training need, as British Rail has an ageing workforce, to which new staff will have to be recruited, and electrification of the rail network will create additional training needs. The demand for training may then decline. British Rail is also aware that simulators can centralise training, with resultant costs.

British Rail's civil engineering function is responsible for maintenance of track, bridges, stations and tunnels, and employs a total of around 30 000 staff. The Training and Education Officer and his assistant took the lead in piloting CBT. In 1984, they used *Mentor II* and a Sirius microcomputer to develop a short course, *Entry into Confined Spaces*, which was subsequently evaluated. The course is for employees required in the course of their work to go into confined spaces such as culverts, tunnels and passages under station platforms, and covers the potential hazards of working in such environments. It combines other media and learning aids with the CBT. Trainees look at photographs and printed text in folders, as well as handling oxygen meters, respirators, current detector tubes, goggles and helmets at appropriate points in the course.

Entry into Confined Spaces could replace conventional material, and has the potential advantage of being available for standardised training needed at spasmodic intervals by up to a thousand employees scattered throughout British Rail's Regions. It was designed to be a half-day course to replace a longer classroom-based course. Regional offices were encouraged to obtain Sirius machines so they could use the training discs, but in the event, this program has not been widely distributed.

A systematic training needs analysis appears to be needed to determine which if any further training should be by CBT within the civil engineering function, although more topics could be selected that 'suit the medium', to gain experience. A program now being developed tests staff knowledge of the British Rail Rule Book through a question and answer session. Another, *Examination of Steel Bridges*, is for use as part of a residential course. Neither has been evaluated yet, except by comparing the performance of a control group of trainees tested after a conventional classroom course with those trained on CBT. The conclusion seemed to be that the standard achieved was not higher, but more consistent. Trainers and trainees both appeared happy with the courseware that had been used at the residential college, although the trainers themselves had not been involved in preparing the programmes. The developers met some resistance elsewhere from trainers, and they felt that British Rail had yet to be persuaded that CBT was cost-effective.

Several other CBT initiatives are being taken elsewhere in the company. For instance, ScotRail is building up expertise in CBT for training staff in rules and regulations and in warning systems. Timesheet skills are taught to British Rail signal and telecommunications personnel via a two hour CBT course developed by Mentor Interactive Training. In 1987, there were plans for Southern Region train and traction crews to be receive CBT (*Mentor News*, Spring 1987).

ROAD TRANSPORT INDUSTRY TRAINING BOARD

The Board serves the British road transport industry by promoting and providing training. It receives funds, through a levy, from companies above a certain size. Its training activities cover management development and craft and operative training, within the motor industry (including dealerships and service stations) and road haulage.

Many employees in the industry are likely to be somewhat wary of training, and their backgrounds are very varied. Any training provided must be accessible and timely.

The Board has 90 training advisors in the field who are linked by a videotex system to the Board's ICL mainframe computer in London. As yet, this system has been used solely for electronic mail and not for training the advisors. The Board is considering setting up a pilot videotex-based training project in two regions, but sees reliability of the system as a potential problem. Access to the system outside working hours is possible, but the ICL mainframe is not manned then.

Since dealerships often have terminals with access to networks based on other mainframe computers, the Board may consider a videotex-based training scheme for dealers and their employees. Technically, it is possible to link up the Board's ICL to these networks.

In response to a demonstrated need, the Board has acquired support from the EEC (European Social Fund) for developing software for management information systems to be used by small transport companies. The software would include embedded training.

Heavy goods vehicle (heavy truck) drivers are in a few instances initially trained on a simulator, but this is one of the few examples so far of CBT in the industry.

The Board recognises that in dealerships and service stations, technicians need well-standardised training, particularly since in the United Kingdom the old apprenticeship system had disappeared. Possibly the Board will produce CBT to standardise technician training, along the same lines as some of the car manufacturers. Audi-VAG, the Germany car company, has prepared an interactive videodisc for technicians repairing and servicing its cars. This disc is most valuable in dealing with upmarket models that have complex systems, for which centralised training courses are not always available. Similarly, Jaguar Cars has its series of six discs for dealers' employees who repair and maintain the new XJ-6 (see Chapter 8).

CBT for managers is under discussion by the Board. Managers of small companies could receive training in how to use spreadsheets and accounting software that would increase company efficiency and profitability.

THE LOCAL GOVERNMENT TRAINING BOARD

Bus crews in Britain were until recently employed chiefly by local government bodies. According to Rushby (1986), the Local Government Training Board, with responsibility for training these crews in England and Wales, decided to develop an interactive videodisc on how to deal with potentially difficult passengers. The disc, entitled *Who Do You Think You're Talking To?*, was commissioned from the University of London's Centre for Staff Development partly to improve customer relations but also because of the large number of attacks on bus crews.

Rushby says that the disc uses the 'trigger' video technique, in which the trainee is asked to respond to a very short incident shot straight to camera. An analysis of incidents encountered by bus crews led to selection of eight scenarios. Each one illustrates a typical incident faced by drivers of one-man buses, and was designed to help the driver to explore possible responses, by presenting about six credible outcomes in further scenarios reached through the program's branching. The disc's content is built on a model of transactional analysis, and ends by using the pattern of responses to give a commentary on the trainee's actions and on what other actions they might take to calm rather than inflame difficult situations (Rushby et al., 1987).

When the disc had been made, drivers and inspectors reported their views on its use and value. The cost of developing it was estimated by Rushby to be £30 000 for the 60 minute package. The long-term benefits, such as reduced numbers of complaints or reduced numbers of assaults by passengers on drivers, cannot yet be judged.

THE AUTOMOBILE ASSOCIATION

The Automobile Association (AA) is the largest motorists'

organisation in the United Kingdom, with several million members. It is a non-profit institution that aims at offering a very efficient service to its members, at a low annual cost per member. The AA's Training Services decided to carry out a pilot study in 1985 to explore the cost-effectiveness of CBT. The AA's Patrol Force consists of a large number of drivers of cars and vans who patrol the roads and answer calls for help received by radio through the breakdown centre. These patrolmen must be trained in mechanical skills and first aid. Topics within these two areas are suitable for CBT, and the trainers selected a topic taught to new recruits, *How to Diagnose and Repair Faults in Alternators* (Dutton, 1985).

The AA chose the authoring system *TenCORE*, but found that its trainers needed help from a programmer and coder. The system worked satisfactorily during the pilot.

The package was tried out on eleven recruits, who used rented IBM personal computers for the occasion. To the trainers' surprise, pretesting showed that two trainees needed no training at all on this topic and another four others needed to study only half the course. Less surprisingly, perhaps, this limited trial suggested that training time could be cut by 50 per cent and administrative costs reduced. Trainee reaction was very positive and the trainers, after early doubts, saw CBT as a useful additional training technique.

On the basis of this pilot, Training Services recommended that CBT should be applied when large numbers of employees had to be trained concurrently but were geographically dispersed, when training could not disrupt normal work commitments, when extensive practice and feedback were required, with remedial training, when existing knowledge and skills varied widely among trainees, or when they learned at widely varying speeds. And, of course, when mistakes by trainees could be expensive, dangerous or both. Further topics were proposed.

Organisational changes in the AA after the pilot held up consideration of wider implementation of CBT, with no lead being given by top management. On the other hand, the AA Training Centre acquired twelve screens and terminals for training insurance employees. The Membership Department bought in a Fraser Nash system for training in keyboard skills, computers and information retrieval. This system paces the student automatically.

Despite some setbacks for CBT within the AA, a learning centre was set up at the end of 1986 to provide workstations for trainees who need access to off-the-shelf CBT packages.

TEXACO TANKERSHIPS

Texaco Tankerships is a company operating a fleet of oil super-tankers around the world. These ships are sailed by small crews, each member of which is usually trained to carry out more than one function. Crew training is difficult by conventional means, since training on board can only be carried out by trainers who move from ship to ship, and training on land implies providing replacement crew. These forms of conventional training are also very expensive.

Partly because one of its managers had used a computer during his Open University studies, the company decided some years ago to develop CBT, with the help of the Marine Studies Department at the University of Wales Institute of Science and Technology. The original programs were mainly for inexpensive Commodore PET microcomputers that could be carried on board. Crew now use the *TOPCAT* (*Texaco Onboard Programme of Computer-Assisted Training*) series to learn, for example, how to load oil cargo correctly and how to carry out maintenance welding. Through a type of arcade game, they learn which fire extinguisher to use for different types of fire on the ship. By means of a large-scale simulator, they learn to navigate the ship in coastal waters.

Loading oil cargo must be done quickly and safely, to reduce time in port. Crew members can refresh their knowledge of pumping procedures the day before docking. With the Texaco *TOPCAT* microbased simulation, they can test the limits of the pumping system, and discover what will happen if they exceed those limits. For example, if they allow the pumping speed to drop, cavitation (appearance of bubbles) occurs in the oil. Similarly, the simulator enables them to appreciate the stresses that build up in a ship while its various tanks are being loaded.

Overall, tankership repairs at sea are considerably cheaper, as a rule, than repairs in dock. *Maintenance Welding* is a *TOPCAT* package dealing with powder welding of bearings. Texaco say that it cost about £3000 to prepare, about the saving on a single repair to a bearing at sea.

The computer-based arcade game *ALARM* not only provides spare time entertainment. It also teaches thoroughly the kind of extinguisher required for various types of fire. This knowledge is essential for all crew: they must instantly know which kind to pick up and use. The game has a time factor built in, so that crew try to choose the right kind quicker and quicker, to beat their opponents.

Texaco's navigation simulator is similar to those used to train airline pilots. A representation of coastline and a port appears on a broad screen which is in fact the 'windows' of the simulated bridge. Trainees learn to steer the ship, which requires considerable skill because of its size and momentum. Crew can practise without the risk of shipwreck and oil spills. The trainer controls what happens in the simulation, which is run by a dedicated mainframe computer.

A novel form of evaluation is used by the company: three months after passing their tests, trainees are asked to complete a form on which they estimate the financial benefit to the company of that training.

Like the nuclear power station simulations, here is another case of a training simulator having an influence on the design of the actual controls. Development of the cargo loading simulation for Texaco led to a redesign of the programs for loading ships (Open University, 1985).

12

Telecommunications

TRAINING NEEDS

By its nature, the telecommunications industry is geographically dispersed, and a single company's operations, serving many millions of people, may be spread across a province, a country or even a hemisphere. American Telephone and Telegraph, and British Telecom, the prime examples quoted in this chapter, are both very large companies, the latter carrying almost all British telecommunications traffic. This kind of traffic is expanding quickly, of course, in all countries.

Typically, training in telecommunications companies needs to be well-standardised and to some extent decentralised. This is true whether the trainees are managers, technicians or sales representatives.

Much of the training must be provided in-house, since trainees must learn to handle many systems and procedures that are unique to their own company. For example, Cable and Wireless, a large telecommunications company with operations in 60 countries, has installed WICAT's S155 processor, with *WISE* and *SMART* authoring and management software systems, at its Telecommunications College at Porthcurno (*Interactive Learning International*, vol. 3, no. 2). Some of the training, on the other hand, is in fields such as electronics where non-CBT courses are likely to be readily available locally outside the company.

New training needs constantly arise in the telecommunications industry as new technology is introduced. In particular, the phasing-in of electronic exchanges (in place of electromechanical ones) and their associated equipment has required substantial retraining of large numbers of engineers, technicians and operators. Increased capabilities provided through this technology result in new services being offered to the public, and sales personnel must be trained to sell these services.

AMERICAN TELEPHONE AND TELEGRAPH

American Telephone and Telegraph (AT&T) is a very large company with offices throughout the United States. Training is conducted in many centres, but over 130 courses are offered through the company's Santa Clara training centre in California. Of these, eighteen are offered to employees at selected centres for training purposes, via Optel's Telewriter II personal computer Conferencing System. This system needs only one telephone line, instead of two, to carry voice and data.

Using bridges (electronic connectors), in the telephone system, AT&T set up small networks of workstations, each consisting of a microcomputer equipped with a normal keyboard, an electronic drawing tablet and pen, plus a standard or loudspeaker telephone. Training programs, including graphics, were developed in advance, stored on floppy or hard disc and transmitted to the other work-stations either during the training or beforehand. Program transmission is not instantaneous, however, and if the instructor draws on the tablet, the picture has to build up on the trainees' screens.

The company has prepared a wide range of short courses for these networks, many them on topics specific to the company's technical operations. For example, three kinds of courses using the system are:

(a) Alliance training courses for AT&T telephone sales representatives who will be selling the service to customers. Alliance is the company's audio teleconferencing network, the largest public teleconferencing system on offer in the United States, which enables up to 80 or more people to conduct a teleconference.

(b) An account planning course to train AT&T account executives in strategic planning.

(c) Training for representatives selling the 800 and 900 services (the 800 'area code' denotes a toll-free number, and the 900 prefix is used for polling opinions).

Using personal computer conferencing for training has definite benefits. The system presents refresher courses, updating information

180

and planning skills much better than classroom instruction, says AT&T. It also requires small groups of no more than ten for good interaction, however, and is tiring, so that half-day sessions with breaks are recommended.

The Santa Clara training centre's experience has shown that this system produces the best training results when there is a ratio of one instructor to no more than three participating branches, with six to twelve people per branch, and when question-and-answer interaction is interspersed with lectures and group activities.

AT&T also has two Individualised Learning Centres, located in Cincinnati (Ohio) and Somerset (New Jersey). The training at these centres is designed primarily for AT&T's own trainees at all levels from managerial downwards. CBT courses are used, running on the AT&T 6300 microcomputer.

The centres produce courses based on requests from other AT&T departments, subject to policy laid down by a centralised training office in the Corporate Services Organisation, which is responsible for setting company-wide policies, including decisions on which media shall be used. One innovative CBT course was designed, following changes in US laws that brought radical changes in AT&T, to orient employees to the new AT&T structure, through a game dealing with basic concepts of divestiture and reducing the size of the organisation.

Details of courses available, including those delivered by CBT or personal computer teleconferencing, are listed in a curriculum book distributed throughout AT&T, so the trainees may come from any-where in the company for teletraining. Many of the courses can be taken on a computer at a learning centre or at an office workstation or at home. Self-development courses such as *Basic Spelling Skills*, and *One Minute Manager* and *How to Use your PC* are also available.

AT&T also acquired generic CBT programs from providers such as Deltak and Advanced Systems Inc. Some providers will prepare courses to meet specific needs in the company. All courses are reviewed within the company to ensure that they teach what is stated.

AT&T's subsidiary, AT&T Information Systems, installed five WICAT interactive terminals at each of ten regional training centres in the United States, with the aim of cutting training time by at least one-third. Each terminal consists of a System 2220 computer and several System 155 computers, linked to five MG8000 graphics terminals with touch panels, and to interactive videodisc players. WICAT developed course materials for AT&T.

BRITISH TELECOM

British Telecommunications plc, otherwise known as British Telecom or BT was created as a private company in 1984 by the sale by the British Government of the telecommunications sector of the Post Office. The Government retains a 49 per cent shareholding in the company, which is one of three licensed telecommunications operators in the United Kingdom. The company is split into a number of operating divisions. The largest, Local Communications Services (LCS), carries out the operation of most of the UK inland network, and in 1986 employed 92 458 technicians. A further 5870 are employed by National Networks Division (NND), which provides trunk services in the UK inland network.

The scale of the training requirement and commitment of BT means that training has a high profile throughout the organisation and some 1330 staff are employed by the British Telecom Technical College alone, over half of these at its main college site at Stone in Staffordshire. The main task of BTTC is system planning, installation and maintenance training for technicians in both NND and LCS. In addition, it does some technical training for other operating divisions and management technical training for all of BT. Ongoing training is regarded as essential and integral in a high-tech, rapidly developing industry.

BT was one of the earliest British companies to venture into the field of CBT (Lamb, 1986). The company's interest stemmed from a 1975 British Government initiative to encourage the application of computers to training. A four-week course on the maintenance of telephone equipment and exchange line circuits was converted to CBT and ran experimentally at the Bristol Training Centre. The experiment was viewed as successful in terms of meeting the training need, but was not financially viable. It served however to generate interest in CBT and in 1980 at a time, as Rothwell (1983a) reports, when the introduction of new technology such as digital signal switching and transmission was placing established training under strain through the need to train large numbers of technical staff in the new technologies, BT itself decided to fund a two year trial evaluation of CBT.

The aims of this trial were to establish whether CBT could shorten courses, as a cost-effective form of training delivery, acceptable to trainees, and to investigate design methods. Five courses, two for technical managers and three for technicians, were designed using Control Data's *PLATO* system as this at the time appeared to be the most comprehensive system available. Alternative systems for CBT were evaluated as they became available — Modcomp's *Simpler*, Regency's *USE*, Hazeltine's *TICCIT*, and WICAT's *WISE/SMART* systems. These were compared against 72 features, in particular the ease of programming by non-experts.

CBT in general was acceptable to BT trainees, and an effective way of training. It reduced course lengths on average by more than 30 per cent, offering potential savings over conventional training delivery. Yet CBT required more rigorous training design than conventional training and the development to delivery ratios at BT ranged from 70:1 to 141:1.

As a result of the two year trial period the WICAT *WISE/SMART* system was adopted in 1983, largely on the grounds of ease of input of training material into the system and superiority of graphics. Early difficulties with the 32 terminal WICAT system were resolved and the system extended to 48 terminals in 1985, when a second 48 terminal system was also installed at BTTC, Stone and a 24 terminal system installed in BTTC, London. A sixteen-terminal system was also commissioned at one of the management colleges in 1984. Each system is driven by a WICAT Systems 2220 microcomputer coupled to the terminals — WICAT Systems MG8000 units — through a local area network, capable of serving any location on the training site. Programs are held on 80 and 160 Mbyte hard discs. Additional systems are used for authoring. Together with a stand-by 2220, the installation at Stone alone cost over £600 000.

By April 1986 eleven courses had been designed for CBT delivery, including two concerned with aspects of telecommunications transmission, and one with digital switching maintenance. Others were reported as being in various stages of design, including a course for maintenance of AXE10 Exchange Systems and further elements of System X Maintenance.

CBT design is treated as a separate function for BTTC, thus designers concentrate on the creation of courseware while inputting of material onto computer is done by specialist typists. Authoring is done using *WISE/SMART* (System for Managing Authors, Resources and Training) is used at the design stage to set up the structure of the course, integrate the training objectives, and provide the essential managing element at the delivery stage. It steers the trainees through the training from one objective to the next, identifying the resources to be used in achieving the objective, and has a resource management and scheduling capability. It also records and reports on trainees' progress.

All courses developed to date are multi-media courses, involving a training model and some use of documentation; some involve simulation and hands on practical experience of the technology. CBT is not seen as a way of doing away with human tutors, who are constantly available to trainees.

The greatest advantage of CBT is seen by BTTC as being that it is trainee-centred — the trainee sets the pace. CBT certainly shortens the duration of training and hence offers cost savings. Not every BT course is amenable to adaptation to CBT and preparing CBT takes at least four times longer than for conventional training. Increases in design staff at BT may indeed outweigh savings in presentation training staff.

In 1987 BTTC was firmly committed to CBT and plans were advanced for introducing small CBT systems remote from the training centres. Additionally some initial experiments with interactive video had taken place, although there were apparently some doubts whether interactive video could provide a high enough level of simulation for technical training. Interactive video cannot be handled directly by the WICAT system.

British Telecom's Management College (BTMC) with its staff of 250, traditionally had responsibility for provision of management skills training. Its role has recently changed in response to organisational changes following privatisation of the industry in 1984. Management structure has become devolved to 26 districts each of which is a profit centre. Management training has to develop within this ethos of profitability and proven cost-effectiveness, while coupled with a heavy commitment to training. The role of BTMC has changed in response to these organisational changes. Line managers in the field are now responsible for identifying training needs within the Districts and are now free to buy in training. So BTMC has to compete with other potential training providers. This has resulted in a decentralisation of training wherever possible to the workplace. Such factors have provided the organisational push for the development of distance learning and the introduction of new training technologies.

The Management College had already had some experience of CBT (according to Bayard-White, 1985), when it decided to look into the potential of interactive videodisc. It had produced *An Introduction to Financial Statements*, a generic CBT program now for sale. By early 1986 the production of interactive videodisc packages was well advanced. A major push was in progress to get the discs out into the districts and integrated into existing training.

All 26 districts were equipped with workstations going part of the way to achieving the goal of workplace training.

Equipment decisions were made largely on the grounds that equipment should be immediately available, easy to use and relatively inexpensive. The delivery system chosen was the Philips 831 videodisc player, with a Cox *Genlock* board, linked to a microcomputer fitted with the Abbey Audio overlay card and headphones (Bayard-White, 1985). *Microtext Plus* was adopted as the authoring language because it was flexible and could be developed and upgraded by BT staff.

This feasibility study and evaluation of interactive video in British Telecom should therefore be seen in the context of a response to changing organisational structures within the industry and evolving demands for different styles of delivery of training. At the time of our visit five training discs had been developed as well as one 'point of sale' disc which could be used with different software for staff training. Several discs were also under production. The content was developed having regard to the needs of the evaluation exercise and broadly represented the range of courses offered by BTMC. The discs were designed to answer the question 'What kinds of subjects are best suited to the medium of interactive video?'. The preparation of the discs was also seen as a means to identify skills needed and to develop these skills in some of the company's own trainers.

Five interactive video packages had been produced by 1986 with much of the course design and all the programming being done by outside production companies. For new management trainees British Telecom required materials that would give them an appreciation of the national telecommunications network, both as it is in the 1980s and as it will be in the 1990s. EPIC Industrial Communications helped to prepare specifications for two of the first four training discs the college wanted. Development of all four was put out to tender, as the company wished to compare the experience of working with different contractors. Bayard-White (1985) offers a detailed analysis of the complex development procedures followed during pre-production, production and post-production phases. A generic course *Introduction to Marketing*, provides a basic general introduction to marketing as part of a comprehensive induction course for all new managers; this is designed to replace modules of an existing course. For production BT went to Interactive Information Services (IIS), which has subsequently sold the course to other organisations.

Transmission and *Introduction to the Network* were produced for BT by EPIC Industrial Communications and aimed at all new managers within BT. A further program, *Modern Technology Overview*, provides an overview of current telecommunications technology and its use in BT. This is aimed at second line managers who need to update their knowledge of switching systems.

Octara 32, was designed specifically for a new product launch in 1985 of a new telephone key-switching system for exchanges. IIS was contracted to produce this program for use with the salesforce. For the evaluation, half the sales force were to be trained with it, half through conventional means, the aim being to provide a test for effectiveness in terms of quality of performance and relative costs.

There appears to be a firm commitment within BT to the use of new technologies for training and in recently reported developments British Telecom is to use interactive courseware to train 20 000 of its telephone operators to use the new digital System X Operator Service System, starting in 1987 and finishing in about 1992 when the last exchange is converted (*Training Officer*, vol. 22, no. 6, 1986). The CD ROMS will be programmed for sound only, to simulate, in ten modules, all the kinds of situations operators have to handle (*Training Digest*, June 1986).

In a similar training venture, 25 000 managers in British Telecom were scheduled to view a new interactive videodisc about the digital exchanges, entitled *AXE 10 — An Appreciation for Managers*, in 1987 (*Interactive Learning International*, vol. 4, no. 1). The video content and programming were produced by the Moving Picture Company, for British Telecom.

Also in 1987 an interactive video on Service Care was produced to train a wide range of British Telecom staff to support this new British Telecom product. The production company used for this development was VPS who are based in Brighton.

PACIFIC BELL

Pacific Bell is part of the US telecommunications network in Northern California. Its training department has been actively using CBT on a mainframe computer since 1978, starting with *PLATO* as the authoring system because there are many CDC terminals in the company.

In 1980, the company decided against further training on the mainframe. The cost of timesharing was high and the mainframe allowed little use of graphics, colour or training peripherals. In

1981, with the advent of the IBM personal computer, the department chose it for training. Since no personal computer authoring system was yet available, the department began to design its own. This proved more difficult than expected.

In early 1983, when several authoring systems were available, the department chose *SAM*, with the agreement that the producer, Learncom, would change it to meet Pacific Bell's needs. The company wanted a system that did not require a programmer to implement it, and one with extremely good graphics capability. *SAM* uses VideoLogic's *MIC 2000* (see Chapter 6), which allows separate control of audio, video and computer data, so that text and graphics can be faded in and out, independently. The board can be used to drive other peripherals, too.

Most of Pacific Bell's training is of its own employees, although the company has developed (with a programming language) CBT for customers that simulates the software used to operate a large corporate Centrex telephone system. Examples of CBT for employees are *Touch Typing*, which is a professional-level typing course, and *The EXAMiner*, a program for developing tests. The latter program offers a choice of nine different question types and handles grading and record-keeping.

Most interactive videodisc courses have been purchased off-the-shelf for use by the company's marketing department. Others such as *Defensive Driving* and *Management Skills* were developed by the training department. All new employees who drive any vehicle on company time are required to take the *Initial Defensive Driving* course, which, together with *Refresher Defensive Driving*, was developed in-house. The Pacific Bell video department videotaped actual driving situations, showing how to handle routine and emergency conditions, including stops and lane changes. This personal computer-based course is supplemented with graphics, and uses two-channel audio in addition to the video on the videodisc.

The training department is now using a cross-section of authoring systems to meet its needs. *PHOENIX* is on the mainframe and *SAM* is used for non-programmer authoring on personal computers. *PASCAL*, *BASIC* and *PC-PILOT* (an authoring language that falls somewhere between a programming language and an authoring system) are available for special programs.

Pacific Bell use a concurrent authoring system for applications software programs. This is a system that runs with the software it teaches, effectively 'wrapping' the software program to control trainee interaction (see Chapter 4). Concurrent systems save

187

considerable development time by eliminating the need to recreate the entire application program for a simulation. In 1987, at the time of writing, the training department was leaning towards using *CAS* (*Concurrent Authoring System*) by Evergreen Technologies. This was considered to have a longer record of effective use than other concurrent systems and consultants are available if needed. One of the first uses of concurrent authoring will be in the VIP (Voucher Improvement Project). Trainees will be able to learn about the software and use it for processing at the same time.

13

Energy

TRAINING NEEDS

The energy sector includes companies that obtain, refine and market primary energy supplies such as gas, oil and coal, as well as those generating electrical energy. The operations of the former are frequently international, those of the latter seldom so. Nevertheless the companies concerned tend to be large or very large, with employees scattered in many locations. If they are public utilities they have very large numbers of customers, even tens of millions.

The training needs of companies in this sector cover a wide range, from general management to highly specialised technical procedures. Training in safety and emergency procedures is particularly important. Training and retraining needs also arise when new technology is introduced, although the pace of change is not as fast in most parts of the energy sector as it is in telecommunications.

These training needs, and their wide variety, are nowhere better exemplified than in the nuclear power industry (whether in the United States or Britain), as the case study of the Central Electricity Generating Board shows. We noted that British Nuclear Fuels purchased the Marconi *Mandarin* CBT system, with 36 software packages covering training needs ranging from induction of new employees to training of 'professional groups' (*Training Digest*, June 1986). Toledo Edison introduced *PLATO* to train its nuclear power plant employees who had to take the National Regulatory Commission's periodic examinations. The training included simulation on *PLATO* of complex systems in the plant. Evaluation showed that CBT was accepted enthusiastically by trainees and trainers, saved training time and cost less.

189

CENTRAL ELECTRICITY GENERATING BOARD

Central Electricity Generating Board (CEGB) generates and distributes electricity in England and Wales. It has 48 000 employees and a number of training centres. The manpower total of the industry has been progressively reduced due to the lower manning levels required by newer plant. For example, generators now being installed produce more than 20 times as much electricity as those installed 40 years ago. The scope for off the job training is thus more restricted especially if employees have to attend distant training establishments. Distance learning materials have been delivered by means of text, video and slide/tape.

The Board is a major user of computers in training where employees are trained to operate power stations safely and efficiently. The Board has three training establishments using simulators based on computers. Littlebrook and Whitehall Road centres provide simulators of fossil-fired (oil and coal) plant. The Nuclear Power Training Centre (NPTC) uses simulators (see below) in addition to the traditional lecture style face to face instruction, supplemented by text, slide/tape and video.

The Nuclear Power Training Centre runs courses providing training and updating to enable employees to meet safety standards agreed by the Nuclear Installation Inspectorate. Standard specifications detail the exact training requirement to enable the technical and managerial staff to meet those standards. The use of computers to provide simulation for nuclear training dates from 1957. Simulators provide a form of training for which there is no alternative, as we shall explain.

The simulators at the Centre range from a generic analogue computer, through a range of specific reactor simulators to the latest model of the Heysham 2 reactor. Each simulator represents as faithfully as possible the man/machine interface in the control room of one of the nuclear power stations. In each, the computer enables the instructor to simulate a wide variety of states, wider even than those normally experienced in operating stations. The control panels exactly mimic the real plant and provide the operator with his information of conditions. As in an aircraft simulator, the instructor can simulate accidents or other incidents to which the trainees are required to respond. The computer is capable of providing all the necessary conditions that a trainee would meet in power station operation, and, by means of additional monitors or screens, the instructor can not only transmit details of the incident but also make

190

teaching points about the reasons behind the incident.

The simulator for Heysham 2, the latest advanced gas-cooled reactor (AGR), was used as an engineering development tool, up to the time the power station was commissioned in 1987. The operators have to be trained before the power station actually goes into operation, and they use manuals, including the station manuals, to operate the simulator. The screens can display various states of the system, including states not normally shown at the power station but derived from the mathematical model of how the station behaves. Much of the training consists of drills based on analysis; for example, an abnormal shutdown that might occur after a 'reactor trip'. Such a trip produces a 30 minute automatic sequence which must be closely monitored by the operator. The operator can intervene after the first five minutes, but only through coded buttons. At all times the training intention is to simulate the real control situation as closely as possible; a nuclear power plant is a very complex system and the model built into the simulation is constantly updated to reflect changes made to the plant and minor variations found from operation of the real plant. Although the simulators are computer-based and therefore within the scope of our book, they offer no didactic teaching. Like simulators used by airlines, they would be useless without a tutor sitting at the console.

Each British nuclear power station manager is required to be aware of the competence of his engineers, and Harris and Chapman (1986) describe a system developed at the Nuclear Power Training Centre for advising these managers on the performance of trainees who have passed through the Centre based on a thorough task analysis. This system provides managers with a very detailed report of trainees' achievements while being trained on the control room simulators.

The Central Electricity Generating Board also uses microcomputers for CBT, but first we must explain how the need to do so arose. The CEGB distributes power through a national grid which has seven control centres staffed by system control engineers, who are responsible for the scheduling and safe dispatching of electricity generated by about 70 stations. According to Fisher and Welham (1987), certain training of these engineers cannot be met by conventional training. They require refresher training in selected aspects of electrical engineering, and training in how to manage system disturbances due to plant failure. They also need to be able to operate newly installed multiscreen computerised control systems at the centres.

The CEGB's own Education and Training formation recommended an evaluation of CBT and with the System Operation Branch agreed to conduct a joint one year pilot project using computers to train system control engineers in dealing with system transient stability. This topic was chosen because it is important in operating the national grid and because the package developed might be of interest to other companies distributing electricity.

A working group was established to review CBT authoring systems and to visit other CBT users to learn from their experience. The group observed that most of the training materials made little use of graphics, yet sophisticated graphics seemed essential for training system control engineers. In fact, the group identified a need for high resolution graphics on two screens simultaneously, with video material displayed on a third screen, in parallel. Only with such facilities would it be possible to provide trainees with a realistic model of the system, in which interactions could be properly displayed. Following a call for tenders, the Board chose Rediffusion Simulation's Regency RC-2+ system.

CEGB subject matter experts and the provider's staff collaborated to produce the program, which contains some novel features. For example, vector diagrams and response curves are generated by the model under trainee control. This is a form of simulation, based on a mathematical model, and the high resolution colour displays change on the screens, according to the inputs, thus depicting the effects of certain changes in the system. Fisher and Welham (1987) claim that trainees, the system control engineers, achieve an immensely improved understanding of the system. They also affirm that trainees gain considerably from the video, which contains examples of the theory being applied: one clip shows changes occurring in control 'dials and gauges', the other a fault occurring in a transmission line.

The CEGB wanted a proper evaluation of the pilot program, which was offered to about 150 trainees out of a potential audience of 350. Built into the system were the usual records of trainees' progress, which showed that trainees took about six hours to work through it, but their concentration flagged after an hour or so. The training was broken up into shorter one hour sessions. The trainees were generally enthusiastic about the CBT and wanted to have further programs available. No statistics have yet been published of trainees' achievement, although Welham, Fisher and Rudge (1986) report that trainees required a score of 80 per cent on each module end test before they could proceed. Overall, the project was judged very successful.

CHEVRON INFORMATION TECHNOLOGY COMPANY

This company is a division of Chevron Industries, which is best known as one of the largest US oil producers. Within Chevron Information Technology is the Computer Services Department, of which the training section provides data processing training throughout the corporation, primarily on a mainframe system.

The section has been using CBT since 1983 as a logical method for teaching data processing concepts and applications, and a good means of training shift workers, since it is not bound by time constraints. CBT began in the company by using IBM's *IIS* authoring system. Later the section was able to experiment with one of the first microcomputer authoring systems, Bell and Howell's *PASS* for the Apple II, with interactive video.

By 1985 it was clear that neither of these CBT systems was able to produce the types of training required for a widening training audience of people who were not data processing professionals. The mainframe *IIS* system allowed direct access to the mainframe for training, but was considered too inflexible as an authoring system. It was totally text-oriented, lacking the ability to incorporate a colour display, interactive video or audio. *IIS* also required time-sharing of the mainframe, which was not cost-effective for training. Although the *PASS* system allowed for more interactive components, it had become obsolete, primarily because Bell and Howell stopped supporting *PASS* in early 1985.

A search was started in 1985 to find a new system, one that met the company's specific requirements, but nothing suitable was found. Another search was undertaken in 1986, with less strict guidelines. This second study included a review of authoring systems on the market for mainframes (*PHOENIX* and *Scholar/Teach*) and microcomputers (*ADROIT, TRAINER 4000* and *PILOT*). *ADROIT* was chosen because it met the need for interactivity on a microcomputer, and was able to capture screens directly from the mainframe system, wrapping instruction round the mainframe program. Once captured, screens could be changed with an automatic help available for each frame. Since *ADROIT* was still under development, Chevron was able to have some of its specific needs incorporated into the final version of the authoring system.

The training section of Chevron Information Technology has begun development with *ADROIT* of their first courses in data processing topics. These will eventually be marketed to other parts of the corporation to meet their training needs. Potential new training areas for the section include employee orientation packages, through which new employees can be taken on a visual tour of operational sections, and an electronic mail training program in which employees are given a simulated trial in using the system.

As with other CBT experiments at Chevron Information Technology, evaluation of program success will be measured in decreased length of training time and performance on the job. In a previous CBT course on payroll entry, training time was reduced from three months to one. This reduction was especially helpful at a time when cutbacks in the company caused retraining of a large number of employees as they changed jobs or took on wider responsibilities.

EAST MIDLANDS ELECTRICITY GENERATING BOARD

This public utility company has a large IBM mainframe, which is used in part for embedded CBT, to train data processing employees. Heaford (1983) writes about the Board's experience in developing a computerised system for management of its training effort. He also touches on how it used *PHOENIX*, a US system, with its *EASE* language (see Chapter 5), to develop a course to introduce a new computer terminal to data processing employees, and a course to introduce technicians to the Board and to CBT.

SHELL EXPLORATION AND PRODUCTION

Video Media made an award-winning interactive videodisc, *Slips, Trips and Falls*, for Shell Exploration and Production, to raise the level of awareness of hazards that cause accidents onshore and on North Sea offshore oil-rigs. Trainees can prevent depicted accidents from happening by their responses to questions on the computer screen. In a sense, they control the destiny of characters appearing in the video. Several thousand workers are being trained with the disc, which is played on a Sony Laserdisc LDP1500P player controlled by a Compaq 286 microcomputer via a VideoLogic *MIC2000* interface. The program is activated by mouse or touch-sensitive screen, therefore there is no need for use of the keyboard. Each workstation is housed in a special cabinet to withstand conditions on the oilrigs.

194

Part Four

Issues

14

Marketing and Adoption

In this chapter we consider the relationships between providers and their clients. The providers market goods and services, and we discuss what they have to offer. Their clients adopt these by purchase or occasionally rental. We asked many questions about how client companies made their decisions to adopt the products of a particular vendor, and we report our findings here, within a framework provided by a model of how innovations spread.

MARKETING: PRODUCTS AND SERVICES ON OFFER

Vendors sell computer hardware, software and advice, often in combination. The hardware may be their own, as in the case of IBM or it may be another company's.

Between them, they offer four or five kinds of software (see Chapter 4).

(a) Some sell operating systems software, to run the hardware at the most basic level, and authoring systems.
(b) Many sell CBT software developed specifically for their client companies.
(c) Some sell generic CBT software, suitable for use in many companies and dealing with topics common to these companies, such as telephone skills, interview skills and time management. They are meeting general training needs.
(d) Some sell interface software to link other devices, such as videodisc players, to computers.
(e) Some are also ready to sell a range of applications programs, such as financial, word-processing and spreadsheet packages, that will run on the company's computers.

If a provider is selling hardware, the training software is likely to run only on that hardware and none other. Vendors selling generic software are likely to have products that run on several computers.

Most providers also sell advice. For a price, they will agree to send consultants to analyse a company's training needs and draw up a proposal for introducing CBT into that company. These tasks can range from almost trivial to very substantial indeed, depending on the size of the company and its own awareness of its training needs. As Gery (1982) says, some companies abdicate to a consultant when they know very little about the technology and have no experience of it, although to do so is not wise.

The best providers will not offer a readymade solution, but will tailor the system to the company's structure and needs, taking into account existing training facilities and equipment. Even the best providers, however, have their prejudices about training strategies and solutions. Knowledgeable consultants who are not linked in some way to a particular provider do exist but are hard to find.

MARKETING: CLAIMS MADE BY VENDORS

Understandably, most providers are in business to make a profit, and they operate in a highly competitive and crowded marketplace, where there were in 1987 only a few user companies per provider, on average.

What claims do providers make, and are these valid? The fact is that many providers are properly cautious in their printed publicity, but companies considering CBT, with or without interactive video, should scrutinise carefully claims such as these:

(a) CBT can be delivered at any time and any place.
(b) Trainees don't have to wait for a place on a course.
(c) Trainees can go at their own rate with CBT, therefore able ones don't get bored.
(d) Slow trainees with problems can be identified early on and helped.
(e) Immediate and individualised feedback on mistakes is available.
(f) CBT offers consistent quality (it standardises training).
(g) Changing CBT is quick and easy, therefore it is always up to date.

198

(h) CBT enables trainers to keep detailed records of trainees' progress.

Of course, not all of these so-called advantages are exclusive to CBT. Many of them can apply, for instance, to printed training materials, too. And not all can be realised in every CBT installation. It is easy enough to draw up a list of disadvantages, too, and respected vendors mention at least some of these, with any necessary provisos.

(a) CBT is not suitable for all training tasks.
(b) Older trainees are resistant to communicating with a computer.
(c) CBT is not as easy to use or transport as the printed word.
(d) CBT cannot be modified as quickly as face-to-face training.
(e) CBT needs experts to develop it.
(f) CBT requires 50–200 hours of development time per hour.
(g) CBT programs can only be used on hardware they were written for.
(h) CBT hardware can be expensive and is not always reliable.

MARKETING: STRATEGIES ADOPTED BY VENDORS

In Chapter 3 we described how companies try, often in rather haphazard ways, to find out about CBT, and we discussed five basic exploratory strategies, the first two of which particularly involved vendors or providers.

Vendors are constantly searching for selling 'leads' in companies where they believe their products may be effective. Because of the complexity of the selling task they face, however, they may well be on the horns of a dilemma. On the one hand, if they provide too little information they may lose the sale, or, worse, make an inappropriate sale that eventually backfires on them. On the other, if they commit too much time and effort to providing a proper analysis of a company's needs before pushing the sale of their products, they may win the sale but lose the profits.

In our opinion, the best providers try to negotiate with their clients, using a staged approach, with each stage being contracted and paid for separately. In this way, providers and clients can gain confidence in each other and in their working relationship. It is true that in some large client companies a point may be quickly reached, after only one or two preliminary stages, at which a major decision must be taken to invest in hardware and software for CBT, and that once the decision is taken there is no easy way to dispense with the CBT. This is not the case in many companies, however, particularly since the advent of microcomputers. Unlike mainframe systems, microcomputers permit small-scale trials that can be extended into general implementation once success has been assured.

In Britain, though not as far as we know in the United States, vendors are also in contact with sources of subsidy, particularly the Manpower Services Commission. The Commission's policy has been to foster development and implementation of CBT in companies by paying part of the costs of demonstration projects and by facilitating advances in the technology by, for instance, subsidising the training of CBT trainer-authors. The exact nature of the MSC's programme has varied from year to year. Vendors have been able to bid, directly or indirectly in association with client companies, to provide their products to this programme, which has therefore to some extent subsidised a number of them, whether US or British in origin.

ADOPTION: AWARENESS

The classic model of how innovations spread has four stages: awareness, interest, inquiry, and commitment. There is no firm evidence that this model applies in the case of CBT. Some experts in this field see no distinct adoption process. One told us of a company in which an enthusiastic executive persuaded the data processing manager to obtain a consultant on CBT hardware and software, then ran a small CBT training project with a clerk/typist who could not cope, and ended by fighting a rearguard action against the data processing management. The model is still useful, however, to analyse the stages many companies might reasonably pass through.

During the first stage, a company merely becomes aware of the existence of CBT, without anyone in the company knowing very much about it. Many companies in the United States and Britain have gone no further than this first stage, as our enquiries showed. For example, when we telephoned the training manager of one British manufacturing company, he said he knew what computer-based training was, of course, but it was not in use in his company nor did he think the company would be investigating its use in the near future.

200

In one large retail company we visited, opinions were elicited before awareness had been raised properly. Although a few of the people consulted had some knowledge and experience of CBT, most of them had not, and Barbara (as we shall call her), who was doing the study, may have done some damage by asking the latter what they thought. Her report on attitudes within the company was rather pessimistic. She began by consulting an area director who thought computers should be kept for managers to use (he may be right!). His view of training was that 'it's a supervisors' function, to help them to develop relations with their staff'.

Next, Barbara talked to the Head of Operations, who saw CBT as 'valuable because it can standardise training', but didn't sound as though he had ever touched a computer. The Training Manager of Management Services was also somewhat positive. He thought the cost of originating programs would be too high, however, so buying them in would be better, but for the fact that very few suitable ones were available. He pointed out the dangers of technophobia and worried about 'staff seeing computers as fun'. At least he had a few CBT programs and he invited Barbara to view two of them with him. They were among the first she had seen.

Barbara heard from the Manager of Operations Technology how he once used professionally-produced CBT in his department and found it unsuccessful. He thought the programs were boring ('especially when they were presented to trainees of differing abilities') and said there was technophobia among the older employees, at least at first.

Barbara moved on to talk to managers at lower levels, and found more scepticism. One told her that

> if paper and video can't motivate staff to train, computers won't either. And the computers won't be available, anyway. Even if they were, they would have to be moved, which would be difficult, and there'd be security problems, with staff getting to know the manager's code.

He thought a separate computer would have to be provided for training in each store, because otherwise training would get pushed off the computers. He also thought EPOS electronic point of sale technology was coming, with more training needs, but was sure 'face-to-face methods can handle them'.

Finally, Barbara talked to two training officers. The first knew nothing about CBT except that she was probably prejudiced against it. She believed supervisors must put something into the training, which 'they wouldn't be able to with CBT'. The second said a new medium would be welcome, particularly one that is self-instructional, 'because things can't get much worse in training, with the supervisors taking so little interest'.

A large number of US companies that use microcomputers extensively still have only trainer-led classroom training for employees in how to use them and the applications packages available. For example, in training employees to work with a spreadsheet program like *Lotus 1-2-3*, they do not even use the CBT tutorials provided. On one of our visits, we met the training manager of a large US manufacturing company, and he was surprised to realise that off-the-shelf tutorials of this type were considered to be CBT, which could be customised to meet his company's needs and still remain self-paced. In fact, he seemed to find the entire idea of self-paced training rather novel, and said he would look into it someday!

It would be foolish to ignore the fear of CBT that exists among some trainers and managers. Even companies that use computers daily may have employees who suffer from such fears, and they have to be understood and dealt with.

ADOPTION: INTEREST

At this stage, a company may be willing to try to find out more about CBT. Sometimes the initiative comes from trainers, but not always. At the Standard Chartered Bank, Ward (1986) says that the *Mentor II* system is in use for basic banking skills training in the Bank's United Kingdom Training Department. The initiative came from data processing employees (Technical Services Division), who collaborated with trainers to evaluate CBT systems and, with Mentor Interactive, developed the first course, *Foreign Exchange*, in 1985.

Even though interest in CBT may be sparked in the company by an article in a training magazine or by what a manager saw at an exhibition, there is bound to be uncertainty at this stage. What is CBT good for? Hirschbuhl (1985) tries to give some help to those who are not sure which 'delivery system' to use for a given training task. He draws up lists of skills commonly included in training programmes, such as time management and communication skills. For each he provides his own judgement about which of four systems to use: classroom, text, video or CBT. His main criterion is whether the subject-matter is 'rational' or in the 'emotional' domain. Thus he sees interpersonal skills as best taught by classroom and video, but time management as suitable for CBT. Inevitably, such a simple classification scheme is open to criticism, if only because most trainers and trainees like to use a mixture of approaches. There is no simple procedure for deciding that a given training task demands a particular medium. Much depends on circumstances, which are usually complex. An interactive videodisc, for example, has been used by British Airways to improve problem-solving skills *and* to change attitudes of ground-staff, yet one of the first videodiscs was about how to repair a bicycle! At this stage of interest, Nissan Motor (see Chapter 8) conducted a survey in the United States of what other car manufacturers were doing with CBT for sales personnel. As a consequence, the company continued to use videocassettes and its interest in CBT declined.

If CBT is introduced into a company, with positive results in terms of performance of trainees, other uses for this training method are more readily considered and attempted by the managers and trainers. Pacific Bell's successful use of mainframe CBT with data processing employees led to consideration of CBT on personal computers for training other employees, and that led to the introduction of authoring systems for the trainers, rather than the company's programmers. In turn, that led to interactive video training and on to a concurrent authoring system for developing training in more sophisticated software.

ADOPTION: INQUIRY

At the third stage, a company is ready to assess, in a systematic way, the feasibility of CBT for its purposes. Finch and Labinger (1986) suggest that any feasibility study of CBT should include thorough investigation of company policy, attitudes of all the people likely to be involved, immediate problems, long-term potential, resources and budget available and required, and benefits expected. This is a counsel of perfection: we did not find a single feasibility study that covered all these aspects.

Finch and Labinger also suggest that a proper cost-benefit analysis should be carried out before adoption. Our view is that such an analysis is feasible in very few companies, because the majority find it difficult to estimate costs of CBT compared with other

203

methods, and because all companies have difficulties in predicting the benefits. Certainly Finch and Labinger's lists of cost factors are inadequate, although they admit that there are hidden costs in all methods of training.

Finch and Labinger propose that a case for CBT should be based on identification of an appropriate training requirement and on consideration of alternatives to CBT. They suggest the case should include discussion of attitudes of staff and relevant company policy, an analysis of facilities required and those available, a budget for capital and recurrent costs and a statement of achievable benefits with timescales. Again, we did not find anything quite so systematic, although some companies have carried out feasibility studies along the lines Kearsley (1983) proposes. He merely suggests that instructional, organisational, technical and economic aspects should be considered.

We do not plan here to provide a checklist of considerations, but assuming that a company is fairly convinced that it ought to adopt CBT, it should ask whether it needs generic software or whether it will have to develop (or commission development of) specific programs to suit its special needs. For many companies, starting CBT with generic software need not be very expensive, whereas specific software is always expensive. The cost of hardware is usually somewhat greater in the latter case.

A company faced with the challenge of evaluating several competing CBT providers could do well to consider Kearsley's (1983) checklists or the factors more recently listed by O'Neal (1986b):

(a) *Range of services*: if hardware, software, courseware and follow-up support are bought from different providers, clearly there are dangers of incompatibility. On the other hand, if these all come from the same vendor, risks are not spread.

(b) *Experience*: providers with long experience do not always have new systems available, but providers with new systems may have been in business too short a time to have a good track record. Experienced provider companies should be able to show their newer systems are more advanced, and on more up-to-date computers, than their older ones.

(c) *Commitment to CBT*: providers should show their commitment through research and development activity.

(d) *Financial status*: providers should be able to prove that their financial status is sound, lest a company adopting their CBT finds the provider has disappeared shortly after delivery, or, still worse, before delivery.

The US accounting firm of Ernst and Whinney spent two years on an initial needs assessment, including interviews with 23 providers, before deciding to bring in Pinnacle Software to develop the *EDP for Accountants* program. The company considers this initial investment was time and money well spent, since it resulted in the type of training it wanted, with the bonus of being able to sell the program to a wider business audience.

ADOPTION: COMMITMENT

The fourth stage involves the company committing itself to change. How does a company decide whether to adopt or reject the technology? O'Neal (1986b) suggests that most CBT programme failures within organisations 'can be attributed to organisational deficiencies. Even when the direct cause can be traced to either inadequate hardware, software or courseware, the indirect cause was an organisational slip-up in evaluation and selection which resulted in the problem'. We think O'Neal is right, but the processes by which companies decide to adopt or reject the technology are worth examining.

What are commonly the first signs that a company is seriously committed to developing its own CBT? First, companies that nominate a strong CBT team leader are probably in earnest. If the job is left to a junior member of staff, or to somebody about to retire, then probably CBT will fail in that company.

Next, where new company-specific CBT is to be developed, qualified staff must be appointed to carry out the work, even if these staff have to be recruited from outside the company. When conventionally trained trainers are simply told to try their hand, the risk of failure is increased, though they may do well if they are given proper CBT training.

As part of a proper plan for CBT, the team of developers must be allocated sufficient non-staff resources. A company that puts its CBT development team in the worst offices, for instance, with no telephones and little contact with other staff, is likely to get a poor quality product. CBT development and testing is not a 'backroom' activity.

Finally, a company that wants to commit itself to development should be ready to agree a schedule leading to delivery of the CBT products. This schedule should predict times for designing, testing, modifying and copying each component.

At a British bank we visited, the new training technology is seen as integral to bank training, not peripheral, but the bank in 1987 was at a crossroads, undecided about which forms of the technology to adopt for the immediate future. It seemed to us that the bank was having trouble committing itself to further change. As we mentioned in Chapter 2, this bank introduced videotex for training purposes into a large number of its branches, but within five years came to see videotex as a 'zero-stretch' technology, therefore not a long-term proposition. The bank's criterion for replacing the videotex system, however, is whether further new training technology will replace the old at the same or lower cost? It is not whether the trade unions have been positive, apathetic, or hostile. It is simply a matter of cost-effectiveness. If the bank could obtain the data that would 'prove' one particular new system to be more cost-effective than the old, then a decision would be taken to implement the new system.

By contrast, when the US retail jewellery chain, Zales, committed itself to interactive video for training in each credit centre and store, they chose the most advanced technology compatible with their needs, which at that time was interactive videotape. The system has worked well since about 1981. Although the company has looked at newer systems, the cost of converting to a new system in all branches is too high. The trainers at Zales also feel that current training techniques do not yet match the sophisticated technology available, and until they do investing in videodisc equipment would be overkill.

At another company we visited, we were told that when the management announced that there would be a trial of CBT, there was resistance from employees, but not from the trainers. In part it was perhaps a matter of branch offices not wanting to follow headquarters' policy, a common enough problem. In part, it was resistance to the unknown. Following extensive trials, this company has installed CBT on a large scale.

Finally, we noted that commitment is particularly hard to obtain when many partners are involved, as in the case of the Association of British Travel Agents.

15

Development and Testing

ORGANISATIONAL ISSUES

Adoption of CBT as a chosen solution, probably among several, to a set of training problems is only the first step. Any company introducing CBT faces organisational issues. As Gery (1983) says, somebody has to decide where the hardware is to be located, what organisational structure the CBT is to fit into, who will have control over the hardware and over the standards and content of the software, and how much autonomy can be granted to trainers and trainees when they are actually using company resources (such as a mainframe computer) that others have to use as well.

The physical and organisational location of CBT can be difficult to decide. Data processing and training departments are often both involved. The former may be ambivalent. Its employees may claim that because computers are being used, CBT belongs to them, particularly if a mainframe is being used. Or they may take the line that the training department had better run and maintain its own computers and related hardware, since training is not their function. Data processing departments are not usually very interested in computers that are different from the ones they use, or in interactive videodisc applications that are outside the mainstream of their work. At worst, they may try to stop the purchase of equipment for training. Training departments often want the technology, not least because it adds to their prestige. They are seldom well-placed to program it, still less to repair and maintain it.

User departments may not be prepared to leave the new technology to data processing or training departments. They may prefer to treat these as service departments. They may demand direct control over hardware and software. This is particularly likely when microcomputers are brought in. The data processing department, on the other hand, may want to control access to them, perhaps in a network within which the microcomputers function chiefly as mainframe terminals.

This kind of conflict can deter people from using CBT, with or without interactive video. Often the trouble is compounded by lack of space on an outdated mainframe system that has not expanded fast enough to keep up with the needs of the company. Since timesharing (allotted computer time based on assigned priority of need) is the rule for access to most mainframe systems, networking can mean long waits and undesirable hours for training. Trainees understandably get impatient.

To settle battles between their departments, some companies adopt a team approach, drawing on staff from several departments. This can be very fruitful, since developing and managing CBT demands a combination of skills.

Whatever organisational approach they choose, companies should recognise that CBT may break the mould of their conventional training practices. Conventional practices are a mixture of centralised and on-the-job training, but seldom provide as much autonomy to the trainee as CBT does. CBT depends on centralised development and production of training software (not necessarily within the company), and decentralised use thereafter, possibly far away from the training department. The rest of this chapter deals with processes of CBT development and testing in companies that decided to do their own, though possibly in association with a provider. Raven (1986) offers helpful checklists that lead to development of a plan and budget for the project, and he stresses the need to secure appropriate human resources and physical facilities.

DEVELOPMENT PROCESSES

Most companies and providers in this field adopt the systems approach to developing conventional training materials, and, as Rothwell (1983b) points out in her useful analysis of CBT design processes, CBT deserves similar treatment. Her emphasis on *systematic* development needs enlarging, however, because the systems approach requires not only working in methodical and thorough ways but also thinking about the whole system. *Systemic* development is what is needed, with careful integration of the various processes. These are laid out below one after the other, but in fact a great deal of iteration is usually demanded. In other words, objectives may be clarified, somewhat late in the day, by the developmental testing. This is true, of course, in producing conventional training materials.

Clarifying training needs and the audience

There should be first-class 'front-end design'. In other words, as for all training, considerable work has to go into identifying the audience, analysing needs and selecting training strategies. In some companies, before training needs can be identified an analysis of the company may be necessary.

Such work is desirable for any kind of training, but we believe that developing company-specific CBT actually obliges trainers to undertake more thorough design than they might need to for other kinds of training. Trainers using friendly non-programming authoring languages may underestimate the prior planning and design required, though this is less likely with complete authoring systems such as *PLATO* (Gery, 1982), which prompt authors to consider these matters.

In identifying the audience, it is not simply a matter of saying that the CBT will be aimed at a particular group of employees. Once identified, that group should be studied to find out what they bring to the CBT course. It may be worthwhile to start the course with a test that will sort out those who can leap over some segments because they already know the content. Trainers will know what questions to put into the test only if they have a sound knowledge of the trainee group and of the content. This knowledge of the group will also be a guide to choosing appropriate training strategies. Will trainees require lengthy practice sessions? Should they be expected to 'explore' the content, rather than being taught it didactically by rule and example? How much should they be expected to memorise and how much will be incorporated in job aids they can turn to if they cannot recall certain facts or procedures? And so on.

Specifying objectives and content

Here again, the processes of developing training based on computers and other new technology are similar to those for developing any other kind of training (see, for example, Richey, 1986, for a good theoretical discussion, and Rowntree, 1981, for a practical guide). Assuming that a training needs analysis has been conducted, the next step is to define training objectives in some detail. So far as possible, these should be stated in behavioural terms: what is the trainee expected to be able to do, to what standard and under what conditions? With objectives clearly specified, trainers will want to move on to design learning activities. Designing these activities and choosing appropriate media should be guided by the underlying training strategies. Materials, including computer programs, must then be produced and, if possible, put through developmental testing in prototype (see below) before the final version is prepared for distribution.

Selecting an authoring system

We discussed in Chapters 4 and 6 the characteristics of authoring systems and what an ideal one might look like. The first consideration is whether or not it must run on existing hardware in the company. This may limit the choice of systems. If new hardware is being purchased for CBT, then many more options are open, particularly if IBM PC-compatible computers and laser-read videodisc equipment are favoured. Each authoring system has a unique set of capabilities, although many of these are held in common, such as text editing.

Well over 100 different authoring languages and systems have been developed. Choosing one to meet the training needs of a particular company involves a complex set of criteria. We agree with Kearsley (1983) that software should get more attention than hardware, but of course the company has to take into account its hardware requirements. Some providers, such as WICAT, sell their hardware with a particular authoring system, as a package.

Selecting a particular language or system is difficult (see Rothwell, 1983b, for detailed analysis of several options), and often involves a process of elimination. Tools that do not provide for implementation of the desired training strategies can be rejected. The strategies selected can range from very simple question-and-answer ones, which deploy the computer merely as a sophisticated quiz machine, to very elaborately designed strategies that approach the training task from many angles, possibly with knowledge of the individual trainees' characteristics and record, therefore fully exploiting the computer's capabilities. Unfortunately, authoring

210

systems do not yet offer a wide range of strategies. Instead, most limit the options available.

Probably the biggest decision will be over whether the company wants to do without programming skills. If so, this will eliminate many authoring tools which require at least some programming. Is a programmer needed? Beech (1984) takes a programmer's line in favouring a system that allows authors to drop into a programming language if they wish (Pascal in the case of *WISE*), and proceeds to show how to use *SuperPILOT* to design your own authoring system. His approach assumes programming skill on the part of the trainer-author.

Tools that are difficult to learn to use should not necessarily be eliminated. As Nordberg (1986) clearly demonstrates, more power-ful authoring languages, which permit somewhat more elaborate strategies, are usually more difficult to learn. CDC's *TUTOR* started as a very simple language with 20–30 easily learned commands. Now it is much more powerful, but its 350 commands demand too much of the average solitary trainer-author.

Some tools may be eliminated because they are deemed to require too much support from professionals other than programmers. Nordberg suggests that all but the most simple training programs should be produced by a team consisting of subject-matter experts, instructional designers, graphics designers, programmers and evaluators. Some companies have such teams available and are will-ing to pay the cost. Yet Nordberg is right in saying that authoring languages now available do not recognise the need for all these skills.

Finally, choosing among the few tools that have not been eliminated may depend on what they cost. As a general rule, more costly authoring systems contain more features and have been more carefully developed. The initial cost is small in relation to the cost of authoring, therefore the final choice should depend more on features required and the reputation of the providers' products than on price. Low-cost products from new suppliers without good finan-cial backing should be avoided, because the risk is high of the supplier going out of business and no longer being able to support the products.

This process of elimination may lead a company to feel that no single authoring language or system suits its needs. Certainly the state of the art is not yet very advanced. We discuss likely future developments in Part Five.

Writing the text

Once an authoring system has been chosen, the business of compiling the text must start. Guided by the statements of content and objectives, and by ideas about training strategies, trainers will write the text into the computer, probably adding graphics, or introducing audio, or linking the training program to video. In Chapter 6 we listed Rothwell's (1983c) classification of authoring systems, from which it is apparent that many then available somewhat limited the options open to trainer-authors. When it comes to the actual frames that trainees will see, we can discuss briefly Beech's (1983) four frame types for writing traditional tutorial CBT, bearing in mind the wider choice of training strategy now accessible through the latest authoring systems:

(a) *Presentation*: a presentation frame contains text and/or graphics, and when the trainee presses RETURN (or some other designated key), leads to another single frame. Chains of these frames, presented in linear fashion, may make up the program. Beech asserts that a presentation frame can extend over several screenfuls, but we have not found that view among others in the field. Naturally, in designing the course it may be necessary to have several presentation frames in succession. There is no obvious interaction between trainee and computer, though the trainers' intention is certainly that the trainee should understand what is on the screen.

(b) *Menu*: a menu frame offers trainees a number of choices, usually between two and five. By pressing a single key corresponding to their choice, they move on to the next frame, which may or may not contain another menu. This structure is similar to that of a branching programmed learning text, through which an individual chooses his or her own route.

(c) *Question*: a question frame usually poses a multiple-choice question, although the more sophisticated authoring systems permit trainers to include open-ended questions for which trainees must construct an answer. From a multiple-choice question, trainees' choices will take them to appropriate further frames, just like the menu frame. For the open-ended questions, the software will attempt to match words in the answers to those that the trainer has inserted into it as acceptable, with or without spelling errors. Rothwell (1983b) lists the full range of types, with advantages and disadvantages.

(d) *Calculation*: a calculation frame asks trainees to key in data to be used in calculating a figure which then becomes part of the training. So, for example, trainees might be asked to read a graph, insert the values on the screen. The computer may then compute a further value. If trainees have read the graph correctly, the program will continue to the next teaching point, possibly using the further value. If not, the program will repeat its teaching, possibly in modified form, until the trainees can answer correctly.

Preparing graphics

Few trainer-authors know much about design matters such as electronic text display, but this is not the place to go into detail. Fortunately there is good advice available (see, for example, Jonassen, 1985). Bhugra (1986) stresses good use of graphics, with the aid of a graphic designer.

Producing interactive video

Producing an interactive videotape is well within the capacity of video units in larger companies. Linking together the computer-based training and the video in an effective way is probably the most difficult part, but many authoring systems provide for the programming aspects of this.

Producing the script for interactive videodisc takes the combined efforts of both training and video production personnel, and even this may not provide sufficient expertise. Norman Powell (1986 personal communication) suggests that trainers and others moving from conventional video production need to learn about transferring their storyboard and scripting techniques, as well as knowing about how to select existing film and video material. They, or others in the team, must be trained in how to introduce still photographs (including slides) and artwork, and in how to prepare computer-generated graphics and effects. Somebody must know about highly technical matters such as time code screening and logging, specifications for videotape masters, online videotape editing and decision-listing, dubbing and editing dual language sound tracks, videodisc mastering and, finally, merging of videodisc and computer outputs. No wonder companies prefer to contract for this work with specialist production houses. Parsloe (1984a), Iuppa

213

(1984), Iuppa and Anderson (1987) and Lambert and Sallis (1986) discuss the details.

Preparing the audio

One inexpensive and relatively simple aspect of CBT that is often neglected during development is use of interactive audio, as Barker (1986a) points out. Sound, including synthetic speech and possibly speech recognition, can be used to very good effect in training. Integrating sound within CBT need not be very difficult and Barker provides details of hardware systems and authoring languages. CD-ROM discs offer fast access to large stores of audio.

Designing the tests

Most CBT programs contain many questions, so that trainees are tested on their understanding or skills frequently throughout the training. Kelly Services' Kee simulator, for example, provides scores for each segment of training, and provides an overall score. Except for the simpler ones, authoring systems now usually include a trainee management program that will automatically collect such data and tabulate it for each trainee and for the whole group. For example, Llewellyn and Kahn (1986) write about using an authoring system, such as WICAT's *WISE*, that provides for both generation of the training program and management of the trainees.

Some companies will want a separate test at the end of each module or perhaps at the end of the course, to be sure that trainees have remembered what they learned earlier. Others may want to test recall and understanding a month later. To keep such a test within reasonable bounds, it will probably be necessary to do no more than sample the knowledge and skills learned, therefore trainers will have to select the parts of the course that are most important and then design searching questions based on those parts.

TESTING THE PROGRAM

Testing the program is sometimes called validating it. Strictly speaking, there are two forms of validation: internal and external. In the case of a CBT program, internal validation is what the developer carries out when he or she looks at its internal consistency. Does it hang together? Does the program run as intended? Is everything in the right order? And so on. External validation is itself of two kinds. On the one hand, it is conducted through other subject-matter experts who agree that the content and techniques of the program are valid. On the other, it is sustained through trainees who show that they can learn from the program what it is intended to teach. Trainers and trainees are both helpful, therefore, in the testing and validation process. Rothwell (1983b) also suggests that trainees' supervisors and employers should participate in this process, but we cover this under evaluation (see Chapter 17).

With trainers

Once the program is at an advanced stage, the first trials are often carried out with the help of other trainers, who work through the material on the computer, with video if that is included. There should be two groups: from one, their comments will be most valuable if they know very little about the topic beforehand, because they will behave much like trainees, with the advantage of their knowledge of training. From the other group, their comments will be most valuable if they know at least as much about the topic as the author. They will be checking the content for accuracy as well as commenting on techniques. Those who developed the program will have to be prepared, however, for conflicting feedback on some aspects, or feedback that only points out that something is wrong, without saying why or what should be done about it.

With trainees

The most important trials are those with trainees who are similar to the target audience for the program. First, it is best if there is tutorial testing with feedback. That is to say, trainers who developed the program should sit with individual trainees while the latter work through the program, commenting on and discussing the program as they go. Then there should be developmental testing, during which small groups of trainees go through the material, right through to taking the tests, and comment on it during and/or after the course. Trainees' detailed comments need to be assessed carefully, of course, because one or two comments about a particular point do not necessarily mean that it is wrong. Any revisions must be made cautiously. If necessary, the test-and-revise cycle should be repeated, though the payoff is normally less each time. The test may include an assessment of performance on the job, of course. This is especially valuable in large, costly CBT projects, where such performance criteria are the basis for judging whether CBT works or not.

One common problem that occurs after developmental testing is connected with the discipline with which the authoring language or system has been used. Revision of part of the training may prove very difficult if the original programming was not well documented (annotated), because recording the program requires a full understanding of what was done. Kearsley (1982) warns that this kind of revision is a source of considerable extra expense in many CBT projects.

Final testing

The final trial comes when the program first goes into regular use. By this time, it may be too late to make further changes, although we know of companies that found many errors. As we have pointed out, CBT programs can range from the simple to the extremely complex, and, like other kinds of computer programs, they need careful debugging. In addition, trainees may have unanticipated problems with parts of the training, just as they do with other forms of training. The final trial should therefore be viewed as a constructive part of the development process.

EVALUATION

Developmental testing may show that the material trains well, but further evaluation may be desirable, along the lines we discuss in more detail in Chapter 17. Sometimes it is absolutely unavoidable, as in the case of CBT for chemical plant operators. No chemical company can take the risk of installing CBT that sometimes does not train such operators extremely well, therefore its CBT must be evaluated and if necessary modified yet again. Trainees' performance on the job, not during trials or on tests, is the ultimate criterion for evaluating CBT.

216

16

Implementation

Implementation of CBT means running it on a day-to-day basis, possibly for thousands of trainees in many locations, who will use a large number of CBT programs, including interactive video. It also means running CBT on a single microcomputer with only a few off-the-shelf programs serving the needs of half a dozen trainees each year within a fairly small company.

None of the companies we talked to seemed to have underestimated the problems of implementing CBT. Nor do the few CBT specialists who have written on this topic. Kearsley (1983) says it is an extremely difficult undertaking. We would prefer to describe the implementation of the larger-scale projects as a complex management task, although that sounds somewhat euphemistic. The smaller-scale projects cannot possibly be judged, as a class, to be extremely difficult undertakings, although each one may have its own problems.

Our study of CBT ranges mainly through large companies, and it is successful implementation in these that we now discuss briefly. The technical details of implementation are dealt with more fully by Kearsley (1983) for US companies and Heaford (1983) for British companies.

RESOURCES

Consider a large company that has decided, for its own employees, to adopt CBT through commissioned production of company-specific interactive videodiscs and the purchase of off-the-shelf CBT programs for microcomputers. Immediately the adoption decision has been taken, resources must be identified and set aside for implementation. Naturally, the resources take the form of cash to pay for the videodiscs and programs, but they also take the form of the hardware to support use of these. Beyond that, they consist of buildings and people.

Buildings

We wrote earlier that finding space for CBT can be a problem. Banks and building societies (see Chapter 7) say their branches do not usually have suitable rooms for CBT, with the result that the hardware is often placed in a room that is either noisy or inconvenient.

American Express chose to set up regional centres. Manufacturing companies (including computer companies) sometimes install the CBT terminals on the assembly line, as at General Motors, but more frequently have training centres, as for example at Austin Rover, Eastman Kodak, Hewlett-Packard and IBM. Retail companies struggle to find space in their shops and service centres: B&Q mounted the sets on trolleys, but British travel agents felt they had no room for new terminals. In the transport industry, training centres seem essential except where embedded CBT is in use, to go by the experience of companies like British Airways and FlightSafety International, but Texaco Tankerships put the training on board. American Telephone and Telegraph, as well as British Telecom, use training centres, but companies in the energy sector use a combination of centres (as in the Central Electricity Generating Board's operations) and localised training (as at Eastman Kodak).

There is no doubt that CBT and interactive video is more demanding on buildings than most other forms of training. The space should be clean (free of dust, which damages the equipment), quiet and sufficiently spacious to house the hardware, with a suitable store for the software. Its electricity supply must be dependable. Special office furniture may be needed, ergonomically suited to the training task.

People

For implementation, many people become involved and they must be trained for and orientated to CBT as appropriate in each case. During adoption, development and testing the whole project was

218

probably the concern of people in the training department, and a few managers. They were the human resource for getting it started. Now every manager within whose department the interactive video and CBT will be used, and every employee likely to be trained with it, must be concerned. They too become human resources for the project. Beyond them, cleaners, technicians, catering staff and many others become secondarily involved.

All these people must be given a lead and enthused about the project, lest it should founder on poor management of human relationships. On the other hand, as Laurillard and Lefrere (1985) point out in their CBT manual,

> CBT will have the greatest impact if it is introduced to several interacting levels of staff at the same time. If line managers are being updated via CBT, and their personnel are being retrained or inducted via CBT, there is a better chance that it will be properly integrated into the work of that group of staff.

When CBT is first available, the project managers will be responsible for ensuring that trainees can use it at times convenient to them. Scheduling may be a complicated task, because the work is self-paced, though it is broken into suitably sized modules. Training managers are frequently embattled with line managers over training time. As Thirkettle (1986) puts it, if the training manager estimates five days for a particular package, the line manager will try to reduce it to two days, and they may compromise on three. Getting line managers' support when CBT is involved is no easier than when conventional methods are to be used.

The trainee management program will keep track of individual trainees' progress, but a system is still needed to sign trainees and others onto the system and off again. Kearsley (1983) has a useful listing of priorities for a large system with terminals: he gives highest priority to trainees taking scheduled courses, followed by trainers or monitors assisting trainees with problems, authors creating or revising courseware, trainers and managers carrying out management activities, trainees taking unscheduled courses, programmers working on software. He gives lowest priority to time for occasional demonstrations of the courseware or systems.

INNOVATION STRATEGIES

Not surprisingly, many companies adopt and implement CBT because a senior manager has noted its potential, perhaps by observing a worthwhile CBT installation in another company. Without managerial support, however, innovation of this kind is always difficult and the chances of failure are high. A successful pilot is a powerful way to convince managers that wider implementation would be in the company's interest. As Gery (1982) says, bringing in new training technology requires careful planning.

Needless to say, employee support is equally vital. Barclays Bank perceives implementation as resting on employee appreciation of how new training technology can help them in their work (Mortimer, 1983). The Bank first sent a member of the project team to each of the chosen branches to discuss where the terminal should be sited. Then seminars were held in district offices for selected branch employees, who were given a live demonstration after discussing the concept. Finally, every branch had a demonstration once its terminal was installed. Later, the central training staff visited branches from time to time as a follow-up, and a few branch trainers visited the training centre to see the computers and meet the program writing teams.

Getting trainers' support may be necessary, too. If the new technology destroys their work patterns, makes them highly accountable to a machine and requires them to learn new skills for which they see little future use, then implementation is likely to fail. If the training manager does not convince the trainers, they will avoid using CBT whenever possible and dampen any enthusiasm trainees may have for it.

Support from people in the company is more likely to be forthcoming if there is a clear plan for implementation, with targets and deadlines, and a means of reporting progress, perhaps through a newsletter and noticeboards. The manager of implementation will have the task of ensuring that progress is maintained. At some points, to keep the project on time, this may mean sacrificing additions and changes that the trainers would like to make.

TECHNOLOGY MANAGEMENT

Installation of hardware and software on a large scale for CBT carries implications for staffing. Technicians must be available to

220

service and repair the equipment, either through a contracted outside service or through the company's own departments.

The company must also set aside resources for replacing the hardware. As in the case of other computer-based office equipment, the problem of obsolescence is difficult and managers must consider carefully the time-scale over which replacement is likely. The CBT courseware, developed at considerable cost, may not run on a new generation of hardware. Some of this courseware may itself become obsolete, of course, and need replacement. It is therefore important to plan replacement about two or three years ahead. Five-year plans are likely to be upset, because predictions of future training needs may not be borne out, and predictions of changes in the technology are even more risky.

POLICY REVIEW

Apart from overall evaluation of the implementation (see next chapter), there should be proper structures for regular review of policy on CBT. If a company gets bogged down with an inadequate implementation, perhaps of a videotex system, then its training will suffer.

One of the few companies to have wide experience of using videotex for training, considered videotex to bring these benefits:

(a) Trainees can be trained as the need arises and do not have to wait for a place on a course at a distant training centre; this allows for more flexible manning in branches.

(b) The system, once established, runs at low cost and saves costs of travel to training centre, accommodation there, trainers' costs, etc.

(c) Because it is centrally controlled, reference material in the system can be easily and cheaply updated and corrected.

(d) Trainees can work through it at their own pace, repeating sections if they wish to until they achieve mastery; significantly less supervision of on-the-job training is needed.

(e) Trainers in branches are kept informed of trainees' progress, and automatically receive the test results of trainees who score less than 75 per cent.

Unfortunately, these claimed benefits for the system were not enough to sustain it over the years. Policy reviews led to the judgement that the system should be replaced, although at the time of writing this book no decisions had been reached about what would replace it and when.

There needs to be a body that reviews policy, in the light of reports from managers. In a few companies, the main board becomes involved. More often, a smaller group exists, made up of the training manager and several heads of user departments. Regrettably, other companies appear to have no formal means of reviewing their policy, once the financial decisions have been taken to invest in the hardware and software.

IMPLEMENTATION AT THE ABBEY NATIONAL

In her report on the pilot projects at the Abbey National Building Society, Hitchcock (1986) proposed a gradual implementation strategy for CBT at the Society, and many of her recommendations were acted upon. In the short term, she suggested that the Society should perform a detailed training needs analysis, more comprehensive than that which preceded the pilot study. It should continue developing its expertise in production of CBT, through training and actual production. A climate of interest in CBT should be created in the Society's regions, which should be educated in its applications. The Society should keep up to date on what hardware was available and assess generic off-the-shelf courseware for possible inclusion in its training. She also proposed that responsibilities for distribution, monitoring and support of the Society's CBT should be established, through Head Office's training department, and that there should be close liaison between that department and the marketing section, so that CBT could be considered whenever the need to train employees arose through the introduction of a new Society product or procedure. In the longer term, she considered that the introduction of microcomputers into the Society's branches would offer opportunities for bringing in CBT. By the time this book appears, Abbey National will be installing 200 Olivetti microcomputers in its branches, and a wide implementation of CBT should be well under way.

IMPLEMENTATION AT B&Q

In mid-1987, B&Q was about to upgrade its videodisc players to full interactivity by adding IBM personal computers (Dobson, 1987). The company had already obtained its first interactive disc and expected to make one or two more in 1987. It planned to commission and develop company-specific CBT programs for the personal computers. On the basis of its successful trials of generic CBT, B&Q was planning to use more, because the cost of training was less than £4 per trainee per program. This story of implementation speaks for itself.

17

Evaluation of Costs and Benefits

Dobson (1987) reports that his company, B&Q, tried to obtain evaluation data from other organisations and from published sources but without any great success. This book will not solve the problem. Dobson quotes a CBT course producer, 'As soon as people start using the technology they tend to forget about evaluation and concentrate on implementation'. Here we look at the evaluation of costs, with some examples, and then go on to discuss evaluation of benefits, again with examples.

EVALUATION OF COSTS

How much does a computer-based training system cost to set up and operate? The answer to this question depends on what a company wants to count towards the cost. Companies are notoriously bad at identifying their training costs (see Chapter 1). For instance, does the company want to include the cost of the learning its trainers have to do? Trainer-authors often need to learn how to design and program a new technology system, before any employee training with the technology can take place.

Heaford (1983) analyses training costs into categories. First he looks at costs of facilities. He divides the annual overhead cost for buildings by the number of days of training in the year, to get an average overhead cost per training day. He multiplies this figure by the number of days of training and the number of students to get a total facilities cost. Unfortunately, this is not how facilities are usually costed. Training facilities in particular are seldom used for other purposes, therefore their total cost is more or less fixed regardless of the number of students using them or how many days they stand idle. Moreover, the overhead charged to training budgets by the company is often fixed arbitrarily, ranging from zero to something close to the real cost including amortisation of capital over a period agreed by accountants to be reasonable.

Heaford looks then at trainer costs. He multiplies the number of trainers by the trainers' total salaries per day to obtain a total cost for salaries. For salary, we would read gross costs to the company, including all fringe benefits. To this figure he adds the cost of trainers' accommodation and subsistence. This is reasonable, of course, only if the training is being held away from the trainers' normal place of work. Similarly, he adds the cost of trainers' travel, which may range from zero to quite a large sum, depending on where the training is being done. Strictly speaking, to the cost of travel should be added the cost of travel time, if the travelling is done inside business hours. Finally, he adds the 'lost opportunity' cost. Though Heaford does not say so, this is the cost of having the trainers doing training rather than doing some other job for the company, perhaps a job like selling that makes a direct profit. Together, all these figures add up to the total trainer-related costs.

Trainee costs come next. Multiply the number of trainees by the number of training days, and multiply again by the average trainee salary (gross costs to the company), to get Heaford's total cost for trainee salaries. Add to that the total cost, if any, of accommodation and subsistence and/or travel for each student each day multiplied by the number of training days. Finally, add the 'lost opportunity' cost, if any, of having the trainees in training rather than on the job. Together, these costs add up to the total trainee-related costs.

Lastly, Heaford analyses administrative costs. He takes the number of administrative staff and multiplies that figure by the average cost of administrative staff salaries for one day. This figure is multiplied by the number of days they are involved with training matters. This gives the total administrative costs, unless the company wishes to include overheads and opportunity costs for these employees as well.

The fact is that Heaford has identified the main costs associated with training. It is also a fact, however, that there is no agreement about how the figures should be derived. For example, calculating the salary of an administrator for one working day can be done several ways, each one taking into account different factors such as holidays, medical leave, training time and so on.

Perryman and Freshwater (1987) provide a brief discussion of training costs at Austin Rover and Lucas, both of which use CBT

225

within open learning schemes. They note that training time is difficult to define when trainees are expected to go at their own pace, and may take anything from half to double the expected time for a given program. Centre (or computer) use is not easy to measure: high occupancy of the terminals or microcomputers seems important to maximise use of the capital, but learning depends on what trainees actually do there. The companies encountered problems in deciding what elements to include in running costs and in agreeing on a basis for comparison of conventional and open learning. Austin Rover includes depreciation costs of CBT hardware, but excludes opportunity costs and travel and subsistence, which happen to be lower for open learning. On development costs, Austin Rover use a figure of 100 hours for one hour of CBT, compared with fifteen hours for one hour of conventional training. To us, the former seems low, the latter high.

We think the most important consideration in costing training, including CBT, is to use a similar base when making comparisons. We found that many companies could not undertake a proper comparison of costs because they had no figures on costs of non-CBT, or could not agree internally on the basis for these. Because companies expect their decision-making to be rational and founded on statements backed by figures, there is a strong temptation to hide costs to make a case look better. These difficulties in costing hinder cost-benefit analysis. Companies wishing to compare the costs of different kinds of training cannot do so, nor can they obtain suitable cost data for comparisons between different CBT systems.

CONVENTIONAL TRAINING COSTS VERSUS CBT COSTS

The greatest difference between conventional training costs and CBT costs, in our opinion, lies in the cost of 'front-end' design. Conventional training is done face-to-face by trainers, the front-end cost for whom lay in their original training and in any preparation work they do before meeting the trainees. The cost of this training is not negligible (although Heaford omits it from his trainer costs), but it is small in comparison with the front-end cost for developing CBT, which may be a hundred times as much.

When companies develop their own CBT, front-end design is where the largest investment must be made. Getting the courseware right is a difficult and often lengthy process, as we showed in Chapters 15 and 16. Once the courseware is made, it may be used to train large numbers of trainees, at considerable savings over conventional training. Or it may be used to train operators to avoid potentially costly mistakes. Or it may do a training job that would have been far more costly, for geographical reasons, by conventional means. Or it may provide training that simply cannot be provided any other way. A large front-end investment can be justified, economically, in situations where the benefits are very valuable.

Of course, company attitudes towards spending money on CBT might change if it were actually regarded as a financial investment. Burnett (1987) claims that current British accounting conventions make training an overhead rather than an investment producing a measurable return. He suggests that training expenditure should often be treated as capital expenditure, because it creates an asset bringing benefit to the company over a long period, just like research and development expenditure. Admittedly, it is not easy to measure the return in increased employee effectiveness (see below), but this change in the accounting system might result in better training of personnel, the most valuable asset of any company.

COSTS OF THE BARCLAYS BANK PROJECT

Mortimer (1983) quotes the cost of the Barclays Bank videotex project Phase I as at least £130 000, with Phase II costing £620 000 up to July 1983. Of these totals, £480 000 was capital expenditure. His list includes costs of using telephone lines, and of an evaluation survey conducted by an external agency. He looks at comparative costs, in an effort to arrive at an assessment of CBT's cost-effectiveness. Not counting the cost of accommodation for face-to-face sessions at the bank's training centre, he finds that usage of the videotex system would have to rise well above 50 000 trainee/hours a year before its costs per trainee/hour was lower than for face-to-face training. In fact, videotex usage never reached anything like this figure, therefore videotex apparently did not prove cost-effective. It is not clear, however, what factors are included in the costings, and his report illustrates the difficulty of determining cost-effectiveness of training, even in a financial institution like a large bank. If he could show that costs were equal, Mortimer's claim that videotex results in bank employees being more fully trained in bank procedures would still need to be supported by statistical data, and probably cannot be.

Mortimer identifies an important problem, however, when he asks whether cost-effectiveness comparisons can be valid while the old and new systems run side by side. If the new is introduced only into part of a national network of branches, as was the case for the Barclays Bank videotex system, then the old training system has to be retained to cater for employees from the rest of the network. The true level of savings in the event of full implementation of Barclays' videotex, nationally, is very difficult to estimate.

EVALUATION OF BENEFITS

What are the benefits of a computer-based training system? This is not a simple question. In any form of training, benefits are usually thought of in terms of whether or not trainees have achieved the objectives of that training. Yet every trainer knows that objectives can shift, even during a trial. Stating them precisely, in a way agreed by all concerned, is difficult enough, but changing circumstances easily change training objectives, rendering evaluation difficult. Some US experts even suggest 'content-free' evaluation, in which no assumptions are made about the original objectives of training, and evaluation rests entirely on judgements of what trainees do during training (process evaluation) and on what they can do at the end of training (product evaluation).

As Smidchens's (1986) review of interactive videodisc training shows, evaluative studies are often based on poor experimental design, which renders suspect the results obtained. Good experimental design demands that proper comparisons are made, on common assumptions. If training is aimed at changing trainees' behaviour in certain desired ways, then a CBT system is more effective if it produces change in a shorter time, or more change, or produces more lasting change, than conventional systems. In other words, the three criteria are usually time, achievement and retention, and no proper evaluation can be made without comparing CBT costs and results with those from conventional training.

Of the three criteria, time seems straightforward to measure. In real life, however, training sessions are frequently interrupted. In pilot studies it may be possible to measure CBT time accurately enough. The snag lies in getting a fair comparison with conventional training. The onset of fatigue while training is seldom assessed, for CBT or conventional training, presumably because the time taken is influenced by fatigue. Yet fatigue can have a significant effect on achievement.

228

Achievement is more difficult to measure. Training can be roughly classified into three kinds of 'improving': of knowledge, skills, and attitudes. The only way a company can find out whether a trainee's knowledge and skills have improved is by testing. This means asking the trainee to show that he or she can behave in certain ways, whether by exhibiting a manual skill correctly or writing down a solution to a problem. Similarly, attitude change can only be confirmed by observing behaviour, probably on the job. Being able to behave in the 'correct' way immediately after training is not sufficient. Trainees must be able to behave the same way after a week or a month or more (and want to).

The tests used by companies for achievement and retention are often inadequate, and do not predict well which trainees will be able to do the job better. This is equally true for CBT and for conventional training. What is not equally true for both kinds of training is that some types of test are easier for people who have been trained one way rather than the other. For example, CBT includes plenty of multiple-choice questions: tests made up of this kind of question can be rather difficult for British conventionally trained employees who have seldom seen one, although they are not for Americans, who are used to this kind of test.

Often companies give a test before training and the same one again afterwards, then compare the scores. The difference between the scores represents the learning. The figures may be impressive, but again a comparison with conventional training is usually needed for a proper evaluation. Rae (1986) offers a practical guide.

Collecting statements from trainees is another form of evaluation. For example, Thirkettle (1986) gives some typical reactions of trainees who used the British Airways interactive videodisc *Who Owns the Problem?*: 'It taught me that I keep looking for things that are not there.' 'I must learn to deal with the facts.' 'I didn't realise I was so inconsiderate.' 'I totally forgot where I was, it was so real.' These statements may be useful for judging what may need to be changed in the disc, but they are not very meaningful to outside observers who have not been through the training experience but who have to judge its worth.

CBT BENEFITS TO TARGET STORES

A particularly interesting evaluation, involving stores in Denver, Minneapolis and Duluth, is reported by Johnson (1986). Target

229

Stores, a company operating a chain of stores, decided to try CBT. To evaluate their own product, the trainers set up a comparison, with 108 employees being trained by conventional lectures and 57 through CBT. The two groups, although randomised, were not perfectly matched on previous experience with computers (67 per cent in lectures group, 53 per cent in CBT group), but they were taught exactly the same topics, dealing with price changes and credit authorisation within the company's new online mainframe information system. The trainers predicted that both groups would achieve similar levels, but that the CBT group would take 25 per cent less time.

After training, the time for which was carefully recorded, all trainees took a paper-and-pencil test of knowledge or procedures and applications. This method of testing may have favoured the lectures group. All trainees also completed a questionnaire about their attitudes. The test was repeated after two weeks, to see whether the knowledge had been retained. In addition, an 'execution' test, involving tasks on the real system, was given to the groups that took the credit authorisation course, three days after they had finished.

The data showed that the CBT group had taken one-third less time to cover equivalent material. The CBT group learned as much as or more than the lectures group, as shown by test scores straight afterwards and two weeks later. The scatter of test scores was narrower for the CBT group. The CBT group also held more positive attitudes towards their training format. Even the Duluth CBT group, which had not had any orientation session, did very well. Only on the execution test did the lectures group do slightly better, perhaps because they had had more experience with computers beforehand, or because the CBT program had provided insufficient practice in one topic, 'system menu transversals', or even because the CBT practice keyboard was slightly different from the real system's.

Target Stores were well-pleased with the results of this thorough evaluation, and proceeded to implement CBT throughout the chain.

COST-EFFECTIVENESS AT BARCLAYCARD

In an attempt to determine cost-effectiveness of the embedded CBT installed at Barclaycard, Rothwell (1983a) reports that costs were analysed in four categories:

230

(a) *Hardware*: this included the costs of central processor (main-frame resources), dedicated disk drives, the network and depreciation of video display units.

(b) *Software*: IBM's charges were counted here, plus the cost of CBT authors' development time.

(c) *Administration*: the costs of student registration and records, and of clerical support, were included here (but not managerial time).

(d) *Students*: Rothwell was uncertain whether the costs of students' salaries should be charged to the project. Certainly they were not charged against Barclaycard's training budget.

In 1981, the year being scrutinised, the total training budget was £400 000. CBT absorbed a quarter of this sum, providing for 1200 trainees, of whom 1050 were muster trainees and 150 keyboard trainees. The average cost was £8 per student hour, much the same as the cost for conventional classroom training. Was CBT therefore cost-effective? Yes, it was, because training was completed in much less time (see Chapter 7) and to higher standards.

BENEFITS TO EASTMAN KODAK

Over a fairly short period, Eastman Kodak (see Chapter 8) gained positive results from CBT and interactive videodiscs for its field engineers. The benefits included savings obtained by eliminating the need for district-level training personnel, and substantially reducing the number of visits employees have to make to a central office for training. Field engineers also save time on repairs by using visual product-shooting references, available at a local office, to back up their training. Less tangible benefits to the company derive from the satisfaction of customers who see repairs done quickly.

A SCEPTICAL EVALUATOR

Cullen (1985) was asked to evaluate a well-known US CBT system, with US training content, with a view to introducing it into a British training context. The advantages were far outweighed, he felt, by disadvantages. Sometimes a sceptical eye detects a great deal.

Cullen starts by noting that the trainees concerned were highly selected and apparently very well-motivated. Despite this, he observed four trainees sitting in front of four interactive videotape terminals, all of them asleep! Clearly, measures of their time taken to train would not be a reliable guide. Trainees spent only 10 per cent of the 30 hour week actually on the computer, so perhaps CBT should not take all the blame. At one point, Cullen says, the computer was being used (expensively) to simulate a cheap electronic test instrument, the multimeter. Students' records were being kept on cards instead of disks, because sometimes the computer corrupted the disks and records were lost. When he asked the CBT supplier for data to support claims of 30 per cent time saved and 50 per cent saving in staff salaries, no such evidence was produced. On the other hand, Cullen himself offers no data on how the trainees performed.

A MODEL FOR COST-EFFECTIVENESS

It would be useful to have models for determining CBT's cost-effectiveness, but all such models so far derived suffer from defects. Beech (1983) makes several suggestions, but he recognises them as probably contentious. For example, he proposes:

(a) That a figure can be arrived at for the number of hours of trainer time required to produce one hour of CBT.
(b) That the effectiveness of this one hour of CBT is equal to or greater than conventional training.
(c) That the average monthly cost of a mainframe system can be calculated, taking into account capital cost, operating, maintenance and depreciation for the mainframe and terminals.
(d) That the cost of developing one hour of CBT can be derived from the cost of trainer time on and off the system.

In place of such a model, we prefer to state the conditions under which cost-effective use of CBT is likely to occur. Companies with stable products or services are more likely to be able to succeed with CBT than those whose products and services are changing very rapidly. Training that has a high technical content is more suitable for CBT than training with a low technical content, although there are examples of successful CBT in fields such as managerial skills where technical content is quite low. CBT thrives on large numbers of trainees, therefore companies that have opportunities to achieve economies of scale (such as reaching thousands of trainees with the same program), are usually in a strong position to exploit CBT, especially if the employees are widely scattered. If the training audience is more or less homogeneous, CBT may be easier to use than if there is wide diversity. Younger trainees are more likely to succeed with CBT than older ones.

Where a company has only a few trainees within each speciality, perhaps with widely differing training needs, or where the content of training is likely to change rapidly, CBT has less chance of success, unless fortuitously suitable off-the-shelf programs can be brought in for use on microcomputers. Small companies can certainly benefit from CBT, including videodisc training, of this type.

Part Five

Trends

18

Trends in Training

In this chapter we observe the main trends in company training as they affect CBT. The relationship between these trends and further development is indirect in the sense that accelerating needs, say, do not necessarily lead to greater investment in CBT, although they may well do so. Nevertheless, the first part of this chapter discusses trends that are probably favourable to CBT, while in the second part are those that are likely to inhibit it.

ACCELERATING NEEDS

The accelerating rate of change in industry and commerce implies accelerating needs for training and retraining. These needs are slowly being recognised slowly in Britain, more quickly in the United States. Geoffrey Holland, Director of the Manpower Services Commission, said (quoted by Parkes, 1987): 'We in Britain must develop our human resources: that is the clear lesson from our overseas competitors who regard the development of their workforces as an investment rather than an overhead'.

This kind of statement of increasing needs in Britain is perhaps reflected in the National Computing Centre (*Training Digest*, February 1987) forecast that spending by companies on CBT would increase fourfold by 1990 to £230 million per annum, or 12 per cent of British spending on training, with an increased proportion spent on software and less on hardware. The Centre also predicted that retailing would be an important growth sector for CBT, although banking and finance companies held the lead in 1986.

In the United States, training has often been given high priority, verbally, but low priority in practice, when money is allocated. This seems to be changing, in some economic sectors, not necessarily for people-oriented reasons, but because senior managers are finally realising that training is a marketing tool. Good customer training helps sell products and services. A well-trained workforce produces these more cost-effectively. Trainers are realising these facts too.

Once time and effort have been invested in training an employee, it then become more cost-effective to retrain that employee if new needs arise than it is to hire and train another. Even those very large industries and businesses that have traditionally offered the most stable employment, such as farming and steel and car manufacturing, have become unstable and the need for retraining at all levels can no longer be ignored.

MERGING OF TRAINING AND JOB

A merging of training and the job is occurring. That is to say, many jobs now require less initial training than before, because further training is available on the job, often in the form of job-aids. Specialised training away from the job may not be required.

One of the best examples of this merging is in word-processing and desktop publishing. We described in Chapter 6 the training at Kelly Girl, a large recruitment agency for temporary secretarial and clerical staff. It needs to train secretaries in the skills of word processing and it needs to evaluate quickly the skills already possessed by would-be word-processor operators. Kelly Girl uses in all its branches a computer-based simulation of IBM, Wang, AES, DEC and Xerox word processors, that trains operators and evaluates their skills. On going to work as word-processing secretaries, however, all these trainees have instant access, on their computers or dedicated word processors, to a wide range of 'help' menus. Should they be drawn into desktop publishing, the software they will use is even more helpful: for example, programs such as Ready, Set, Go and PageMaker provide many options as well as having printed manuals. Of course, training in aesthetic page design is still required.

We support Fisher's (1985 personal communication) idea that information technology of this kind should enable people to 'work smart' instead of 'work ignorant'. CBT can and should enable them to do so, whether it is for initial training or is embedded in the technology, accessible for everyday reference. Apple has in mind a videodisc-based technical reference manual, and Eastman Kodak has its Parts Locator and Index of Adjustments and Removals. At present, these are primarily for technical personnel who must check product references. With development of expert systems, it seems likely that highly sophisticated job aids will appear (see Chapters 19 and 20) to help managers solve problems and make decision, and there is no reason why there should not ultimately be aids for accountants, sales personnel and many others.

As training becomes a more integral part of job performance, instead of something rather divorced from it, trainers in their role as 'knowledge engineers' should become more involved to contributing to major decisions on product planning and updating. Trainers' standing in companies may then improve, with greater resources being placed in training as its central importance is realised. The traditional view may change: departments nearest to the operational end of a business usually have more clout in staffing and funding than those in the administrative area, where training is usually located. CBT is likely to aid and abet such change.

DEMANDS FOR FLEXIBILITY

In some sectors, it seems likely that employees will be required to be more specialised in their jobs, therefore they will require specialised training. In others, however, the demand may be for increased flexibility, with employees being expected to switch between several specialised areas during a working day. For instance, Smith and Wield (1986) suggest that banking institutions may have to retreat from the present specialisation of jobs, especially in smaller branch offices, and that computers may help them to do so. Individuals will find themselves 'picking up' the training necessary to take on other tasks.

If Smith and Wield are right, then CBT may be the convenient way to train these staff and afterwards to offer them readily accessible job-aids.

There are signs that training generally is becoming more diverse to meet the increased demand for flexibility in jobs. Companies have used for many years a variety of training media (printed manuals, videotapes, audiocassettes, slides, and so on) in addition to classroom instruction. In some of the larger companies with CBT and interactive video, a new trend is emerging as they turn to using simultaneously more than one system. Routine mainframe CBT is in use alongside, say, microcomputer-based CBT and level 3 interactive video, with plans being laid to bring in level 4 plus CD/I.

An example of this trend is Pacific Bell (see Chapter 12). *PHOENIX* programs run on the mainframe to train data processing employees. An authoring system, *SAM*, is used to develop and deliver training throughout the company on a personal computer interactive video system. The company also purchased and adapts for its own purposes off-the-shelf interactive videodisc courses for its marketing personnel. In addition, the company is working with a personal computer-based concurrent authoring system in developing CBT that 'wraps' certain applications programs. Finally, Pacific Bell uses standard programming languages to develop special training or for segments of training programs that the authoring systems cannot handle.

INCREASED COMPLEXITY OF TRAINING TASK

For increasing numbers of employees, their future training is likely to be for higher level and more complex tasks. This is because there is a general drift towards larger and more complex systems in companies, whether for manufacturing, banking, retail trade or some other sector of our economy.

This trend probably favours development of CBT, since it includes some tasks that can only be taught through simulation. Singh (1986) suggests that as manufacturing plants become more complex, they become more inaccessible for training purposes, making some kind of simulation essential. He thinks the control panels of processing plants such as paper mills, steel rolling mills, chemical works and oil refineries will be reproduced on videodisc. This would limit the range of states that could be represented, however, and it seems likely to us that computer simulations, with high resolution graphics, will be more useful. Then emergencies and states beyond the normal operating range can be represented accurately.

Interactive video will have its place in training operators and their supervisors for such plants. As Singh (1986) optimistically puts it, this medium can 'bring reality and urgency to the training . . . testing the supervisor's speed of reaction as well as the quality of the technical decisions taken'. Whereas a computer screen can represent dials and gauges clearly enough, the videodisc can present realistic sequences of action and reaction, of humans and machines, that would follow each decision taken by a supervisor.

240

Interactive video is also an excellent medium for learning problem-solving, specific to an industry or to a particular company. When used in supervisor training the trainees, in groups or individually, can view these discs and attempt to solve the technical, personnel and other problems presented to them. The British Airways' disc for ground crew training, *Who Owns the Problem?* is a leader in this field (see Chapter 11). Another example is Digital Equipment Corporation's (DEC's) *Account Chronology* for training its own employees to manage customers' accounts and sell them the company's products and services.

In 1986, 60 per cent of the non-consumer videodisc sales in the United States were for training applications (*Screen Digest*, February 1987). It seems very likely that company training will make greater use of this technology in years to come.

We should make one further point. As training meets the challenge of increased job complexity, more updating information must be placed at trainees' disposal. The self-paced, do-it-yourself mode of CBT and/or interactive video is well-suited to meet this need. FlightSafety International's pilot training is a good example. Although initial training is in the classroom, reviews, simulations and self-tests are presented in an interactive video format which enables trainees to update their knowledge and practise skills at their own pace, and in a less threatening context than a classroom.

COMMERCIAL PRESSURE

Commercial pressure is building up as greater investments are made in training companies. This investment has not yet assumed mammoth proportions, but the signs are there and the investors will be looking for returns. The journal *Training and Development* reported in December 1986 that Deltak, suppliers of CBT software in both the United States and the United Kingdom, had been acquired by National Education Corporation, the United States' largest industrial and vocational training company. Takeovers of this kind probably herald increased efforts to persuade companies to incorporate CBT into their training plans.

Similarly, the Provident Financial Group, parent company to Mentor Interactive Training, announced in early 1987 that it would invest a further £1 million in the light of Mentor's established leadership in interactive training and the growth forecast for this market, conservatively estimated at more than £100 million per annum by 1992. From our contacts with providers we are aware that this is not the only case of increased capitalisation of provider companies.

Another sign of commercial pressure in this field (or at least of perceived markets) is that Datasolve Education, a British provider and part of the Thorn-EMI group of companies, increased its offerings of generic CBT from fifteen courses in 1986 to over 60 in 1987. These include courses produced by Datasolve and those bought in from other providers. The curriculum covers microcomputer applications training, understanding computers, and training in sales, management, financial, business and technical skills.

SLOWNESS OF RESPONSE

Unfortunately, in many British companies there is no concerted effort to train, let alone use new technology for training. The Manpower Services Commission aptly titled its 1986 report *A Challenge to Complacency*. Doulton (1986), Director of the National Interactive Video Centre in London, paints a gloomy picture:

> Not enough organisations are prepared to consider their interactive video requirements at a high enough level. In . . . training the Centre is . . . dealing with committed individuals, often working very hard to crack entrenched attitudes in their organisation, rather than with coherent groups intent on a major improvement programme. Not enough organisations have seen the need to plan a long term strategy that is owned and driven at a very senior level and which considers, from the outset, future goals and requirements.

Much depends on attitudes. For example, one company trainer wrote:

> We are not very keen on computer-assisted learning because it is too impersonal. I am afraid the whole phrase 'New Training Technologies' is too much like a new-fangled buzz word. We believe in Training but not in gimmicks. If we are not into CBT we are not progressive — perhaps even worse, the more we are into it the more 'with it' we will consider ourselves. Such an attitude is putting far too much faith in CBT. The best training

results from the personal inspiration of a good trainer, from his or her ability to communicate with the trainee and whet the appetite for further knowledge and the ways to use that knowledge to good effect on the shop floor, in everyday ways.

SHRINKING RESOURCES FOR TRAINING

In some companies, management makes clear that resources available for training are fixed or even likely to shrink, and that therefore increased cost-effectiveness is the key to any increased training provision.

Inevitably the question is asked: Are the new technologies going to help because they are more cost-effective than the old? We have already addressed this issue, indicating how tricky evaluation can be. It is easy for companies to underestimate true costs if they set out to develop their own CBT. Overall, the high development costs of CBT must militate against its widespread adoption. Fisher (1987) asserts that US companies cannot be expected to bear the whole burden of these costs and proposes greater government support.

Some spinoffs are likely, however, from military training. The US armed services are investing heavily in new training technology. For example, the US Army, after lengthy evaluation, selected interactive videodisc as an important training medium and as a job-aid on the battlefield. Other services are expected to follow this example. Whether or not the Miller and Sayers (1986) forecast of 57 000 players for the US armed services by 1990 is accurate, it seems certain that a great deal of training on interactive videodisc will have to be developed in the next few years. One of the consequences will be that developers will gain experience, and development work paid for by the services will benefit the industrial and commercial training sector. On a much smaller scale, the same effect is likely in Britain, where cuts in conventional defence spending are likely to reduce training expenditure on the armed services.

WHAT IBM SAYS

Dowsey (1987) summarises the IBM point of view, saying that there are more clients for his company to train than ever before, ranging downwards from the chief executive of a customer company, and more IBM products to introduce to these clients. IBM's Education section trains agents and dealers, too, as well as its own staff. These are dramatic changes in training, and they have occurred in many other companies besides IBM.

Dowsey also points out that trainees now expect more variety in media used in the course, and want to study at their own pace, omitting topics they already know about. We might say they have become more demanding.

19

Technological Trends

THE INTERFACE BETWEEN HUMANS AND MACHINES

Despite several decades of research on educational television, and recent work on educational video, little is yet known about how trainees interact with dynamic video images. Even less is known about how they interact with these images integrated with text, as in interactive video. British research has begun in this field, with stress on how pointing can be used effectively, but this is only one small aspect of a wide field of study. More research is greatly needed, as there is no doubt that 'imaging' (the presentation of images of many kinds on the screen) is going to be a very important development in CBT over the next decade. The work we have reported in Part Three already includes many examples of graphic simulation and animation, and the power of authoring systems, such as *VW/I* and *CreationStation*, to present complex graphics is increasing rapidly. For a time, the capabilities of the technology may outrun the experience and expertise of the creative trainers who want to exploit the software. Hints about what is most likely to be effective in training come from several project evaluations.

In the United States, evaluation by Foodmaker (see Chapter 10) showed that trainees in the 18–21 age-bracket reacted positively to visual training connected to a 'storyline' as opposed to conventional procedures training, and they enjoyed interacting with the videodisc medium. Texaco Tankerships (see Chapter 11) found that the computer game format was ideal in teaching trainees to distinguish between various fire-fighting appliances. Eastman Kodak (see Chapter 10) obtained very positive reactions to interactive video from its trainee field engineers, who learned quickly from it. Syntex (see Chapter 10), with sales representatives, and Ford (see Chapter

8), with machine operators, obtained similar results. Learning from moving images is clearly going to be very important in the future of CBT.

With regard to static images, such as text, Waller (1986) points out that reading text on a computer screen is rather like reading a scroll, and scrolls went out of regular use in the fourth century AD. Bound books offer information in much more accessible form. 'Electronic text' does not yet match a book in presenting developed arguments in a linear and coherent fashion, or in providing for skimming, scanning and browsing. Research is proceeding in this field. Frames of text on the computer can, however, be easily integrated electronically with sound, animation, graphics, spreadsheets, databases and so on.

Unfortunately, much CBT is still limited in its screen presentation format by the developers' perceptions and the systems' capabilities. As Isaacs (1987) shows, many developers are still concerned with relatively trivial details such as lower-case versus upper-case text, underlining versus italics, and use of background colour. To some extent this is because of the capabilities of the basic (unenhanced) IBM personal computer hardware and software standard that Isaacs and many others still feel obliged to work to.

This state of affairs is not likely to continue, however, because hardware and software capabilities are increasing very quickly indeed. For example, the Apple Macintosh series of microcomputers introduced in 1985 vastly enhanced opportunities to integrate black-and-white graphics and text on the screen, with a wider range of fonts, using an easy-to-learn authoring system. By the time this book is published, very high resolution graphics, in colour, should be available on the next generation of medium-priced microcomputers, together with all the facilities of windows, pop-up and pull-down menus (these are temporary displays occupying part of the screen) offered by the Macintosh. In other words, developers of authoring systems and of CBT itself will have better tools at their fingertips. The level of their technical discussion will be raised accordingly. This will not mean that they forget matters such as line length and justified text: these items will be considered within the overall display for each screen. The display will be much closer in some respects to the static printed work than it is at present, but it will also be dynamic where appropriate, integrating text with videodisc images on the computer monitor, as some of the more costly systems already do.

AUTHORING ENVIRONMENT

O'Neal (1986b) suggests that authoring systems will evolve to address the full range of authoring functions and activities rather than merely the problems of coding and debugging (remove errors in coding).

Important developments are occurring that will bring the power of electronic publishing software to bear in authoring CBT. At present, the word-processing capabilities of many authoring systems are primitive when compared with the facilities available in electronic publishing for creating text and graphics displays. For example, the *Guide* interactive text system software, developed by Office Work Stations of Edinburgh, enables a trainer-author to store definitions, footnotes and other reference material as 'pop-up' items, to be called into view by the trainee as needed.

Similarly, CBT authors have not yet been able to take advantage of prototype software such as the *Alternate Reality Kit* developed in the United States by Xerox. The kit, implemented in a Xerox programming language called Smalltalk-80, is defined by Scanlon and Smith (1987) as a graphical animated environment for building microworlds or interactive simulations. They discuss using it for teaching an aspect of physics. Guided by a mouse, which is a familiar input device on some modern microcomputers, a 'hand' grabs and manipulates objects on the screen. What happens on the screen also depends on conditions, such as the strength of a magnetic field, which are established by the hand pressing buttons, flipping switches and setting controls, again all on the screen. Programming the simulation is relatively straightforward because the kit uses 'object-oriented programming' (see Chapter 20).

Along the same lines, CBT trainer-authors have not yet been able to use, within authoring systems, what Malik (1985) calls 'mindware'. This is software that assists individuals to organise their thoughts. It aids logical and ordered structuring of concepts. Malik lists programs such as *Brainstorm, Brainstormer, Maxthink* and *The Idea Processor*, saying that they help because humans cannot hold more than a few concepts in their minds simultaneously. They offer an electronic back-of-an-envelope, so to speak. More advanced mindware is under development.

INTEGRATING DATABASES

Work is proceeding on the problems of integrating textual, graphical and video training material. The task is easier as hardware memory and speed increase, although it is still an open question whether large amounts of memory will aid the CBT design process. If so, Compact Disc Read Only Memory (CD-ROM) and Compact Disc Interactive (CD-I) technology may become rather important. CD-ROM technology employs a compact disc player. Each disc can store very large amounts of digitised information (in 1987, up to 600 Mbytes, the equivalent of 200 000 typed pages) that could be searched by a trainee using a microcomputer. Lotus, the software company, launched CD-ROM databases in 1987 (Cross, 1987). Like CD-ROM, CD-I is being marketed in Britain and the United States by Philips and Sony and is an extension of this compact disc technology. A CD-I player connects with a television set to provide video, text and sound. An onboard computer gives the trainee full control over the disc's content, making the system interactive. CD-ROM is made in a standard format, unusual in this field where lack of standardisation is the rule but extremely beneficial to those who wish to use CDs in training.

Digital Video Interactive (DVI), developed by RCA, is a set of microcomputer chips that enables a compact disc to hold up to 72 minutes of real time colour video, as opposed to the seven or so minutes available on a CD-I disc used for this purpose (Dvorak, 1987). Each frame of video is compressed into only 5K (kilobytes, Kbytes) by a mainframe computer (as opposed to the usual 500K), then written onto a compact disc and decoded when needed, by the chips. As the name implies, DVI is also interactive, in the sense that it could be used in the same way as interactive videodisc for training.

As of 1987, however, neither this new CD technology nor DVI had been tried out in the industrial training field. In the face of compact discs, what is the role of conventional text? How will trainees find what they need out of such a vast store? What design principles should be followed in merging CD technology with computers, videodiscs and authoring software? These and many other questions must still be answered.

The LaserVision Read Only Memory (LV-ROM) format is used for the Domesday and Ecodisc videodiscs, produced and marketed for educational use by the British Broadcasting Corporation. Up to 648 Mbytes of digital data and 54 000 analogue video frames can be stored on a single disc in this format. The disc can only be played

248

on a specially adapted Philips LaserVision player, linked to Acorn's BBC Master Advanced Interactive Video Microcomputer, an enhancement of the Master 128. Logica wrote the unique software that enables users to move around easily among the data and pictures held on the discs.

This format has considerable potential for CBT applications, because very large digital databases of industrial or commercial information can be stored, searched, analysed, transformed and displayed, in association with the video.

Beyond LV-ROM, other laser disc technology is being developed for large-scale data storage. The Optical Digital Data Disc (ODDD) offers up to a gigabyte (Gbyte) of memory, and the Eastman Kodak 14 inch (35 cm) Write Once, Read Many times (WORM) system carries 6.8 Gbytes. There is no sign yet that these advanced systems will be used for training applications, but they could be.

INCREASING COMPLEXITY OF SOFTWARE

As Melmed (1987) has pointed out, CBT systems developed to date are generally rather unsophisticated in their capacity to analyse trainee responses. It is certainly true that they can do little more than carry out a rough matching of the trainees' responses against a range of 'legal' responses defined by trainers and held in the system memories. Once this matching is done, the systems do not behave intelligently. That is to say, they merely refer trainees to further instruction, without detailed analysis of individuals' previous record of learning.

VideoLogic's *MIC 3000* is an example of modern interactive video software. But it appears that now the need is for authoring tools that handle interactive video scripting, flowcharting and storyboarding. Llewellyn and Kahn (1986) estimate that developing an authoring system such as *WISE* takes more than 25 person-years and requires extensive specialist knowledge. Since authoring systems are likely to become more complex rather than less so, will the development time increase? The answer probably depends on the extent to which artificial intelligence can be brought to bear.

Some take the somewhat pessimistic view that the future of interactive videodisc depends on the professional brilliance of commercially made generic training materials. Unless such materials are produced, along the lines of widely used training films (such as those produced in the United Kingdom by Video Arts), the high cost of interactive videodisc production will not be recouped. Interactive videodisc is even more complex, as a training medium, than film, and makes greater demands on producers. Without large sales of high-quality generic products, the interactive videodisc producers will be defeated while trying to make a profit in a fragmented market.

ARTIFICIAL INTELLIGENCE AND CBT

Is there great potential in artificial intelligence for improving computer-based training by making it possible for computers to be more or less intelligent tutors? Will computers and trainees be able to engage, say, in collaborative problem-solving? At its lowest level, this collaboration consists of the computer building up a simple model of the trainee in its memory at the same time as the trainee is building up a model of what the computer knows about the problem being solved. At a higher level, the computer uses its admittedly incomplete knowledge of the trainee and the problem area to propose approaches to the trainee, who in turn may propose approaches to the computer.

The idea of this sort of collaboration raises questions about how a model of the trainee can be constructed. Elsom-Cook (1986) sketches the process (Figure 19.1), suggesting that instead of attempting to build a precise model of what the trainee knows, it is better to start by estimating upper and lower bounds on that knowledge. This is his 'bounded user model'. He further suggests that concrete observations about the trainee's behaviour, made by the computer's equipment and recorded in its memory, under control of its programs, can contribute to this model, through inductive reasoning. There has to be a model of such reasoning in the computer's programs, too. A further model, this time of deductive reasoning, enables the computer to offer concrete predictions about how the trainee will behave next, based on what he or she knows. Elsom-Cook acknowledges that these models of reasoning processes are not yet well-developed, but clearly considers that future progress lies in this direction.

If, as Ennals (1986) suggests, computers can contain a description of a problem area, through use of logic programming (such as LISP and PROLOG) rather than a sequence of instructions as in ordinary programming (such as BASIC), then training becomes a process of knowledge exploration rather than reading successive preordered frames. He points out that already a number of providers

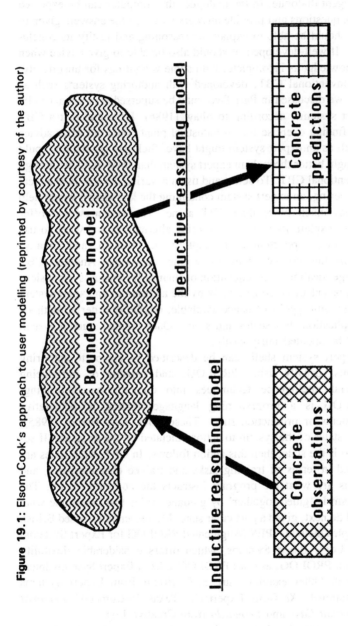

Figure 19.1: Elsom-Cook's approach to user modelling (reprinted by courtesy of the author)

offer 'expert system shells'. An expert system contains knowledge about a subject, rules of inference and the means for conducting an intelligent dialogue. In the dialogue, the computer can be expected to ask questions and provide answers based on the answers given to it. It should be able to explain its reasoning and justify its conclusions. If well-developed, it should also be able to give advice when its knowledge is incomplete, with some weightings for uncertainty.

Conventional CBT, developed with authoring systems such as those we discussed in Part Two, may be superseded or enhanced by expert systems, according to Shaw (1986). He found that a CBT fault-finding exercise for an industrial plant could not offer advice as well as an expert system might have. Sick pay regulations could be taught better through an expert system than they could be through conventional CBT. To select and use measuring devices in chemical engineering, an expert system containing the knowledge would help trainees much more than CBT alone. The system would offer advice, explain its reasons, prescribe alternatives and when to use them, offer opportunities to explore the problem, and, finally, explain the consequences of wrong decisions. Another CBT package, dealing with acquisition of finance for business expansion, could be enhanced considerably by the addition of an expert system dealing with types of finance available, eligibility criteria, methods of application, timescales and so on. Once created, such a system could be updated fairly easily.

Expert system shells can be described as elaborate authoring systems, usually using PROLOG, and capable of introducing artificial intelligence techniques into computer-based training. PROLOG is a programming language dealing in declarative statements or production rules. These rules, says Heines (1985), relate states of the system to actions dictated by the program. If so-and-so is the state, then this action follows. In CBT, such states are defined in terms of training tasks and trainee characteristics, and actions are what the program instructs the computer to do. The program is 'glued together' by guidance rules that determine what it will do next, given a particular state. Microcomputer-based British examples include APES (Augmented PROLOG for Expert Systems) from Logic Based Systems, which offers considerable flexibility through PROLOG, as does PROLOG-2 from Expert Systems International. Other examples are *ESP-Advisor* from Expert Systems International, *Xi* from Expertech, Texas Instruments' *Personal Consultant Easy* and *Leonardo* from Creative Logic.

Claims that the shells can be used by novices should be treated with caution, says Shaw (1986). Like several others, *Expert Edge*, from Helix Expert Systems, is a shell that the developers declare can be used without a knowledge of programming. It is menu-driven, in natural language, and can control an interactive videodisc player. It has been used to develop a series of expert systems for advising employees in fields such as credit rating, stock record conciliation and engineering fault analysis. These 'advisers' are perhaps more like on-the-job aids than training systems.

Technical differences between conventional frame-based authoring systems and expert system shells are emphasised by Judd (1986). He thinks the latter have considerable potential, but notes constraints they place on the author. Examples are easily created in a frame-based system, while in a shell the task is more complicated. An authoring system (like *ADROIT*) can capture programs from other computers for insertion in the CBT. A shell takes a more roundabout route to do the same.

Expert systems are worth considering seriously if only because there is a shortage of experts who know how to design high-quality training programs. Theoretically, expert systems can be built that codify the knowledge of training experts and/or that of experts in the training topic under consideration. In practice, there are few examples so far of expert systems being developed for company training purposes. The main problem with the first generation of expert systems was that the expertise was generalised and not really useful in specific situations. Developers of the systems attempted to teach topics such as communication and management skills, without considering whether the medium was appropriate, given the relatively unsophisticated level of development of expert systems technology.

Pipe (1986) asserts that although expert systems may be a potential boon to training, task analysis using decision tables is considerably cheaper and just as effective for many kinds of training. Decision tables are the basis for algorithms such as flowcharts and decision trees, and for 'if-then' rules of the sort used in building expert systems. Pipe has developed the (microcomputer) software needed to produce decision tables for tasks, including larger tasks that were more difficult to analyse. His approach is promising, we think, and deserves attention.

AN EXPERT SYSTEM FOR TRAINING FARMERS

Imperial Chemical Industries (ICI) is one of the world's largest companies. Among its many products are fungicides for wheat crops. Dealers in these fungicides lack sufficient expert agricultural sales employees. Now they can 'train' their farmer customers to select the appropriate fungicides through a videotex program, *Wheat Counsellor* (McCarten, 1985). The program is available only through videotex sets in dealers' stores, to encourage farmers to visit them. Dealers already had these sets for business management purposes, linked to ICI's mainframe computers.

The program asks the farmer for his name, the name of his farm and of the field to be analysed. ICI's database holds geochemical and farming information about this field. Next, the program asks the farmer for details of seeds and fertilisers used and how the latter were applied. All these facts are needed, because complex decisions depend on them.

With this information available, the program weighs up the risks of various fungal diseases and explains them. It recommends fungicidal treatments and shows costs and benefits, pinpointing the most favourable. Its recommendations are balanced and in terms credible to the farmer. Its advice is based on the computer's dialogue with that individual.

Wheat Counsellor was produced using the *Savoir* expert system shell developed by Isis, a software production house. It is an expert system because it integrates knowledge from the user with expert knowledge it already holds and arrives at decisions through expert-like reasoning that can take into account some kinds of uncertainty.

FUTURE INTELLIGENT TUTORING SYSTEMS

Logica Tutor, a prototype intelligent computer-assisted instruction system has been developed by Logica Cambridge, a British provider (Ford, 1986). It builds up a trainee model by recording and integrating what it has taught the trainee and what level of skill the trainee is displaying. It holds a database covering the domain of knowledge and skills being taught, in the form of production rules and an interpreter. And it chooses a teaching strategy from its repertoire by examining the differences between the trainee model and what is to be taught. The strategy is translated into the appropriate topics and level of instruction. The knowledge database can be

254

updated independently of the rest of the system, and the trainee can ask the system to explain further any statement it makes. At the time of writing (1987), Logica Tutor was being incorporated into development of an interactive video training package for CNC (computer numerical control) milling machine operators.

Various experimental tutoring systems are discussed by Elsom-Cook (1986), who points out that they have differing forms of inter-action with the trainee. Some simply react to what the trainee does, others define rigidly the trainee's activities. The best-designed do attempt to recognise responses that indicate the trainee is trying to obtain control, and allow this taking over to occur. None yet support a variety of interaction styles. Many only plan ahead to the extent of acting on a single response from the trainee, although a few main-tain a plan built up over many interactive steps.

IMPROVING TELECOMMUNICATIONS

Opportunities for delivering standardised CBT to large numbers of geographically scattered employees are improving. As we showed in Chapter 12, American Telephone and Telegraph is actively pursuing the development and installation of conferencing systems for train-ing, with the help of a modem that transmits voice and data signals over a single telephone line. These systems incorporate micro-computers, with CBT graphics and text being transmitted between them.

There is no technical reason why CBT should not be transmitted by satellite as well as terrestrial networks. If the network is simply used to send CBT software to a distant location, where it is downloaded onto a local microcomputer, then the costs are likely to be reasonable. Where interactive CBT is online, however, costs will be relatively high, as we showed for several videotex users discussed in Part Three. Dowsey (1987) mentions that in the United States, the Interactive Satellite Education Network has been used by IBM to teach over 100 customer students in as many as eight remote loca-tions for up to three years, and that IBM Europe is planning to use satellite technology for advanced technical training of its own employees.

A UNIQUE KIND OF JOB-AID?

As a tailpiece to this chapter, we mention a new technology that may prove helpful if used for job-aids. The optical memory card, Laser-Card, produced by Drexler Technology Corporation in California is the size of a credit card. It contains a reflective laser-read optical recording stripe that can store up to 2 Mbytes of digital information, the equivalent of about 800 pages of text. Its capacity is due to be increased to two to five times as much. A system in a small box reads and 'writes' the data, and can be linked to a microcomputer.

Such a card, although not yet used for training, has immense potential as a job-aid, especially for situations where quick access is needed to a large amount of reference material for troubleshooting, as when a field engineer visits a customer and needs full details of the equipment being repaired. The reader should cost no more than about $100 when produced in quantity, making widespread use financially feasible.

20

Forecast to 2000 AD

Somebody once said that prediction costs nothing and commits nobody to anything. In writing a forecast to the year 2000, we risk being wrong! We did consider approaching 20 or so experts in this field to obtain their views, but eventually decided to quote several published opinions and state our own.

THE STATE-OF-THE-ART

We set out to undertake a critical analysis of developments in this field, based on our understanding of company experience in the two countries. Our book does not reach conclusions in the experimental sense, but it does review the state-of-the-art, and includes a large number of company case studies.

On the positive side, it shows clearly that many British and US companies have succeeded in making cost-effective use of computer-based training, that others have found that computer-based training is the only solution to a specific training problem and that the trend is towards rapidly increasing use of microcomputers and interactive videodisc for training, while mainframe systems decline.

On the negative side, our study shows that over the last 25 years money has probably been wasted on comparatively primitive systems that could not satisfy certain companies' medium-term and long-term training needs, that the problems of upgrading and updating these systems were significant until the technology improved and that companies experienced difficulties in introducing such distinctive innovations. The need to integrate computer-based training with other means of training is clear: no company has moved to training entirely with computers and computer-related equipment. CBT for part of the training task is common.

If this is an accurate summary of the state-of-the-art of CBT, what can we predict up to 2000 AD?

FORECASTING

As humans, our main forecasting method is extrapolation. After 25 years of CBT, it may not seem too difficult to extrapolate the trends for another decade or so. In fact, there are large grey areas, particularly in relation to the potential of artificial intelligence.

Rushby (1986) offers an agenda for knowledge engineering research applied to instructional design, stemming from a 1986 meeting sponsored by the British Computer Society. Although the items are not mutually exclusive, they do represent the areas in which more work is likely to support the development of CBT. The eight items were:

(a) models of learning and learners,
(b) structures of knowledge and guides for learners through these structures,
(c) explanatory and evaluation systems to test understanding,
(d) knowledge elicitation, elucidation and representation,
(e) curriculum mapping,
(f) ways of handling and querying complex information databases,
(g) tools for designing and producing CBT,
(h) how to improve communication between people and computers (human interface problems).

Regrettably, the amount of money going into research in these areas is totally inadequate to produce substantial changes in CBT by 2000. It is reasonable to predict that by that date prototypes and experimental projects will exist, dealing with narrowly defined topics.

By 2000, a few general purpose tools are likely to be on the market to assist trainers in building models of learners. Progress in building structures of knowledge is going to be slow, despite the existence of some software that can help. Knowledge elicitation and representation will move ahead fast on a few narrow fronts, some potentially very valuable in terms of training. New authoring tools for designing and producing CBT may well appear, but their use will be limited to a small number of companies, while the rest use older

258

tried-and-tested systems. Human interface problems may well have diminished by 2000: in fact, this is the area where most progress is likely.

Barker's (1986b) predictions, made in April 1985, were that the future of CBT will be influenced by research into (a) human–machine interaction, (b) artificial intelligence, and (c) computer communications networks. He predicted that from (a) will come 'techniques to enable detailed scientific studies based upon behavioural observation of the interaction between a student and an expert tutor, and dialogue engineering methods that permit the construction of highly effective learning conversations between a student and a computer system'. From (b) will come 'techniques for modelling the student and student teacher behaviour, and easy-to-use methods for the construction and handling of knowledge bases relating to the universe of discourse with which the instruction deals'. From (c), he said, will come 'means whereby instruction may take place at virtually any geographical location'.

Again, our comment is that, up to 2000, resources for research in these fields are likely to be insufficient for great strides to be made in CBT, despite the optimism of providers such as the company where Lindsay (1987) works. This is not to deny that her company may develop some excellent systems for particular clients.

ARTIFICIAL INTELLIGENCE AND CBT

Is artificial intelligence going to be important? Opinions vary about artificial intelligence. Malik (1986) says, referring to Star Wars: 'Artificial intelligence is not a solution: it has the same relationship to intelligence as artificial flowers have to flowers'. Developing and controlling computer-based training is a far easier task for artificial intelligence than controlling a US strategic defence system, but the signs to date are not hopeful.

Naughton (1986) acknowledges that forecasts of the impact of artificial intelligence are speculative because of the lack of established products and conventional markets. He also notes that, although development work is being done on the supply side of the market, hardly any is being done on the demand side. That is to say, companies have little idea of how their training needs might be better met through incorporating artificial intelligence techniques into their CBT. Naughton cites the example of British Telecom, whose field technicians may now require a computer-based expert system on the

259

spot when installing or repairing state-of-the-art electronic telephone equipment, but if supplied this would be more a very sophisticated job-aid or an intelligent assistant than a training device.

Mayer (1987) discusses the advanced example of *DEFT* (*Diagnostic Expert — Final Test*) at IBM. *DEFT* consists of software that encapsulates the expertise of two senior technicians and presents this expertise in a way that enables testers to diagnose very quickly the faults in disk drives. This is an expert system, developed using IBM's Expert System Environment, which runs on the IBM VM operating system. *DEFT* is a considerable aid to training. Preliminary results in three manufacturing plants, says Mayer, show very considerable savings on labour and a 50 per cent reduction in wasted parts. Mayer also mentions that Ford has an expert system for use when repairing robots. A maintenance worker need only press the return, cursor up and cursor down keys and the system diagnoses the fault and explains how to cure it.

These are examples of one of the most practical applications of artificial intelligence, in that they enable constant and consistent transfer of expertise, at levels that normally take years of work to acquire. When used to produce more products with fewer defects, expert systems like these are extremely cost-effective, even though the cost of design and development is high.

Expert systems as intelligent assistants can be applied not only in production but also in technical areas responsible for product and service improvement and updating. An expert system could quickly update employees concerning the successes and failures of their initial development efforts, so helping them to avoid making the same mistakes again.

Conventional training techniques are weak in transferring such expertise to a new and constantly changing audience of trainees. The appropriate technical experts are often not available to conduct the training, or may not be among the best communicators in the company. When trainees try to absorb and comprehend the expertise in the classroom, something gets lost in the translation, so to speak. Expert systems do not entirely remove this problem of varying degrees of understanding, of course, but they can be at hand to explain yet again the advice they offer to a trainee who did not understand at first.

If such intelligent assistants are developed for many company settings, then naturally the training needs in these companies will be affected. Deskilling need not follow: just as word-processing software has led to increased skills on the part of secretaries, the same

260

may well happen in other fields. There will be a merging of training and what Fisher (1987) calls 'information acquisition' at work, provided through embedded instructions and accessible advice. There will be less emphasis on initial training and more on learning-as-you-go.

Elsom-Cook (1986) specifies several potential ways of using artificial intelligence techniques to improve authoring systems. He foresees 'automation' of some of the processes by which knowledge is represented and transformed into complex training. More sophisticated processing of trainee responses will lead to better selection of the next sequence of training. In simple domains, examples of problems will be generated automatically. More adaptive interactions will be possible through using improved models of trainees. Again, however, funds are required to support the necessary research. According to Mayer (1987), one analyst predicts a surge in the US market for artificial intelligence, from $400 million in 1986 to over $1.7 billion in 1990, with much of this growth due to applications in factories. Training is not likely to be entirely left out of any such growth.

A particularly interesting product of research in this field is the five-component model formulated by O'Shea (O'Shea and Bornat, 1986). The five components are the student model, teaching strategy, teaching generator, teaching administrator, and student history (Figure 20.1).

Each of these components can be expressed in production rules, according to O'Shea (1979), whose purpose in developing the model is to constrain designers to one of a number of models, thus keeping down CBT development costs. He suggests that it is possible to create ten courseware development templates that enable trainers without programming skills to create CBT materials of different types. The templates and their interrelationships are illustrated in Figure 20.2. O'Shea and Bornat developed prototype sets of production rules for three topics, one of them photocopier maintenance. The five-component model is to be exploited commercially for CBT by Advanced Technology Training Associates, a British company.

Overall, however, it looks as though the dearth of trained workers in artificial intelligence research in Britain and the United States will slow down this kind of work. Mayer (1987) notes that 'companies are finding that the skills required to solicit information from an expert, organise it, and structure it are extremely diverse and difficult to find'. He also says that the relatively high development costs and an 'immature technology' are putting off managers and trainers.

261

Figure 20.1: The components of O'Shea's five component model (reprinted by courtesy of the author)

THE TEN COURSEWARE DEVELOPMENT TEMPLATES

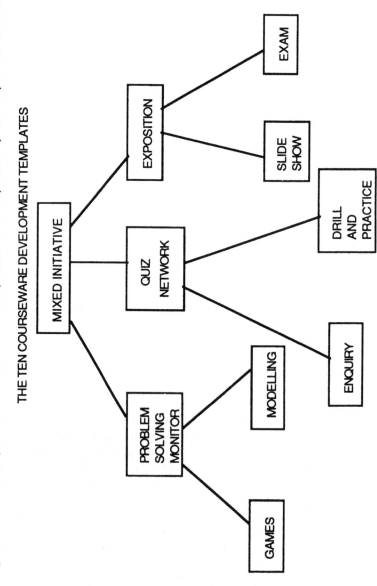

Figure 20.2: The Courseware Development Templates for O'Shea's five component model (reprinted by courtesy of the author)

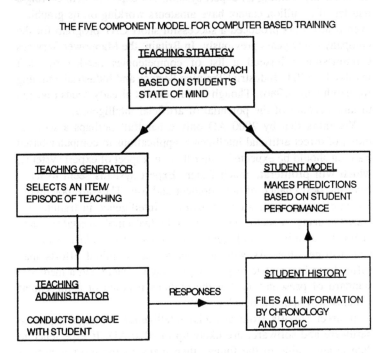

THE FIVE COMPONENT MODEL FOR COMPUTER BASED TRAINING

Without doubt, progress in this field of applying artificial intelligence to company training will require a working partnership between researchers, software developers, subject matter experts and trainers. Among the skills essential to the teamwork is a particular form of knowledge elicitation, peculiar to training. Trainers already have some experience in developing the right number and type of questions to be asked during the elicitation process, through their interviews of subject matter experts. These interviews, originally conducted to obtain information on new products and services for which conventional training was required, must now be adapted and refined to yield the detailed data needed for building expert systems, in which exact and concise description and identification of relationships is more vital than ever before.

The team will also require of some of its members significant abilities in writing texts and scripts and in conceiving visual explanations. Trainer training already includes development of these abilities, but they are likely to be in demand at a higher than ever level, because of the significantly greater investment being made by the company wanting an expert system. An expert system costing a quarter of a million cannot have amateurs working on its graphics, even if amateurs produced a successful short CBT program for the company a few years previously. In Britain, the Manpower Services Commission published a list of competencies needed by staff involved in CBT (Industrial Training Service and Industrial Training Research Unit, 1986). Though useful, the list already needs revision to take account of the potential of artificial intelligence.

We think that by 2000 AD only a handful, perhaps a score at most, of direct artificial intelligence applications to computer-based training should be expected, other than in respect of expert systems, which will proliferate much faster. Expert systems seem to us to have the best chance of development and use. They are potentially a cost-effective application of artificial intelligence in training for manufacturing, a sector where an individual employee takes many years to acquire a full range of skills. The *DEFT* example demonstrates this. As with interactive video, initial efforts may suffer from incomplete or poorly presented content and a mediocre standard of presentation, but the obvious benefits of using expert systems will spur on development.

Indirect payoffs from artificial intelligence, through improved hardware and software, are likely up to 2000 AD. If experience to date is any guide to the future, then many of the most important developments in artificial intelligence research will come from the military sphere. Adaptations for civil purposes, including training, will follow within a decade of these developments being declassified.

PROVISION OF CAPITAL

Laurillard (1986) suggests that CBT is a kind of manufacturing industry, producing as a marketable product the CBT programs. Its objective is to increase training efficiency. For it to be successful, it needs a national context in which there is collaboration between it and the hardware manufacturers, trainers of software developers and providers of capital (private and public). These kinds of collaboration are beginning to emerge. Much of the hardware is still not specifically geared to CBT. There are still shortages of well-trained trainer-authors. Private and public capital has moved towards this fledgling industry, however, particularly in the United States. Even in Britain, Mentor Interactive Training recently estimated the market for CBT at £100 million a year.

We certainly hope that the next few years will see changes in tax legislation in Britain and America that will promote training. As Fisher (1987) points out for America, current policies give preference to investment in physical capital goods rather than to investment in human resources.

A simpler kind of extrapolation is made by Miller and Sayers (1986) about the growth of interactive videodisc, but they do so in the context of the total US market for all purposes. They forecast that the number of players will increase by 32 per cent a year, 1985–90, resulting in over 400 000 players by the end of 1990. They consider that by then training will be the largest single sector of use, with nearly a quarter of the players. Miller and Sayers say that the cost of videodisc technology and of production of videodiscs is dropping. According to Austin (1987), Pioneer expects that about two-thirds of the industrial-quality videodisc players it sells will go to training, and one US market analyst predicts that CD-I players will cost only $300 by 1989.

THE CHALLENGE TO CBT DESIGNERS

Pritchard (1986) says, on behalf of IBM:

We expect to see the emergence of the PC as a key piece in the delivery systems jigsaw. The development of interactive PC/videodisc technology offers enormous potential to the whole industrial training marketplace. The limitation is no longer the delivery system but rather how skilled and innovative course designers and developers must be to take full advantage of the facilities available.

We agree with Pritchard's assessment. Skilful and innovative design will be at the heart of successes in company training using computers, as it has been to date. Training the trainers is going to be vital in the next decade. Bringing artificial intelligence techniques to bear may yet offer the trainers the breakthrough they need.

265

A SCENARIO FOR 2000 AD

At New Century Corporation, a training needs analysis led to installation of a network of the new generation of high-speed mega-memory microcomputers, which makes computer-based training and interactive audio and video available throughout the company. Most of the training programs are developed with a combination of concurrent and interactive audio/video authoring systems. Expert systems have been designed and implemented as job-aids for several important aspects of company production, and the training department itself has an expert system to aid development of new CBT programs.

The new microcomputers enable even the training of data processing employees to be moved off the mainframe, which is a supercomputer, far too expensive to use for routine training. Concurrent data processing training on the microcomputers effectively simulates the mainframe applications.

Training of production personnel is aimed almost exclusively at a fairly small cadre of operators and technicians. CBT trains them to operate, maintain and troubleshoot the full range of process controllers and robotic equipment used by New Century. Most of it is microcomputer-based and accessible at all times on the production floor. The equipment programs were originally developed by the equipment manufacturers and then modified and expanded by New Century's training department as necessary. Videodisc reference manuals stand near each workstation. Most programs have at least a partial expert system built into them, so that users can question the system when solving problems.

Sales and marketing personnel train with a level 4 interactive video system that carries video and audio. The training is mainly product knowledge updating, but salespeople learn new selling skills through use of a type of expert system that enables them to observe and comment verbally on simulated situations, then to try using various techniques on a simulated customer.

Within New Century's administration, employees in the finance division receive much of their training through a program prepared with a concurrent authoring system, combined with an expert system. This teaches them about new procedures, suggests ways of solving problems, and offers a facility for keyed in or spoken questions about a range of financial topics. In the personnel division, employees have access to a data bank of resumes, categorised by job, as well as an expert system component to question when they

266

want to update information about employee benefits.

Secretarial and clerical employees are trained with off-the-shelf programs that introduce them to new software. Most of these programs were created with concurrent authoring systems that also allow users to create their own examples for practice.

Managers use their own expert system to obtain suggestions and options when they have to make decisions or predict trends. Top-level and middle-level managers are required to update regularly their management and supervisory skills by, among other training, responding to and commenting on simulations of typical employee problems, recorded on videodisc.

All training, whether CBT or not, at New Century is monitored through a joint effort of the data processing department (called Management Information Services, like many were in the 1980s) and the training department. These two groups like to call themselves the software engineers and the knowledge engineers. Both are held responsible for developing, producing and updating the specialised software to meet new training needs, and they collaborate well in carrying out this important task for the company. They believe they are making cost-effective use of computers in company training.

References

American Society for Training and Development (1986) *Employee training in America: a comparative assessment of training and development*. The Society, Baltimore

Austin, S. (1987) Interactive video: state of the art, state of the market. *Data Training*, March

Barker, P.G. (1986a) A practical introduction to authoring for computer-assisted instruction. Part 6: interactive audio. *British Journal of Educational Technoogy*, 17(2)

Barker, P.G. (1986b) Information technology, education and training. In Rushby, N. and Howe, A. (eds), *Aspects of educational technology XIX*. Kogan Page, London

Barker, P.G. (1987) A practical introduction to authoring for computer-assisted instruction. Part 8: multi-media CAL. *British Journal of Educational Technology*, 17(2)

Barker, P.G. and Singh, R. (1984) A practical introduction to authoring for computer-assisted instruction. Part 3: Microtext. *British Journal of Educational Technology*, 15(2)

Barker, P.G. and Skipper, T. (1986) Authoring for CAL. Part 7: graphic support. *British Journal of Educational Technology*, 17(3)

Bayard-White, C. (1985) *Interactive Video Case Studies and Directory*. National Interactive Video Centre, Council for Educational Technology, London

Bazeley, J.A. (1985) Boots and CBT. Mimeo report. Boots Retail Training Department, Nottingham

Beaumont, G. (1985) Domino. *Bulletin of the British Psychological Society*, 38, August

Beech, G. (1983) *Computer-based learning: Practical microcomputer methods*. Sigma Technical Press, Wilmslow

Beech, G. (1984) Low cost author language program generators. *Interactive Learning International*, 1(1)

Beech, G. (1985) Two contrasting approaches to authoring on the IBM-PC. *Interactive Learning International*, 2(2)

Bentley, T. (1986) New technology solutions to training problems. *Interactive Training International*, 3(2), October

Bhugra, A. (1986) Computer-based training: a case for creative skills within development teams. *Programmed Learning and Educational Technology*, 23(3)

Bitzer, D. (1977) The million terminal system of 1985. In Seidel, R.J. and Rubin, M. (eds) *Computers and communication: implications for education*. Academic Press, New York

Blackburn, L. (1986) Do it yourself CBT: a systems approach to training. *Interactive Learning International*, 3(1)

Boyer, E.L. (1985) Foreword, in Eurich, N.P., *Corporate classrooms: the learning business*. Carnegie Foundation for the Advancement of Teaching, Princeton, New Jersey

268

Brady, T. (1984) *New technology and skills in British industry*. Research and Development Report No. 32. Manpower Services Commission, Bradford

Branscomb, L.M. (1980) CBT at IBM. *ADCIS SIGCBT Newsletter*, 2(3), January. (Quoted by Kearsley, 1983.)

British Steel Corporation (1986) *Basic electrical knowledge: a computer-based training course with video laser disc support*. The Corporation, Sheffield

Burnett, M. (1987) Accounting for training: a true and fair view? *Training and Development*, 5(9)

Butterfield Communications Group (1983) *Potential roles for public television stations in the emerging interactive videodisc industry*. Corporation for Public Broadcasting, Washington, DC

Calvert, R. (1986) *Training America's Bankers*. American Society for Training and Development and American Bankers Association, Washington DC

Carnevale, A.P. and Goldstein, H. (1983) *Employee training: its changing role and an analysis of new data*. American Society for Training and Development, Washington DC

Craig, R.L. and Evers, C. (1981) Employers as educators: the shadow education system. In Gold, G. (ed.), *Business and higher education: toward new alliances*. Jossey Bass, San Francisco

Cross, M. (1987) Compact discs go into business. *The Independent*, 14 April

Cullen, A.M. (1985) An evaluation of a computer-based training package. *Royal Air Force Education Bulletin*, 23

Datasolve Education (1987) *Computer based training: the way ahead for 1987*. Datasolve Education, London

Dean, C. and Whitlock, Q. (1982) *A handbook of computer based training*. Kogan Page and Nichols, London and New York

Dobson, R. (1986) Paper read at 'Support the Economy' Conference, Winchester, 3 July

Dobson, R. (1987) The application of technology to training in retail. Paper read at a conference on Computer Assisted Approaches to Training, Lugano, 25–26 May

Dorsman, M. and Griffith, J. (1986) *Small and medium-sized firms, new technology and training: a case for change*. Centre for Educational Development and Training, Manchester Polytechnic, Manchester

Doulton, A. (1986) *National Interactive Video Centre: final report*. The Centre, London

Dowsey, M. (1987) Using new technologies in training at IBM. *Interactive Learning Interational*, 4(1)

Drinkall, B. (1985) How to get started. Paper read at Second International New Technologies in Training Conference, London, 2–4 October

Duc Quy, N. and Covington, J. (1982) The microcomputer in industry training. *THE Journal*, March. (Quoted by Kearsley.)

Duke, J. (1983) *Interactive video: implications for education and training*. Council for Educational Technology, London

Dutton, T.J. (1985) Computer-based training — pilot project. Internal report (mimeo). AA National Training Centre, Widmerpool Hall, Nottingham

269

Dvorak, J.C. (1987) Inside track. *PC Magazine*, 12 May

Elsom-Cook, M. (1986) Artificial intelligence and computer assisted instruction (mimeo). The Open University, Milton Keynes: Institute of Educational Technology

Ennals, R. (1986) The Fifth Generation and learning strategies. *Interactive Learning International*, 3(1)

Eurich, N.P. (1985) *Corporate classrooms: the learning business*. The Carnegie Foundation for the Advancement of Teaching, Princeton, New Jersey

Finch, P. and Labinger, M. (1986) Computer-based training: making the case. *Interactive Learning International*, 3(3)

Fisher, F.D. (1987) Redefining training: an American perspective. Paper read at a conference on Computer Assisted Approaches to Training, Lugano, 25–26 May

Fisher, N. and Welham, D. (1987) CBT — a pilot project. *Training Officer*, 23(2)

Foggo, T. (1986) Open learning in ICI. *Open Learning*, 1(1)

Ford, L. (1986) A new intelligent tutoring system. *Interactive Learning International*, 3(4)

Friend, J. (1985) Review of the Microtext CBT authoring system. *Programmed Learning and Educational Technology*, 22(1)

Further Education Unit (1986) *Interactive video in further education*. Department of Education and Science Further Education Unit, London

Gange, D. (1986) TVI in context: an individual view of distance learning in industry. In Fleetwood-Walker, P. and Fletcher-Campbell, F. (eds), *TVI: a handbook for producers and users of tutored video instruction*. Further Education Unit, London

Gerard, M. and Edwards, P.W. (eds) (1984) White collar productivity and quality issues. Proceedings of the NASA Symposium on productivity and quality: strategies for improving operations in government and industry. National Aeronautics and Space Administration, Washington, DC

Gery, G. (1982) The politics of CAI implementation: how to gain an organizational mandate. *Data Training*, June

Gery, G.J. (1983) Implementation and management of computer assisted instruction. *Proceedings of the conference on computers and instructional technology of the Society of Applied Learning Technology*, 9–11 February, Orlando, Florida

Gery, G. (1987) *Making CBT happen*. Weingarten, Boston

Goodwin, C. (1984) Jostling for position in holiday networks. *Computer*, 22 November

Gooler, D.D. (1986) *The education utility: the power to revitalise education and society*. Educational Technology Publications, Englewood Cliffs, New Jersey

Griffiths, M. (1986) Interactive video at work. *Programmed Learning and Educational Technology*, 23(3)

Harris, D. and Chapman, C. (1986) An assessment of trainees using simulators. In Rushby, N. and Howe, A. (eds), *Aspects of educational technology XIX*. Kogan Page, London

Hart, F. (1983) The future of computers in industrial training. *Journal of*

Instructional Development, 6(2)

Hatfield, J.M. and Howard-Jones, T. (1986) *The place of simulation in training*. Rediffusion Simulation, Crawley

Haukom, R. and Malone, E. (1986) Level III interactive videodisc. In Lambert, S. and Sallis, J. (eds), *Programmer's guide to interactive video and CD/I*. Sams, New York

Hawkridge, D. (1983) *New information technology in education*. Croom Helm and Johns Hopkins University Press, London and Baltimore

Hawkridge, D. and Robinson, J. (1982) *Organising educational broadcasting*. Croom Helm and Unesco, London and Paris

Hawkridge, D., Vincent, T. and Hales, G. (1985) *New information technology in the education of disabled children and adults*. Croom Helm and College-Hill Press, London and San Diego

Heaford, J.M. (1983) *Myth of the learning machine: the theory and practice of computer based training*. Sigma Technical Press, Wilmslow

Heaford, J. (1985) Authoring tools: help or hindrance? *Interactive Learning International*, 2(2)

Heines, J. (1985) Rule-based systems applications in computer-based training. Paper read at the Second International New Technologies in Training Conference, London, 2–4 October

Hickey, M. (1985) A comprehensive CBT system for IBM mainframes: the rise of PHOENIX. Part 1: overview and basic components. *Interactive Learning International*, 2(2), April–June

Hickey, M. (1986) A comprehensive CBT system for IBM mainframes: the rise of PHOENIX. *Interactive Learning International*, 2(3), February

Hirschbuhl, J. (1985) What if . . .? *Interactive Learning International*, 2(1)

Hirschbuhl, J.J. (1986) The impact of training in enlightened countries. *Interactive Learning International*, 3(3)

Hitchcock, C. (1986) Report on the findings of the computer-based training pilot project. Internal report (mimeo). Abbey National Building Society, Milton Keynes

Holland, G. (1986) The investment challenge. *Training Through Technology*

Hutt, G. (1986) Using interactive videodisk. *Interactive Learning International*, 2(4), April

Industrial Training Service and Industrial Training Research Unit (1986). *Deciding, designing, delivering: the competencies of staff involved in computer based training*. Manpower Services Commission, Sheffield

Institution of Production Engineers (1986) *An investigation into the provision of continuing education and training*. Manpower Services Commission, Sheffield

Isaacs, G. (1987) Text screen design for computer-assisted learning. *British Journal of Educational Technology*, 18(1)

Iuppa, N.V. (1984) *A practical guide to interactive video design*. Knowledge Industry Publications, White Plains, New York

Iuppa, N.V. and Anderson, K. (1987) *Interactive videodiscs: new tools and applications*. Knowledge Industry Publications, White Plains, New York

Jay, A. (1985) The use of interactive video in training. Paper read at the Second International New Technologies in Training Conference, London, 2–4 October

Johnson, C.G. (1984) TenCORE and PC PILOT: a comparison of two authoring languages, Part 1. *Interactive Learning International*, 1(2)

Johnson, C.G. (1985) TenCORE and PC PILOT: a comparison of two authoring languages, Part 2. *Interactive Learning International*, 2(1)

Johnson, J. (1986) A CBT field study: productivity gains at Target Stores Inc., USA. *Interactive Learning International*, 1(3), February

Jonassen, D.H. (1985) *The technology of text. Vol. 2: Principles for structuring, designing and displaying text*. Educational Technology Publications, Englewood Cliffs, New Jersey

Judd, W. (1986) Progress in tandem. *Data Training*, May

Kearsley, G. (1982) *Costs, benefits and productivity in training systems*. Addison-Wesley, Reading, Massachusetts

Kearsley, G. (1983) *Computer-based training: a guide to selection and implementation*. Addison-Wesley, Reading, Massachusetts

Lamb, R.T. (1986) *The use of computer based training within the British Telecom Technical College*. The College, Bletchley

Lambert, S. and Sallis, J. (eds) (1986) *Programmer's guide to interactive video and CD/I*. Sams, New York

Laurillard, D.M. (1982) The potential of interactive video. *Journal of Educational Technology*, 8(3)

Laurillard, D.M. (1986) Introducing computer-based learning. *Open Learning*, 1(1)

Laurillard, D.M. and Lefrere, P. (1985) *An introduction to computer-based training (PH515MT)*. The Open University, Milton Keynes

Lindsay, S. (1987) AI and the future of training. *Data Training*, February

Llewellyn, R. and Kahn, J. (1986) Authoring systems and the integrated solution. *Interactive Learning International*, 2(4)

Lloyd, T. (1985) PC authoring as technology comes of age. *Interactive Learning International*, 2(2)

Lusterman, S. (1985) *Trends in corporate education and training*. The Conference Board, New York

Mace, S. (1986) Syntex calls on micros for training. *Infoworld*, 8(16)

Madhavan, S. (1984) Ammonic process simulator. *Plant/Operations Progress*, 3(1)

Malik, R. (1985) Mindware? *Intermedia*, 13(2)

Malik, R. (1986) Star wars: can software ever match the expectations? *Intermedia*, 14(1)

Manpower Services Commission (1985) *Adult training in Britain*. Manpower Services Commission, Sheffield

Manpower Services Commission (1986) *A challenge to complacency*. The Commission, Sheffield

Mayer, J.H. (1987) AI on the threshold. *Data Training*, February

Mayer, S.R. (1967) Computer-based subsystems for training the users of computer systems. *IEEE Transactions on Human Factors in Electronics*. HFE-8. (Quoted by Stammers and Morrisroe, 1986.)

McCarten, J. (1985) Grains of good advice? *Computing*, 5 December

McLean, L. (1985) Seeking information on interactive video: the information sources and strategies used by corporate training developers. *DEd thesis*, Syracuse University, ED 259 719

Melmed, A. (1987) A new educational technology: need and opportunity.

Paper read at the conference on Computer Assisted Approaches to Training, Lugano, 25–26 May

Meyerson, M. and Zemske, R. (1985) *Training policies: public and private reinforcement for the American economy*. University of Pennsylvania, Pittsburgh

Miller, R.L. and Sayers, J.H. (1986) The US videodisc market: analysis and forecasts to 1990. *Interactive Learning International*, 3(2)

Miranker, C.W. (1984) Team effort pays. *San Francisco Examiner*, 4 November

Mortimer, R.J. (1983) Viewdata traning project: report on Phase II. Internal report (mimeo). Barclays Bank Training Centre Viewdata Unit, Teddington

Mortimer, R.J. (1984) Using a viewdata system for training. *Programmed Learning and Educational Technology*, 21(3)

Mudrick, D. (1986) Human factors in the design of user-friendly authoring systems. *Interactive Learning International*, 3(4)

Naughton, J. (1986) *Artificial intelligence and industrial training: a report to the Manpower Services Commission*. Open University, Milton Keynes

Nordberg, S.C. (1986) Authoring tools: a perspective on the future of computer based education author systems. *Interactive Learning International*, 3(1)

O'Neal, A.F. (1986a) The current status of instructional design theories in relation to today's authoring systems. *Interactive Learning International*, 2(4)

O'Neal, A.F. (1986b) Evaluating computer-based training tools. *Interactive Learning International*, 3(3)

Open University (1985) *PH514: an introduction to computer-based training*. Open University, Milton Keynes

O'Shea, T. (1979) *Self-improving teaching systems*. Birkhauser, Basel

O'Shea, T. and Bornat, R. (1986) A five component model for computer based training. In Kearsley, G. (ed.), *Artificial intelligence and instruction: applications and methods*. Addison-Wesley, New York

Parkes, A. (1987) Why managers must take responsibility for training. *Training Officer*, 23(3)

Parsloe, E. (1984a) *Interactive videodisc*. Sigma Technical Press, Wilmslow

Parsloe, E. (1984b) Making video interactive. *Interactive Learning International*, 1(1)

Perryman, S. and Freshwater, M. (1987) Industrial dimension of open learning. In Percival, F., Craig, D. and Buglass, D. (eds), *Aspects of educational technology XX: flexible learning systems*. Kogan Page, London

Pipe, P. (1986) Decision tables: the poor person's answer to 'expert systems'. *Performance and Instruction Journal*, March

Postings, R. (1986) Getting started with authoring software. *Training Officer*, 22(7)

Pritchard, D. (1986) Education delivery systems in IBM United Kingdom. *Training Through Technology*

Rae, L. (1986) *How to measure training effectiveness*. Gower, Aldershot

Rajan, A. (1984) *New technology and employment in insurance, banking and building societies: recent experience and future impact*. Gower, London

Rajan, A. (1985) *Training and recruitment effects of technical change*. Gower, Aldershot

Randall, A.D. (1986) The SEGAS experience. *Interactive Training International*, 3(1)

Raven, B.K. (1986) Managing computer-based training projects. *Interactive Learning International*, 3(4)

Reed, A. (1986) Training for flight. *High Life*, October

Reid, P. (1985) Keeping CBT alive: on use, interest and visibility. *Training News*, 6(5)

Rhodes, D.M. and Azbell, J.W. (1986) Authoring systems to get you started on interactive video design. *TechTrends*, 31(5/6)

Richey, R. (1986) *The theoretical and conceptual bases of instructional design*. Kogan Page and Nichols Publishing, London and New York

Rosenberg, E., Smith, B. and Hoffman, U. (1987) Training human resource personnel at 100 sites in two months on a computerised information system. Paper read at a conference on Computer Assisted Approaches to Training, Lugano, 25–26 May

Rothwell, J. (ed.) (1983a) *CBT case histories*. National Computing Centre, Manchester

Rothwell, J. (ed.) (1983b) *Designing CBT systems*. National Computing Centre, Manchester

Rothwell, J. (ed.) (1983c) *Authoring systems*. National Computing Centre, Manchester

Rothwell, J. (ed.) (1985) *Interactive video*. National Computing Centre, Manchester

Rothwell, J. (1987) Buying and using off-the-shelf courseware. *Training and Development*, 5(9)

Rowntree, D. (1981) *Developing courses for students*. McGraw-Hill, London

Rushby, N.J. (1986) Courseware evaluation. *Interactive Learning International*, 3(3)

Rushby, N.J., Weil, S., Schofield, A. and Delf, G. (1987) The ubiquitous trigger: a flexible resource. In Percival, F., Craig, D. and Buglass, D. (eds), *Aspects of educational technology XX: flexible learning systems*. Kogan Page, London

Scanlon, E. and Smith, R.B. (1987) A rational reconstruction of a bubble chamber simulation using the Alternative Reality Kit. Paper read at the CAL 87 conference, Glasgow

Seabright, J. (1987) Stars and Lemons: some thoughts on retail management training. *Training and Development*, 5(9)

Seaver, D. (1987) Interactive video: yes . . . for technical skills. *Data Training*, March

Seymour, W.D. (1966) *Industrial Skills*. Pitman, London

Shaw, C. (1984) A luxury the travel trade can't afford? *Computing*, 22 November

Shaw, K. (1986) The application of artificial intelligence principles to teaching and training. *Interactive Learning International*, 3(4)

Singh, R. (1985) Low cost interactive video. Paper read at the Second International New Technologies in Training Conference, London, 2–4 October

Singh, R. (1986) Selecting the right application media. *Interactive Learning International*, 3(3)

Siomiak, M. (1987) I did not get where I am today by computer based training, but . . .. Paper read at a conference on Computer Assisted Approaches to Training, Lugano, 25–26 May

Smidchens, U. (1986) An examination of the research methodologies used in evaluating interactive videodisc training results. *Interactive Learning International*, 3(2), October

Smith, S. and Wield, D. (1986) New technologies in banking: revolutionary change? *Telecommunications Policy*, 10(1)

Stammers, R.B. and Morrisroe, G.C. (1986) Varieties of computer-based training and the development of a hybrid technique. *Programmed Learning and Educational Technology*, 23(3)

Stewart, C. (1986) TALENT at Forward Trust Group. *Training Through Technology*

Stretch, J. (1984) Notes on Austin Rover's computer-based training. *Open Tech Newsletter*, Summer

Thirkettle, N. (1986) Technology-based training versus conventional training. *Interactive Learning International*, 3(3)

Treadgold, A.J. (1987) Retraining in the manufacturing sector. Paper read at a conference on Computer Assisted Approaches to Training, Lugano, 25–26 May

US Bureau of Labour Statistics (1982) *Economic Projections to 1990*. The Bureau, Washington DC

Wakeley, J. (1985) Proposal for a computer-based training pilot project. Internal report (mimeo). Abbey National Building Society, Milton Keynes

Wall, L. (1987) Interactive video: training executives explain their votes. *Data Training*, March

Waller, R. (1986) Skimming, scanning and browsing: problems of studying from electronic text. Paper read at a Colloquium on 'Paper versus screen: the human factor issues', organised by the Institution of Electrical Engineers and the Ergonomics Society, 16 October 1985, (revised April 1986)

Ward, N.D. (1986) Standard Chartered Bank on Mentor. *Mentor News*, Summer

Welham, D., Fisher, N. and Rudge, B. (1986) CBT in the Central Generating Board. *Interactive Learning International*, 3(4)

Whiting, J. (1986) Microtext and programming style. *CAL News* 32, February

Wilson, L.S. and Backen, D. (1984) MicroTICCIT: a sophisticated CBT system. *Interactive Learning International*, 1(2)

Yeates, D. (1986) Computer-based training fundamentals: the components of technology based training systems. *Interactive Learning International*, 2(4)

Zani, R. (1987) Interactive video: no . . . if your group is mixed and your content changes. *Data Training*, March

Index

276

For Product Safety Concerns and Information please contact our EU representative GPSR@taylorandfrancis.com Taylor & Francis Verlag GmbH, Kaufingerstraße 24, 80331 München, Germany